BECOMING A WOMAN WHO PLEASES GOD

BECOMING A WOMAN WHO PLEASES GOD

A Guide to Developing Your Biblical Potential

PAT ENNIS & LISA TATLOCK

MOODY PUBLISHERS
CHICAGO

Cover Photography: © Garry Black/Masterfile

Library of Congress Cataloging-in-Publication Data

Ennis, Patricia A.
    Becoming a woman who pleases God : a guide to developing your biblical potential / Patricia A. Ennis and Lisa Tatlock.
        p. cm.
    Includes bibliographical references.
    ISBN 0-8024-1416-8
    1. Christian women--Religious life. 2. Christian life--Biblical teaching.
I. Tatlock, Lisa. II. Title.

BV4527.E56 2003
248.8'43--dc21

2003000481

5 7 9 10 8 6 4

Printed in the United States of America

To John and Shirley Baird,
Lisa's parents,
whose willingness to minister to the
Singles' Sunday school class
at Scott Memorial Baptist Church
laid the foundation for the Titus 2:3–5 relationship
that we share.

CONTENTS

Acknowledgments   9

Foreword   11

Introduction: Becoming a Woman Who Pleases God   15

One: The Wise Woman Builds Her Home   21

Two: The Wise Woman Acknowledges   53
        the Strategic Position of the Home

Three: The Wise Woman Develops a Heart   79
        of Contentment

Four: The Wise Woman Manages Her Home   109

Five: The Wise Woman Creates a Gracious Home   145

Six: The Wise Woman Practices Stewardship   169

Seven: The Wise Woman Practices Biblical Hospitality   209

Eight: The Wise Woman Develops a Worldview   235

Nine: The Wise Woman Accepts Her Unique Position   259
        in the Body of Christ

Ten: The Wise Woman Practices the Titus 2 Principle   289

Scripture Grids   309

Notes   315

ACKNOWLEDGMENTS

W e are indebted to the many individuals who supported the creation of *Becoming a Woman Who Pleases God*. Among them we offer special gratitude to:

Drs. Tim LaHaye and John MacArthur—Your vision to develop a character-based Home Economics curriculum and perpetuate it made this volume possible.

Carella DeVol—Pat's roommate: Your moral support, enthusiasm, and consistent prayer on all aspects of her ministry is a constant source of blessing.

Mark Tatlock—Lisa's husband: Your vision and practical support allowed Lisa the time to write and made working on a book possible. Thank you for your belief in the project and faithfully encouraging us through it.

Dr. Stuart Scott—You provided us with the contact with Elsa Mazon, Acquisitions Editor at Moody Publishers.

Elsa Mazon—Your enthusiasm for *Becoming a Woman Who Pleases God* was evident from our initial contact. Thank you for presenting our proposal to the Editorial Committee, responding to myriad questions, and for seeing the project through to its completion.

Dr. Barbara Schuch—Your unselfish sharing of your editorial skills, thought-provoking comments, and belief in *Becoming a Woman Who Pleases God* provided momentum to keep the project in process.

Cynthia Hilderbrand—Your careful work on the detail part of the book allowed us to present it to Moody Publishers in appropriate format.

Our Endorsers, Verna Birkey, Elizabeth George, and Drs. Tim LaHaye, Richard Mayhue and Henry Morris—All published authors, who not only supported the content of *Becoming a Woman Who Pleases God* but the character of the writers.

Anne Scherich—What a privilege to have you as our editor. Thank you for adhering to a high standard of excellence throughout the editing process.

The Moody Team—Your commitment to excellence made this partnership in the ministry of the written word a joy.

Amy Peterson—We so appreciate your fulfilling your job title of Author Relations Manager to the fullest extent.

Our Students, both at Christian Heritage and The Master's College—Your presence in our classes and completion of our assignments helped in the compilation of the synopsis of your Home Economics education.

Our Heavenly Father—*You* established the criteria for the Christian home in Your Holy Word and then provided the strength to apply it to daily living. Eternity will not be long enough for us to express our love and gratitude to *You!*

FOREWORD

As a pastor for over three decades, I have constantly faced the tragic casualty list in the war against marriage, the family, and the home. Trying to keep marriage together and families healthy has been a necessary concentration through all the years of my ministry.

The culture never lets up the assault and has surely wounded its targets, if not killed them. The future looks worse. In many cases, the church has made peace with the defeat and redefined itself to accommodate the demands of the culture—as if that opened the door to effective evangelism. Without a strong defense from the ranks of pastors and churches, the Enemy is

unopposed. The effects are well known: undisciplined and re-
bellious children diagnosed as victims of a syndrome as if they
had no responsibility for their behavior, absent and worldly,
success-dominated fathers who provide no real spiritual leadership or exemplary presence contribute to conflict, bitterness,
even divorce. The family might survive the problems with children and husband-fathers if the women who are wives and
mothers were faithful to their godly calling. Their influence is
so strong and pervasive in the home that it can mitigate the other
influences. After all, Scripture says the woman is the "home-
keeper" who, if she loves her children and her husband truly,
and is "sensible, pure, . . . kind, being subject to [her] own [hus-
band]," will remove any dishonor or reproach that might fall
upon the Word of God (Titus 2:3–5 NASB; 1 Timothy 5:14). In
these Scriptures, Paul is saying that when a wife and mother fulfills her God-given duty, she acts as a barrier against that family's dishonoring God and His Word. While the woman in the
home is not the leader, she is the dominant influencer.

Tragically, however, the mentality of the modern woman
is to leave home and seek her own fulfillment rather than sacrificially give her life away to her husband and children in the
home. That essential and effective influence is lost. There is,
of course, a whole generation of young women raised in this
mentality who, when they come to Jesus Christ and take His
Word seriously, desire to do what honors God but have had
no model to follow.

When I became president of The Master's College in 1985,
one of my first objectives was to develop the finest training program for young women to shape them into godly and competent home-workers with all the character of a Proverbs 31
woman and the skill required to create a unique and fulfilling
home environment for the family.

Few colleges, even Christian ones, have any interest in a real
Home Economics program that is both challenging in academics

and skills. Even fewer are concerned with the personal mentoring of women toward godly virtue.

To have the finest program requires the finest faculty, and the Lord graciously gave The Master's College Dr. Patricia Ennis. She is one-of-a-kind in her pioneering development of a program that is comprehensive in its building of character and skill. Dr. Lisa Tatlock has served as a partner in the department and brings her own rich input and experience to the preparing of young women to fulfill God's high calling for them.

This exceptional book will give each reader exposure to the heart of the college course, the divine design for the home.

JOHN MACARTHUR

BECOMING A WOMAN WHO PLEASES GOD

The purpose of *Becoming a Woman Who Pleases God* is to encourage you, a twenty-first-century woman, to pursue the biblical mandate found in Titus 2:3–5, a passage that identifies biblical priorities for Christian women. Our book's message focuses on the character and the skills required to implement the Titus 2 mandate.

The content of *Becoming a Woman Who Pleases God* is based on the curriculum of the Home Economics Department at The Master's College and focuses on the topics most frequently requested by individuals who are unable to enroll as students; our curriculum integrates faith and learning into a college level Home Economics major. Responding to the vision of Dr. Tim LaHaye, Pat wrote the original curriculum for Christian Heritage College. Fifteen years later she brought the program to The Master's College because of the deep commitment of Dr. John MacArthur to shape godly and competent workers at home who model the character of the Proverbs 31 woman. The curriculum has matured and been refined over the years to reflect key areas for Christian women to pursue as they practically live out the mandate found in Titus 2. The principles apply to all women whether young or old, single or married, workers at home or professionals in the marketplace. Pat has taught college-level Home Economics for twenty-eight years and Lisa for fifteen.

We have used the phrase "Wise Woman" throughout the book to emphasize that women who practice the principles found in God's Word are women who have both understood and subsequently applied the truths found in God's Word. Wise Women desire not only to know but also to implement the mandates of Scripture.

Though we each could have written this book independently, we collaborated on the volume because we believed that it would be a more useful resource if we each focused on our strengths. We are two very different individuals, but our common commitment to the truths found in Titus 2 and the discipline of Home Economics has resulted in the development of an intimate friendship as well as a unique professional team.

Pat wrote chapters 1, 5, and 10. Chapter 1 identifies key principles from Proverbs 31, and chapter 5 emphasizes the importance of graciousness in today's society. Chapter 10 was written by Pat after we discussed the principles of mentoring we had learned as we applied the Titus 2:3–5 principles to our relationship—it is "our story." Pat is the older woman and Lisa the younger.

Lisa wrote chapters 4, 6, and 7. Chapter 4 discusses home

management, priorities, and decision-making. Chapter 6 addresses principles of stewardship applied to finances, time, and entrepreneurship. Chapter 7 identifies the biblical definition of hospitality and establishes meal-management guidelines.

We collaborated on chapters 2, 3, 8, and 9. In chapter 2, Pat addressed the family as the first institution established by God and statistics concerning family life, and Lisa developed the sections on leaving and cleaving, protection for oneness, and the purposes of marriage. In chapter 3, Pat wrote on the topics of cultivating a welcoming environment, the attributes of the welcoming home, flexibility, and forgiveness, whereas Lisa addressed confidence in God's sovereignty, goodness, and work and practicing the principles of contentment. In chapter 8, Pat developed the principles of "salt and light," while Lisa wrote on the discipleship of children and raising "world" Christians. Finally, in chapter 9 Pat identified the principles related to thriving in singleness and nourishing the single mother, and Lisa addressed content regarding childlessness, caring for widows, and responding to life's demands.

Our students would be disappointed if we wrote a book without "assignments," so each chapter contains follow-up questions or "growth projects" that encourage application of the chapter content. They were created to challenge our readers to become "doers of the word, and not hearers only" (James 1:22). It is our prayer that you will be stimulated to create a home that is a "prepared place" (see John 14:2–3) for you and your family and that it will be a "city that is set on a hill" (Matthew 5:14) for your community. Most important, however, we pray that as you explore the pages of *Becoming a Woman Who Pleases God* you will be encouraged to live out with excellence the mandate of Titus 2.

The vivacious coed nervously grasped a form as she stood at my office door and inquired, "Dr. Ennis, may I talk with you?" "Surely," I replied and invited her to have a seat in one of the rocking chairs. I moved from my desk chair and sat in the rocker opposite hers.

Classes were well under way for the semester, and this young woman was enrolled in the first of the character classes in the Home Economics Department which had as its biblical core Proverbs 31:10–31 and 1 Peter 3:1–7. As her professor, I was pleased with her attentiveness, promptness with assignments, and excellent work. I was, therefore, surprised when she stated, "I am dropping your class, and I need for you to sign this form." Knowing her academic performance, I probed for the reason. Unable to make eye contact with me, she softly responded, "I really like the class, but, well, I am not sure that I have an obligation to embrace what was written hundreds of years ago." Her speed increased and she hastily finished, "And besides, even if it is true, I'm not sure that I want to be so virtuous!"

Realizing further discussion would probably do more harm than good, I sadly accepted the form and signed my *name; as she turned to leave I extended an invitation for her to return to chat at another time—she did not respond. I closed my office door and, with a breaking heart, approached the Throne of Grace. "Dear Father," I prayed, "I just witnessed another young woman succumb to Satan's age-old lie that surely You didn't really mean that she is to take Your Word literally. Please protect her, Father, and create in her a desire to become a godly woman." It was my heartfelt prayer that she learned, before it was too late, that . . .*

THE WISE WOMAN BUILDS HER HOME

The wise woman builds her house,
But the foolish tears it down with her own hands.

PROVERBS 14:1 NASB

V*irtuous, trustworthy, energetic, physically fit, economical, unselfish, prepared, honorable, prudent, lovable,* and *God-fearing* are eleven qualities pictured by the Wise Woman of Proverbs in 31:10–31. Many believe that the woman described in this passage is simply a fantasy rather than a real woman whose life twenty-first-century Christian women are challenged to model in their own lives. However, the immutability (changelessness) of God would be in question if Proverbs 31:10–31 were not timelessly relevant. If we think that God changed His mind about one passage of Scripture, how can we be sure that He has not changed His mind about others? J. I. Packer, in

Knowing God, lists six attributes of God that are helpful to be reminded of before we study the eleven principles suggested in Proverbs 31:10–31 that help the Wise Woman build her home.

1. God's life does not change.
2. God's character does not change.
3. God's truth does not change.
4. God's ways do not change.
5. God's purposes do not change.
6. God's *Son* does not change.[1]

Since God does not change, then fellowship with Him, trust in His Word, living by faith, and embracing His principles are the same realities for twenty-first-century believers as they were for those of the Old and New Testaments. The description of the Wise Woman of Proverbs 31:10–31 is not designed to develop an inferiority complex within us—rather, it provides a biblical foundation for the creation of principles by which we, as Wise Women in progress, live our lives. While the outward historical context has changed since King Lemuel wrote Proverbs 31, the character principles have not.

❦ ❦ ❦

Martha, a college sophomore, was well-known throughout the college community for plainly speaking her mind. She appeared at my office door one afternoon with several forms in her hand, and stated, "I need to see you about changing my major to Home Economics." Since she was already a second-semester sophomore, I had the obligation to tell her that she could delay her graduation by changing majors at this point in her education. "That's all right," she replied, "Titus 2:3–5 says the younger women are to learn from the older, so I am changing my major so I can learn from you—if it takes longer, God will provide the resources for me." As she left my office I

pondered Martha's words; she was right. I enjoyed the price-
less privilege of imparting godly character to the younger
women (though at that time they didn't realize that I was not
that much older than they were), and she was to be commended
on having the strength of character to acknowledge that . . .

THE WISE WOMAN LEARNS
FROM THE WISDOM OF OTHERS

The fear of the Lord is the beginning of wisdom;
A good understanding have all those who do His commandments;
His praise endures forever.
PSALM 111:10 NASB

Biblical wisdom "is both religious and practical. Stemming from the fear of the Lord (Job 28:28; Psalm 111:10; Proverbs 1:7; 9:10), it branches out to touch all of life, as the extended commentary on wisdom in Proverbs indicates. Wisdom takes insights gleaned from the knowledge of God's way and applies them in the daily walk."[2] Scripture provides the basis for wise instruction (2 Timothy 3:16–17). Paul, in 1 Corinthians 10:6, reminds believers that "these things became our examples, to the intent that we should not lust after evil things as they [the Israelites] also lusted." Titus 2:4–5 instructs the older women to "encourage the young women to love their husbands, to love their children, to be sensible, pure, workers at home, kind, being subject to their own husbands, so that the word of God may not be dishonored" (NASB). Solomon taught his son that "fools despise wisdom and instruction" (Proverbs 1:7). Our Wise Woman possesses a heart open to learning from the experience and wisdom of others.

The MacArthur Study Bible introduces the book of "Proverbs" by stating, "The proverbs are short, pithy sayings which express timeless truth and wisdom. They arrest one's thoughts, causing the reader to reflect on how one might apply

divine principles to life situations. . . . To the Hebrew mind, wisdom was not knowledge alone, but the skill of living a godly
life as God intended man to live."[3]

ELEVEN PRINCIPLES OF THE WISE WOMAN

Many daughters have done well,
But you excel them all.
PROVERBS 31:29

Essential to us becoming Wise Women is the personal application of biblical principles that stimulate our decisions and
actions. *Principle* is defined as "an accepted or professed rule
of action or conduct."[4] Pondering the question, "What are my
specific abilities, heritage, and talents that make me unique and
determine my actions or conduct?" will determine the way we
apply the principles to our lives. Their application ultimately
determines our character—and whether we are considered Wise
Women or fools. Let's take a look at eleven principles that will
keep us away from foolish behavior.

ॐ ॐ ॐ

The afternoon sky was dark and rain was pounding against
the windows when the handsome young man entered the Home
Economics Center. He surveyed the now empty building and
paused at my office door. "Are you Dr. Ennis?" he inquired.
"I am, and how may I help you?" "Is it true that the purpose
of Home Economics at The Master's College is to build godly
women?" "Yes, it is," I replied. He probed further, "How many
students do you have in the major?" "As you know, this is the
first semester to offer Home Economics, and I have twenty
women in our introductory character course." "May I have a
list of their names?" Working diligently to maintain a straight
face, I replied, "I think if you observe the students carefully you
will be able to identify them." "You are telling me you won't

*give me their names?" was his response. "Yes, that would vio-
late their privacy." "Well, Dr. Ennis, I do understand, but you
sure would save me a lot of time if you would just give me a
list!" He thanked me for my time;* as the door closed behind
him, I thought, Now there is a young man who values a woman
who embraces . . .

PRINCIPLE ONE: THE PRINCIPLE OF VIRTUOUS

*An excellent wife, who can find? For her worth is far above
jewels.* (Proverbs 31:10 NASB)

Moral excellence, right actions, and thinking that is true,
noble, just, pure, lovely, of good report, possessing virtue, and
praiseworthy (Philippians 4:8–9) describe the *quality of being
virtuous*. Virtue is an effective power that is to fill all the
thoughts, actions, and relationships of our Wise Woman. When
integrated into her life, this quality graciously generates power
and demands respect.

Our Wise Woman establishes godly guidelines for living
according to the Scriptures and determines, through the
strength of the Holy Spirit, to abide by them (Philippians 4:13).
The Old Testament book of Ruth describes such a woman.
Ruth 3:11 is the only scriptural reference to a "virtuous"
woman and explains that Boaz knew of Ruth because of her
reputation for purity; in contrast, Rahab's reputation as a harlot followed her throughout the Scriptures (Joshua 2:1; 6:17;
Hebrews 11:31; James 2:25). Though God saved Rahab and by
His grace allowed her to be included in the messianic line
(Matthew 1:5), her reputation as a harlot lingered.

Our Wise Woman is a crown to her husband. A woman lacking in virtue causes him shame and produces suffering that is like
a painful, incurable disease (Proverbs 12:4). A woman's character prior to marriage determines her quality as a marital spouse—
thus the importance of every Christian woman's embracing virtue

at an early age. To live a life characterized by virtue should be the ambition of every Christian woman (Matthew 5:8).

PRINCIPLE TWO: THE PRINCIPLE OF TRUSTWORTHY

The heart of her husband trusts in her, and he will have no lack of gain. She does him good and not evil all the days of her life. (Proverbs 31:11–12 NASB)

The *quality of being trustworthy* is demonstrated by behaviors that lead to confidence in the honesty, integrity, reliability, justice, and loyalty of an individual. *Integrity,* the quality or state of being complete (Colossians 2:10), is demonstrated through how one handles *prosperity* because abundance tends to reveal our value system (1 Corinthians 10:1–10).

The character of our Wise Woman motivates her husband to respond with trust (Proverbs 31:11). This trustworthy lifestyle includes the nurturing of security, love, service, limits, freedom, enjoyment, faith, and encouragement. Her husband and those under her leadership are challenged to reach their full potential (Proverbs 18:22; 19:14). She understands that she has the ability to feed or starve their character and thus handles this privilege through the strength of the Holy Spirit (Galatians 5:16–26).

Our Wise Woman can live in today's world with or without a husband. My life is an example of such a woman—I am a single woman who, in the words of John MacArthur, God has kept single to allow me to serve Him most effectively (1 Corinthians 7:1–8). I am an orphan, as well, with no earthly relatives—which frees me to serve my heavenly Father without encumbrances. As I implement Psalm 37:3–4; Proverbs 3:5–6; and Jeremiah 29:11–13, my trust in my heavenly Father affirms that He is a sun and shield; He gives grace and glory, and there is *no good thing* that He withholds from me if I walk uprightly (Psalm 84:11). I use this statement frequently when people ask how I can know how to cook, sew, and maintain a well-managed home and not be married! If married, her husband's response to her character is trust. If unmarried, trustworthiness is the evaluation of those closest to her.

The fruit of trustworthiness is an understanding, encouraging, sympathetic, and tactful spirit. A trustworthy woman has the ability to retain another's confidence (Proverbs 10:19). As I counsel with women who experience difficulty in applying the *principle of trustworthy* to their speech, I encourage them to say, "Stop, please do not tell me that—I am not trustworthy!" when someone begins to share information they know they cannot refrain from passing on. I find they do not need to repeat the phrase many times before their speech habits are corrected. Stability in her life, based upon a growing relationship with the Lord rather than circumstances (James 1:5–6), the ability to resist temptation, and dependability (1 Corinthians 10:12–13) describe the trustworthy woman.

PRINCIPLE THREE: THE PRINCIPLE OF ENERGETIC

She looks for wool and flax, and works with her hands in delight. She is like merchant ships; she brings her food from afar. She rises also while it is still night and gives food to her household and portions to her maidens. She considers a field and buys it; from her earnings she plants a vineyard. . . . She stretches out her hands to the distaff, and her hands grasp the spindle. She extends her hand to the poor; And she stretches out her hands to the needy. . . . She makes linen garments and sells them, and supplies belts to the tradesmen. . . . She looks well to the ways of her household, and does not eat the bread of idleness. (Proverbs 31:13–16, 19–20, 24, 27 NASB)

Being *energetic* suggests strength or power efficiently exerted. A Wise Woman knows her assets and liabilities, develops her talents, and is a worker, not a shirker. She works willingly with her hands (the word *hand* is used six times in the twenty-two verses of Proverbs 31:10–31) and sets an example for her children by her personal and physical involvement in the management of her home. The woman described in Proverbs 31 trained her servants and then supervised the tasks they performed. She was actively involved in her well-managed household (v. 27), fabric and garment construction (vv. 13, 24), trading in the marketplace (v. 24), and ministry to others (vv. 19–20).

Application to the twenty-first century finds our Wise Woman training her children and then supervising them to efficiently use their "electrical servants." At the same time, she is involved in Christian services that complement those of her children, rather than neglecting them to perform "her ministries." Because her role model is Christ (Philippians 2:5–11), who cares much more about those under Him than they care about Him, she is not easily discouraged if others do not compliment her endeavors.

PRINCIPLE FOUR: THE PRINCIPLE OF PHYSICALLY FIT

She girds herself with strength, and makes her arms strong.
(Proverbs 31:17 NASB)

Physical fitness, that is, being in good physical condition and healthy, is enthusiastically affirmed by many twenty-first-century women. The biblical application is defined by three words: *suitable, proper,* and *fit;* they describe our Wise Woman's attitude toward the condition of her body. *Suitable* guides her in the selection of physical toning activities that prepare her to fulfill the demands of her life. *Proper* encourages her to select activities that are dictated by good judgment. *Fit* expands the definition to challenge her to possess the qualifications necessary to meet conditions, circumstances, purposes, or demands. Our Wise Woman described in Proverbs 31:17 is physically fit because of the rigorous work she does to maintain a well-run home.

A study of body mechanics helps us understand that much of the movement associated with the care of the home tones the body comparably with hours spent at the gym. First Timothy 4:8 directs Wise Women to the truth that "bodily exercise profits a little, but godliness is profitable for all things"; thus our Wise Woman will be more concerned about her character without neglecting her body tone (1 Peter 3:3–6). The guidelines that follow help our Wise Woman balance her physical and spiritual fitness.

- *She has a realistic attitude toward her personal capabilities.* God provides health boundaries to assist us in being sensible about the responsibilities we assume. Just because she can perform a skill does not mean that she should. Purposely pushing beyond safe health boundaries would be like jumping off a bridge and then praying on the way down that you won't get hurt!
- *She acknowledges that her body is the temple of the Holy Spirit; it is her responsibility to make it a fit dwelling place for Him (1 Corinthians 6:19–20).* It is a sobering thought to acknowledge that the Holy Spirit will not empower a spiritually dirty vessel.
- *She realizes that she must be healthy to perform her duties efficiently.* Applying this guideline requires the freedom from all habits that would injure her physically, mentally, or spiritually (Romans 12:1–2).
- *She understands the importance of recreation to maintain a healthy body.* Mark 6:31 and Luke 9:10 describe our Lord's sensitivity to his disciples' need for rest and privacy from their demanding ministry. Our Wise Woman will adopt our Lord's model.
- *She accepts the fact that sometimes "others can, she cannot."* It is an exercise in futility to compare her capabilities with

those of others, since each woman is "fearfully and wonderfully made" (Psalm 139:14).

- *She has a clear perspective regarding her body cycling and
wisely accommodates its ebb and flow.* The regular physical conditioning of our Wise Woman allows her to be
involved in the lives of others. She balances the care of her
home with the care of her body to avoid becoming a wor-
ried, frazzled, and defensive woman who sacrifices herself
on the altar of domesticity or physical fitness.

PRINCIPLE FIVE: THE PRINCIPLE OF ECONOMICAL

*She senses that her gain is good, her lamp does not go out
at night.* (Proverbs 31:18 NASB)

Budget and *diet*—two words that conjure up visions of eco-
nomic and nutritional deprivation. Each word, however, has
both a positive and negative definition. A budget can be established for either a high or a low income. A diet can consti-
tute a high or a low daily caloric intake. The *quality of being
economical* challenges our Wise Woman to refrain from wasting time, money, fuel, or any other resource. Application of
the principle economical insures that she operates her home
on a budget (a plan for spending) and that monthly it balances
(not too much month at the end of the money).

The Wise Woman of Proverbs 31 perceives that her mer-
chandise is good. As an accomplished seamstress and nutri-
tionist, she recognizes quality. With practiced eye, she seeks out
a bargain that reflects excellence. At the same time, her knowledge and skill allow her to make the best decision of whether
to make the purchase, pay for the service, or personally perform the task.

Most twenty-first-century women can identify with their
"lamp not going out at night" because of the impacted schedules they maintain. However, this verse does not suggest that

our Wise Woman deprives herself of sleep. Just as exercise con-tributes to a physically fit body, so sleep is necessary to a woman's mental, spiritual, and physical well-being.

Several characteristics describe our Wise Woman's attitude toward money and material possessions:

- *All resources are a gift from the Lord to be used carefully* (Deuteronomy 8:18; Acts 4:32–36; 1 Timothy 6:17–19).
- *God does not love the poor and hate the rich.* The Bible reports a number of godly individuals who were exceed-ingly wealthy—Job, Abraham, Joseph, David, Solomon, Josiah, Barnabas, Philemon, and Lydia—to name a few. He does, however, hate false gain (Proverbs 1:19), wrong motives for acquiring wealth (13:11), and a lack of com-passionate generosity among the wealthy (14:20–21; 16:19).
- *There is wisdom in Proverbs 19:17, "One who is gracious to a poor man lends to the Lord" (NASB).* The Wise Woman applies this truth to our life in her generosity to those in need.

Our Wise Woman possesses an attitude of contentment which corresponds with the New Testament teaching found in 1 Timothy 6:6–8: Godliness + contentment = great gain! Evidence that wealth is not the source of her contentment is found in her model of humility patterned after her Lord (Philip-pians 2:8; 1 Peter 5:5). She does not trust in her wealth for se-curity (Psalm 20:7; Proverbs 11:28), and is a gracious (v. 16), generous woman (31:18).

PRINCIPLE SIX: THE PRINCIPLE OF UNSELFISH

She stretches out her hands to the distaff, and her hands grasp the spindle. She extends her hand to the poor, and she stretches out her hands to the needy. (Proverbs 31:19–20 NASB)

Selfish is an adjective our Wise Woman seeks to eliminate from the list of her character qualities. By definition, it means having such regard for one's own interests and advantage that the happiness and welfare of others become of little concern. Selfishness stems from pride and is first in the list of sins most hated by God (Proverbs 6:16–19); according to Scripture, selfishness is a sin.

The body of an ancient woman mummified by the volcanic ashes of Mount Vesuvius was unearthed when the Roman city of Pompeii was excavated. Her position told a tragic story of selfishness—her feet were pointed toward the city gate, but her outreached arms and fingers were straining for something that lay behind her. The treasure for which she was grasping was a bag of pearls. Of her it was written, "Though death was hard at her heels, and life was beckoning to her beyond the city gates, she could not shake off their spell . . . but it was not the eruption of Vesuvius that made her love pearls more than life. It only froze her in this attitude of greed."[5]

Anything can fuel the flames of excessive desire and greed. If not checked, they can destroy women (Proverbs 1:19). The wealthy landowners in Isaiah's day acquired more and more houses and fields until they had a monopoly (Isaiah 5:8). But God said that they would become desolate and their lands would not produce (vv. 9–10). Wise is the woman who lives by the principle that if she is not satisfied with what she has, she will never be satisfied with what she wants.

Our Wise Woman's character is free from selfishness—she is not too busy with her own affairs to take time to assist others. The spindle and distaff—two flat, circular objects used to work textile fibers—were tools of the day. The Woman of Proverbs 31 used them to provide for her family, herself, and the less fortunate. That "she extends her hand to the poor" indicates her response to calls for help (Proverbs 31:20 NASB). Her response is both active and passive—she gives when she is asked and is sensitive to offer assistance when she is not asked. Our Wise Woman has a spiritual attitude toward helping —she is like Dorcas, who was "full of good works and charitable deeds which she did" (Acts 9:36).

Unselfishness is most clearly seen in our Wise Woman's willingness to share her time with others; time is the most precious commodity we have and the highest compliment we pay to another when we unselfishly give it. As Wise Women we are not to favor certain people (James 2:1–13), but are to place before the Lord the requests of all who desire to benefit from our wisdom. Our attitude toward selfless living should mirror the contents of this poem:

> *Lord help me live from day to day*
> *In such a self-forgetful way,*
> *That even when I kneel to pray*
> *My prayers will be for others.*
>
> *Others, Lord, yes others,*
> *Let this my motto be;*
> *Help me to live for others,*
> *That I might live like Thee.*
>
> —Author Unknown

PRINCIPLE SEVEN: THE PRINCIPLE OF PREPARED

She is not afraid of snow for her household, for all her household are clothed with scarlet. She makes a tapestry for herself; her clothing is fine linen and purple. . . . She watches over the ways of her household, and does not eat the bread of idleness. (Proverbs 31:21–22, 27)

Putting events, objects, or people in order, as well as *making suitable and receptive* are phrases that describe the *quality of preparedness in action.* Our Wise Woman demonstrates planning and foresight that equip her for unforeseen circumstances, rather than living from crisis to crisis. Besides being physically prepared, our Wise Woman knows the value of spiritual preparedness; she builds a financial reserve for financial challenges and a spiritual reserve for emotional challenges. The prophet Jeremiah refers to the person who "trusts in the Lord" as being prepared "like a tree planted by the water, that extends its roots by a stream and will not fear when the heat comes; but its leaves will be green, and it will not be anxious in a year of drought nor cease to yield fruit" (Jeremiah 17:7–8 NASB). The heat will come; the drought is certain; however, there is a lack of fear when one is prepared.

Her firm grip on scriptural priorities allows her to be prepared for the future. Charles Hummel, in his classic booklet *Tyranny of the Urgent,* urges his readers to evaluate their priorities daily:

> Sometime ago, Simba bullets killed a young man, Dr. Paul Carlson. In the providence of God his life's work was finished. Most of us will live longer and die more quietly, but when the end comes, what would give us greater joy than being sure that we have finished the work that *God* gave us to do? The grace of the Lord Jesus Christ makes this fulfillment possible. He has promised deliverance from sin and the power to serve God in the tasks of His choice. The way is clear. If we continue in the word of our Lord, we are truly his disciples. And he will free us from the tyranny of the urgent; free us to do the important, which is the will of God.[6]

The Wise Woman will refuse to allow the urgent to take the place of the important in her life.

PRINCIPLE EIGHT: THE PRINCIPLE OF HONORABLE

Strength and dignity are her clothing, and she smiles at the future. (Proverbs 31:25 NASB)

Being honorable is synonymous with having integrity and is seen in others' high regard or respect for our Wise Woman. She possesses a biblical sense of right or wrong, and her moral uprightness is apparent to all. As our Wise Woman applies the *quality of being honorable* to her life, others will note these honorable qualities.

- Her outer adorning complements her inward qualities (1 Peter 3:3–4).
- She abstains from every appearance of evil (1 Thessalonians 5:22).
- She possesses strong convictions of right and wrong (Proverbs 14:12; 16:25; Matthew 7:13–14).
- Her convictions are based upon biblical principles (Psalm 119:11, 105) rather than cultural trends.

If married, the Wise Woman's high standards of behavior make a significant contribution to her husband's position (Proverbs 12:4; 18:22; 19:14; 31:23). She functions as a helpmeet (Genesis 2:18) and determines to never be an embarrassment or a hindrance to her husband. The conduct of Job's wife (Job 2:9) and Potiphar's wife (Genesis 39) stand in stark contrast to the behavior of the woman who chooses to live an honorable lifestyle.

Our Wise Woman acquires a stable, honest reputation. Strength and honor accompany her business practices (Proverbs 31:25). Desiring to walk worthy of her calling (Ephesians 4:1–2), she leads a life that brings glory to God (1 Corinthians 10:31). Humility, unselfishness, gentleness, mildness, patience, bearing with others, and making allowances for others are characteristic of her godly behavior.

Our honorable woman has control of her body—it is presented as a living sacrifice to the Lord (Romans 12:1–2). She refuses to yield her body as an instrument to sin (Romans 6:12–13) and acknowledges that her body belongs to Christ (1 Corinthians 6:15). Realizing that her body is a temple literally inhabited by the Holy Spirit (1 Corinthians 6:15), she chooses to glorify God in her body (1 Corinthians 6:20). She becomes a student of her body so that she knows how to control it in honor (1 Thessalonians 4:4) and understands the need for accountability to the body of Christ to maintain her purity (Galatians 6:1–2; James 5:19–20).

PRINCIPLE NINE: THE PRINCIPLE OF PRUDENT

She opens her mouth in wisdom, and the teaching of kindness is on her tongue. (Proverbs 31:26 NASB)

Mothers frequently remind their children, "If you can't say something nice, don't say anything!" James 3:2, 5 teaches that "if anyone does not stumble in word, he is a perfect man, able also to bridle the whole body. . . . Even so the tongue is a little member and boasts great things. See how great a forest a little fire kindles!" The *quality of being prudent,* implying wisdom and careful consideration of consequences, especially applies to the use of our tongue. Miriam, Moses' sister (Numbers 12:1–15), serves as a graphic illustration of the impact of a sharp, complaining tongue. The entire nation of Israel was delayed for seven days because she chose to use her tongue the wrong way.

Our Wise Woman's speech exhibits good judgment and discretion (Colossians 4:6). Rather than being too aggressive or bossy, gentleness (Proverbs 15:1) and compassion characterize her words (Ecclesiastes 10:12–14). She possesses the ability to be kind, yet very firm, as well as the ability to maintain confidences—remember the question we asked about our speech when we explored the *principle of trustworthy?* (Ecclesiastes 5:2). Truthfulness is evident in her relationships with others (Ephesians 4:15), and she realizes that what she meditates upon will emerge in her speech (Psalm 19:14; Luke 6:45). Within her family relationships, she refuses to discredit her husband's character and speaks with firmness, balanced with kindness and gentleness, when disciplining her children. Desiring the description "she opens her mouth with wisdom, and on her tongue is the law of kindness" (Proverbs 31:26) to characterize her conversations, before speaking she asks . . .

- Is it kind?
- Is it necessary?
- Is it true?
- Is it gossip (sharing private information with those who are not a part of the solution)?
- Am I defending my own opinion rather than listening to the individual?

I recall finishing a class session with these questions one Friday afternoon. As I closed in prayer I asked my heavenly Father to remind everyone in the class, including the professor, to put their conversations during the weekend through the grid of the five questions.

When I returned to class on Monday, I noticed that Melaine, a generally gregarious young woman, was glumly slumped in a chair in the back row of the classroom. I approached her and inquired, "Melaine, is there something the matter?" She responded, "Yes, there is. You ruined my weekend!" Since a major assignment was not due that day, I was curious as to how I so negatively impacted her weekend. "Could you share with me how I ruined your weekend?" "Well, you know how I *love* to talk—but since I asked myself your five questions before speaking, I found that I did not have much to say. That's how you ruined my weekend!" I finished our conversation by affirming my pleasure in her choosing to apply what I was teaching her— she simply sighed as I walked to the front of the classroom.

Having implemented these standards for her speech, our Wise Woman chooses to make encouragement a part of her lifestyle because it is a spiritual concept (Hebrews 10:25). The act of encouragement inspires others with renewed courage, spirit, and hope. It affirms individuals for who they are rather than what they do. Proverbs 25:11 teaches us the value of appropriate words. A number of actions can provide encouragement to others:

- Bestowing notes and small gifts at unexpected times
- Commenting on desirable character qualities (for example, punctuality or a good attitude)
- Calling with specific, encouragement-oriented purposes
- Complimenting a job well done
- Supporting someone who is hurting
- Choosing to use confrontation in the appropriate manner (Matthew 18:15–19) rather than as a Christian way of "telling someone off"

Our Wise Woman cultivates a positive, reassuring attitude, knowing that encouragement does not thrive in a negative atmosphere. She realizes that developing the attribute takes time and does not anticipate repayment (Luke 6:30–31; 1 Timothy 6:17–19).

PRINCIPLE TEN: THE PRINCIPLE OF LOVABLE

Her children rise up and bless her, her husband also, and he praises her, saying: "Many daughters have done nobly, but you excel them all." (Proverbs 31:28–29 NASB)

The sense of kindness and generosity we should possess for others; an intense love for others, including one's husband, children, friends, and relations; and a steadfast commitment to our heavenly Father describe our Wise Woman. She displays a strong liking for others and chooses to apply the Titus 2:3–5 principle of the younger women learning from the older women in her life. Our Wise Woman is approachable by others and resists the temptation to be a "respecter of persons" (Acts 10:34 KJV; see James 2:1–13).

The portrait of our dear woman described in Proverbs 31:10–31 showed that she concentrated her domestic efforts on her family and can be seen in their evaluation of her. Her husband and children spontaneously cheer her on (Proverbs 31:27–29). Every day, when they open their eyes, they rejoice that she belongs to them. She chooses to live a consistent life as a wife and mother as this adaptation of 1 Corinthians 13 by Dianne Lorang suggests:

THE LOVE CHAPTER FOR MOTHERS

If I talk to my children about what is right and what is wrong, but I have not love, I am like a ringing doorbell or pots banging in the kitchen. And though I know what stages they will go through, and understand their growing pains, and can answer all their questions about life, and believe myself to be a devoted mother, but I have not love, I have nothing.

If I give up the fulfillment of a career to make my children's lives better, and stay up all night sewing costumes or baking cookies at short notice, but grumble about lack of sleep, I have not love and accomplish nothing.

A loving mother is patient with her children's immaturity and kind even when they are not; a loving mother is not jealous of their youth nor does she hold it over their heads whenever she has sacrificed for them.

A loving mother believes in her children; she hopes in each one's individual ability to stand out as a light in a dark world; she endures every backache and heartache to accomplish that.

A loving mother never really dies. As for home-baked bread, it will be consumed and forgotten: as for spotless floors, they will soon gather dust and heel marks. As for children, right now toys, friends and food are all-important to them. But when they grow up, it will be their mother's love that they will remember and pass on to others. In that way, she will live on.

So care, training and a loving mother reside in a home, these three, but the greatest of these is a loving mother.[7]

Having made her home her first priority, our Wise Woman works creatively with her husband (Amos 3:3; Ephesians 5:22–24; Colossians 3:8–4:1; 1 Peter 3:1–6). She knows him well enough to respect and honor him (Ephesians 5:33), as well as to be his helpmate and friend (Genesis 2:18). Training her children well by practicing child-rearing principles based on the Word of God (Deuteronomy 6:6–7; 11:18–32; Psalm 78:1–4; Proverbs 22:6; Ephesians 6:4; Colossians 3:21; 2 Timothy 3:14–17) is the focus of her life while her children are at home. An unidentified author paints a vivid picture of the importance of this training process:

Plastic Clay

I took a piece of plastic clay
And idly fashioned it one day,

And as my fingers pressed it still,
It moved and yielded to my will.

I came again when days were past—
The bit of clay was hard at last.

The form I gave it, it still bore,
But I could not change that form no more.

I took a piece of living clay
And gently formed it day by day,
And molded it with my power and art,
A young child's soft and yielding heart.

I came again when years were gone—
It was a man I looked upon;
He still that early impress wore,
And I could change him nevermore.

Finally, she sets an example for the character qualities she wishes to instill in the lives of her children, realizing that they absorb the behaviors she models (1 Corinthians 11:1; Ephesians 5:1–2).

As a spiritual mentor, I am faced with the same decisions as a mother in discerning my level of involvement in professional and ministry opportunities. I chose, on numerous occasions, to decline professional and ministry invitations to be available to the young women God gave me to mentor at both Christian Heritage and The Master's College. The limited time I have for writing is primarily focused on the yearly newsletters I prepare for my students, alumni, and other individuals interested in Home Economics from a Christian perspective. Recently I received the following note from one of my graduates in response to a newsletter:

> Dear Dr. E.,
>
> Thanks for putting the newsletter together and sending edifying materials again this year. It is such a blessing. Thanks for fighting the good fight with endurance and continuing to build up those of us who have children ahead of careers. In today's world we have made all the "wrong" choices. But in the kingdom of God, we are doing right. You continue to support this by your very edifying classes in Home Economics and newsletters. I thank God for you, Dr. E.!!
>
> Christine

Christine's unsolicited response reminded me that the most meaningful affirmation a Christian woman can receive is from those who know her best!

PRINCIPLE ELEVEN: THE PRINCIPLE OF GOD-FEARING

Charm is deceitful and beauty is vain, but a woman who fears the Lord, she shall be praised. (Proverbs 31:30 NASB)

Fearing God means a reverential trust in God, including the hatred of evil. Romans 12:9 challenges our Wise Woman: "Abhor what is evil. Cling to that which is good." The Wise Woman develops values that are based on the Word of God. As she lives out the *principle of God-fearing,* she will honor, respect, worship, and love her Lord with all her heart (Matthew 22:37). There are many practical applications of this godly lifestyle:

- An individual hunger and thirst after God (Psalm 42:1–2)
- A willingness to possess an attitude of submission to God's will and ways (James 4:7)

- A consistent evaluation of her spiritual condition (1 Corinthians 11:31–32)
- A determination to make spiritual principles a priority (Matthew 6:33)
- A refusal to slump into a monotonous devotion routine
- A focus on the strength found in the joy of the Lord (Nehemiah 8:10b)

Exercising 1 Corinthians 10 as a warning, our Wise Woman acknowledges the traps that the ancient Hebrews fell into regarding their spiritual condition:

- They craved evil things (v. 6).
- They were idolatrous (v. 7).
- They began practicing immorality (v. 8).
- They took God's goodness for granted (v. 9).
- They became cynical and negative (v. 10).

In the midst of God's best blessings, they became cool, distant, and indifferent—not suddenly, but slowly, the keen edge of enthusiasm became dull. Applying the wisdom of 1 Corinthians 10:12–13, the Wise Woman is careful to learn from the example of the disobedient and indolent Jews in Moses' time.

THE REWARD

Strength and dignity are her clothing,
And she smiles at the future. . . .
Give her the product of her hands.
And let her works praise her in the gates.
PROVERBS 31:25, 31 NASB

The reward of cultivating these eleven principles is presented in Proverbs 31:31 as our Wise Woman receives her rewards "in the gates," or the public assembly of people. She is often rewarded in this life and always in the hereafter (1 Corinthians

3:10–15, 4:1–51; 2 Corinthians 5:10; Revelation 22:12). A review of these qualities of the Wise Woman bring to mind the earthly rewards that she might receive:

VIRTUOUS

- An unobstructed relationship with her heavenly Father (Matthew 5:8).
- Blessing from the Lord and righteousness from the God of her salvation (Psalm 24:1–5).
- The assurance that her influence will never die (Proverbs 31:28; 2 Timothy 1:3–7).

TRUSTWORTHY

- Her husband trusts her (Proverbs 31:11).
- She has an honorable reputation (Proverbs 31:25).
- She has the confidence that as she walks uprightly her heavenly Father will provide grace, glory, and all the things that are good for her (Psalm 84:11).

ENERGETIC

- Her family benefits from her business endeavors (Proverbs 31:24).
- She enjoys professional and spiritual stimulation (Proverbs 27:17).
- She is exempt from reaping the fruit of slothfulness (Proverbs 19:15).

PHYSICALLY FIT

- She enjoys the tasks she undertakes to their fullest potential (Colossians 3:23).

- Her body is an appropriate dwelling place for the Holy Spirit (1 Corinthians 6:19–20).
- She avoids the type of judgment and denouncement God executed on the women of Judah (Isaiah 3:16–26).

ECONOMICAL

- She embraces a spiritual attitude toward money and material possessions (1 Timothy 6:6–8).
- She experiences the joy of generosity (1 Corinthians 9:6–8).
- She perceives that her purchases are sound choices—no guilt (Proverbs 31:18).

UNSELFISH

- She has the joy of giving to others with the right attitude (2 Corinthians 9:7).
- She is pleasing to the Lord ("lends to the Lord," Proverbs 19:17).
- She enjoys the fruit of giving to others (Acts 9:36–42).

PREPARED

- She meets the design of God's plan for her life (Jeremiah 17:7–8).
- She is an authentic role model for others (1 Corinthians 11:1).
- She is free from frustration and regret (Matthew 25:21, 23).

HONORABLE

- Her moral integrity allows her to reflect fulfillment in later life, rather than a wasted life filled with remorse and sin (2 Corinthians 9:6; Galatians 6:7–9).

- She behaves in a way that reflects her position as a daughter of God's royal family (Genesis 1:26–27).
- She has confidence that her convictions are based upon biblical principles rather than cultural trends (Psalm 119:11, 105).

PRUDENT

- People are willing to confide in her and trust her to retain their confidences (Proverbs 15:1–2).
- Others seek and follow her advice (Colossians 4:6).
- She has the privilege of encouraging and affirming others (Hebrews 10:24–25).

LOVABLE

- She enjoys a healthy, growing, love relationship with the Lord (Matthew 22:37).
- The individuals closest to her love, honor, respect, and praise her (Proverbs 31:28–29).
- She lives in such a way that she is an example for the "younger women" (Titus 2:3–5).

GOD-FEARING

- She is a positive role model because of her faith (the epistle of James in action).
- She enjoys the benefits of learning from the experiences of others (1 Corinthians 10).
- She is counted as a faithful servant (Matthew 25:21).

Realizing that her motive for cultivating these eleven principles is to glorify God (1 Corinthians 10:31), to hear her heavenly Father say, "Well done, good and faithful servant" (Matthew

25:21), and to cast her rewards (crowns) at the feet of her Savior (Revelation 4:10–11), our Wise Woman pursues her eternal crown with vigor!

A FINAL THOUGHT . . .

The inspired description of God's Wise Woman focuses on the development of what is truly permanent and noteworthy . . . the character of the woman. This chapter concludes with the scriptural blueprint for becoming a Wise Woman.

- Begin the process by becoming a new woman in Christ (Romans 3:10, 23; 5:8, 12; 6:23; 10:9–11, 13; 2 Corinthians 5:17).
- Consistently grow into conformity to His image (John 1:12).
- Actively pursue the application of biblical principles into your life (Psalm 19:7).
- Purpose to model godly character (Psalms 86; 145).
- Avoid comparing yourself with others and refuse discouragement with the growth process (Philippians 3:13–14).

It is our prayer that the remaining chapters of *Becoming a Woman Who Pleases God* as well as the "Growth Projects" will provide you with the necessary tools, and challenge you to build your home using the eleven principles introduced in this chapter as its foundation.

GROWING IN WISDOM

1. Using the format below, prepare a chart that allows you to set personal goals for the eleven principles embraced by our Wise Woman.

[YOUR NAME], WISE WOMAN IN PROGRESS		
Principle and Personal Definition	**Verse**	**Personal Goals**
Virtuous Practically wise and careful of the consequences.	Proverbs 31:30	1. Place everything read, viewed, or listened to through the grid of Philippians 4:8–9.

2. Study Jeremiah 17:7–8 in relation to your life, using specific examples that reflect drought or heat. Describe how you can be like the tree described in these verses.

3. How can you apply Proverbs 22:1 to your life?

4. Study the following Scriptures that describe God's love toward you: Jeremiah 31:3, Exodus 19:5, 1 Peter 2:9, Genesis 1:27, Isaiah 43:7, Isaiah 42:1, Deuteronomy 32:10, Isaiah 43:1, 4; Romans 5:8. Prepare a chart following the example on the following page.

GOD'S WORD TELLS ME OF HIS LOVE TOWARD ME	
Verse	Its Message to Me
Jeremiah 31:3: "The Lord has appeared of old to me, saying: 'Yes, I have loved you with an everlasting love; therefore with lovingkindness I have drawn you.'"	Because God loved me, He drew me to Himself.

5.   *Paraphrase Proverbs 31:10–31 using your life as the model.*

As a young teacher and growing Christian I had excitedly caught the vision of my church's newest project—the founding of a Christian liberal arts college. I supported it both financially and prayerfully. I even helped with some curriculum development. However, I encountered a major professional and spiritual challenge when I was asked to leave my "secure" position in the public school system to become a full-time faculty member and department chair for the new Home Economics major. I had designed the curriculum but had no intention of personally implementing it.

The curriculum idea, another of Dr. Tim LaHaye's visions, was to prepare Christian women spiritually, academically, and professionally. A new dimension of Home Economics at the college level, it would help the students to achieve the Christian character described in Colossians 2:10. After giving much prayerful consideration to my pastor's request to launch this program, I resigned my tenured teaching position in January of 1976.

Now, four years later, in January of 1980, I was experiencing significant testing about the validity of my decision. The major had grown and many young women had experienced the fulfillment of its original goals. Yet there were challenges associated with being employed in full-time Christian work that I had not anticipated. The challenges were causing me to question whether I should continue in this ministry.

The week preceding Saturday, January 26, was particularly trying. I was diligently seeking my Lord's direction about where He wanted me to minister for the next academic year; now was the time to send résumés and complete applications if I was going to relocate. Though I arrived on the college/church campus in ample time the afternoon of January 26 to attend the two o'clock wedding of one of my students, I was detained by an individual whose elongated conversation caused me to reach the church auditorium dangerously close to the start of the ceremony. My disappointment was great, realizing that I would undoubtedly have to sit in the back—if I could be seated at all. However, when I arrived at the door, one usher whispered to the other, "There she is," and much to my surprise I found myself escorted to an aisle seat close to the front!

The beautiful wedding served to remind me of the

precious privilege that I was entrusted with to fulfill the Titus 2:3–5 mandate by training the younger women. Concluding with the meaningful unity candle ceremony and the introduction of the bride and groom, the recessional began. It stopped momentarily at the pews of both parents to allow the bride to extract a beautiful red silk rose from her bouquet for her mother and new mother-in-law. "What a lovely gesture," I mused. The recession began again only to stop at my pew. Much to my amazement, the same honor was bestowed upon me to commemorate the part I had played in Susan's maturity as a godly woman. The answer to my prayer was clear—despite the seemingly insurmountable obstacles that my full-time Christian work presented, in light of eternity, they were truly nothing.

Today Kirk and Susan are serving the Lord in a pastorate in southern California. The red rose still has a prominent place on the bookshelf in my office—daily it reminds me to teach the younger women that . . .

THE WISE WOMAN ACKNOWLEDGES THE STRATEGIC POSITION OF THE HOME

And the Lord God caused a deep sleep to fall on Adam,
and he slept; and He took one of his ribs, and closed up the flesh
in its place. Then the rib which the Lord God had taken from man
He made into a woman, and He brought her to the man. And
Adam said: "This is now bone of my bones and flesh of my flesh;
She shall be called Woman, Because she was taken out of Man."
Therefore a man shall leave his father and mother and
be joined to his wife, And they shall become one flesh.

GENESIS 2:21–24

The marriage relationship was established as the first human institution in Genesis 2:24; a reminder of this priority is repeated throughout the Scriptures (Matthew 19:5; Mark 10:6–8; 1 Corinthians 6:16; Ephesians 5:28). The *principle of lovable* presented in chapter 1 challenges our Wise Woman to concentrate on making her home her first priority. Charles Swindoll says, "If you must become over involved—become over involved in your role as a character builder in the home."[1] While addressing a Home Economics class at The Master's College shortly after his mother's death, Dr. John MacArthur said that while he learned many valuable techniques and lessons from his pastor father, he learned about character from his mother. Our Wise Woman implements the *principle of lovable first* in her home, thus creating a nurturing environment that allows her husband and children to spontaneously "call her blessed" and praise her (Proverbs 31:27–29).

A PORTRAIT OF
TWENTY-FIRST-CENTURY FAMILY LIFE

But realize this, that in the last days difficult times will come.
For men will be lovers of self, lovers of money, boastful,
arrogant, revilers, disobedient to parents, ungrateful, unholy,
unloving, irreconcilable, malicious gossips, without self-control,
brutal, haters of good, treacherous, reckless, conceited, lovers of
pleasure rather than lovers of God, holding to a form of godliness,
although they have denied its power; avoid such men as these.
For among them are those who enter into households and
captivate weak women weighed down with sins,
led on by various impulses, always learning and
never able to come to the knowledge of the truth.
2 TIMOTHY 3:1–7 NASB

An understanding of the world that her family encounters daily is critical to the Wise Woman's creating a nurturing environment. Current research predicts that the nuclear family, as we know it, will soon become extinct—and Christian families are not exempt from the predictions! In 1982 Charles Swindoll presented a grim picture of the family:

It comes as a surprise to nobody that the family is under fire these days. When one national periodical did a special report on the American domestic scene, the issue was not entitled "Strengthening the Family" or "Examining the Family" or "Depending on the Family." It was "*Saving* the Family." Like the prairie bison and the sperm whale and the crane, the family is fast becoming an endangered species. For sure, it is a different scene from the quiet, heartwarming scenes of yesteryear when mom was always home, dad was the sole breadwinner, children lived predictable lives of ease and relaxation, and the lifestyle was laid back and simple.[2]

Statistics describing family life at the beginning of the twenty-first century present a somber portrait:

- Since 1950, the percentage of American children living in mother-only families has climbed from 6 percent to 24 percent in 1994.[3]
- Twenty-five percent of children will live in a stepfamily by the age of 18.[4]
- The percentage of children living with one parent has increased from 20 percent in 1980 to 27 percent in 1999.[5]
- The average number of hours per day American children spend in front of a screen of some kind is 4.35.[6]
- The likelihood of a first marriage ending in divorce is 43 percent.[7]
- First marriages last an average of 11 years; remarriages that end in divorce last 7.4 years for men and 7.1 years for women.[8]
- At least 500,000 children are physically abused in the United States each year.[9]
- Nearly two-thirds of men who beat their wives also beat their children.[10]
- According to the National Center for Education Statistics, in 1995 there were approximately 21 million infants, toddlers, and preschool children under the age of 6 in the U.S.; more than 12.9 million of those children were in childcare.[11] In 1993, 1,802 mothers who were considered "below poverty" spent 21 percent of their income on childcare.[12]

- Data recently released by the census bureau show that the median income for married-couple families in 1993 was $43,000 compared to $17,443 for female-headed families.[13]
- There have been 38,010,378 abortions since 1973.[14]
- The number of births to unmarried women increased from 1.17 million to 1.30 million between 1990 and 1999.[15]
- In 1992, 26 of every 1,000 women aged 15–44 had an abortion.[16]
- There were 2.0 million single fathers in 1997, 50 percent more than 1990.[17]
- There are 11.9 million single parents in the U.S. Thirty-eight percent of the children living in a single-parent household live with a divorced parent; 35 percent, with a never-married parent; 19 percent, with a separated parent, and 4 percent, with a widowed parent.[18]

Our Wise Woman creates a nurturing environment that will not perpetuate these statistics because she possesses a biblical perspective on the principles of leaving and cleaving, protection for "oneness," and the purposes of marriage.

LEAVING AND CLEAVING

For this reason a man shall leave his father
and his mother, and be joined to his wife;
and they shall become one flesh.
GENESIS 2:24 NASB

God created the concept of "male" and "female" (Genesis 1:27). God said that it was not good for a man to be alone, so He created a helpmate in the form of woman (2:18–22). He did not create a unisex world, but rather one where man and woman contribute different physical and emotional qualities to create a single unit of oneness. Scripture states, "They shall become one flesh" (v. 24). How do two different people become one? Research suggests that numerous factors in twenty-first-century society detract from the concept of oneness rather than strengthening it. The world promotes independence over dependence, self-preservation over self-sacrifice, leadership over servanthood—the list goes on and on. Society, in general, promotes an isolated existence where one must defend, preserve, and often fight for one's individual rights rather than consider the needs of others. Herein lies the challenge for applying the principles that Scripture gives for developing oneness in marriage. One of the keys to developing oneness in marriage is to practice the concept of "leaving and cleaving" (v. 24 KJV).

Marriage was the first human institution—God's plan for marriage is outlined in Genesis 2:18–25. The first part of God's plan for marriage involves the concept of "leaving" (v. 24). The Hebrew word used for leave is *aw-zab,* which means to loosen, relinquish, or forsake. It implies that one leaves the family and joins or creates another family. This is the first key to establishing oneness in marriage. Complete leaving must occur. Leaving one's family to establish a new union does not imply that the responsibility to honor one's parents ceases (Exodus 20:12). Scripture emphasizes the importance of children honoring their parents (Matthew 19:5; Mark 10:7–8; 1 Corinthians 6:16; Ephesians 5:31). Marriage does, however, represent the beginning of a new and primary responsibility for the man and woman. The phrase "joined together" in the marriage ceremony implies a permanence to the union of marriage. Divorce was not an option or a consideration in God's plan for marriage.

Complete leaving, therefore, is the first key to establishing the unity God intended for marriage. Leaving is practiced in several forms. The most obvious is the physical move from one home to another. When the new bride and groom establish their home together, the leaving and establishment of a new family unit occurs. However, there must be emotional leaving as well. No longer should the man or woman look to his/her parents for his/her source of love, encouragement, or counsel; his/her spouse is to fulfill that role. Does this mean that parental advice or involvement is never solicited? Absolutely not! It would be foolish to dismiss the rich resource of parental counsel, experience, and support. It simply means that the parental relationship is not elevated above the spousal relationship.

Incomplete leaving can create serious problems since it is impossible to cleave if one does not leave. Cleaving is the second key to establishing oneness (Genesis 2:24b KJV). *Daw-bak'* is the Hebrew word used for cleave and means to cling, to adhere, or to hold fast. The cleaving step can be viewed as the glue to establishing one unit; cleaving allows for bonding to occur. As one husband clings to one wife, and vice versa, a marriage unit is established.

Finally, Scripture states the two shall become "one flesh" (Genesis 2:24). While a man and a woman do not literally become one flesh, it does imply unity. MacArthur explains the concept of "one flesh":

> One flesh speaks of a complete unity of parts making a whole, e.g., one cluster, many grapes (Num. 13:23) or one God in three persons (Deut. 6:4); thus marital union was complete and whole with two people. This also implies their sexual completeness. One man and one woman constitute the pair to reproduce. The "one flesh" is primarily seen in the child born of that union, the one perfect result of the union of two. (cf. uses of this verse in Matt. 19:5, 6; Mark 10:8; 1 Cor. 6:16; and Eph. 5:31). Permanent monogamy was and continues to be God's design and law for marriage.[19]

Leaving, cleaving, and becoming one flesh is incomplete without unity. Many couples leave their original family unit and are endeavoring to cleave to one another, while struggling to maintain unity in their marriage. A primary reason for this struggle may be the failure to cultivate unity in all areas of daily life: intellectually, socially, physically, and spiritually. Many families find themselves drowning in the midst of demanding work schedules, hectic school calendars, and abundant church ministry or social opportunities. Frequently the marriage relationship simply survives daily life rather than intentionally developing unity through shared intellectual, social, or spiritual pursuits. Unity, therefore, must become an intentional and planned goal of the marriage relationship.

Genesis 2:25 describes the results of the leaving, cleaving, and becoming one flesh process: "And they were both naked, the man and his wife, and were not ashamed." Genesis 2:25 was written prior to the Fall, when evil was unknown. God's perfect plan intended for men and women to find complete gratification in the joy of their marriage union. Twenty-first-century marriages, however, are marred by sin and evil motives. A majority of married couples struggle to maintain the intimacy, security, and refuge the marriage relationship was designed to provide.

THREATS TO LEAVING AND CLEAVING

Now I exhort you, brethren, by the name of our
Lord Jesus Christ, that you all agree
and there be no divisions among you,
but you be made complete in the same
mind and in the same judgment.
1 CORINTHIANS 1:10 NASB

Many factors contribute to the struggle to apply the principle of "leaving and cleaving"—a struggle that threatens the unity and eventually the stability of the marriage. The most common challenges in this area are the four *I's: ignorance, indecision, influence, and in-laws.*[20]

IGNORANCE

Ignorance implies a lack of knowledge; within marriage, the lack of knowledge is the ignorance of God's Word and His design for the organizational structure of marriage. Scripture is definitive about the organizational structure God intended for the family (Genesis 2:18–25; 3:16–21; Ephesians 5:22–33; 6:1–4; Colossians 3:18–21). God designed the Lord Jesus Christ to be the "Head" of the family. All family members are to submit to and seek to serve Christ as their Lord on a daily basis. The husband is to submit to Christ as his sovereign Lord and then function as the "head" of his wife. He is also the chief authority over any children. He is dependent upon and responsible to God to ensure the family needs are met in all areas: physical, spiritual, and emotional.

The wife is the partner and helpmate who is to willingly submit to the leadership and authority of the husband. She derives her authority over her children through her husband. Within the family unit, she is primarily concerned with the needs of her husband, children, and home. The children are a product of the home and maintain no authority. The family's full potential is realized in the implementation of this organizational structure. Many couples are ignorant of God's design for the family and are therefore not applying God's principles for the organizational structure of the family. This significantly hinders the leaving and cleaving process.

INDECISION

Indecision is the second threat to marital unity and is manifested by failing to leave the original family unit. Indecision implies the matter is not settled; a conclusion or choice has not been made. This vacillation or lack of commitment to begin the new union significantly hinders the secure establishment of an independent family unit. Indecision is especially challenging for women desiring to submit to their husbands. Without deciding to transfer their primary authority from father to husband, they place themselves in the precarious situation of having two authorities in their lives. This may not seem like a challenge until the two authorities have differing views on issues or give differing advice. For men, the indecision may manifest itself in continuing to rely on parental support rather than assuming the leadership of his wife and home. However the indecision is evidenced, it is critical that both the man and the woman decide to implement the organizational structure God designed for the family unit.

INFLUENCE

The third threat to marital unity is influence. Synonyms for *influence* include *sway, authority, control,* or *power.* Influences on a marriage relationship generate from many sources. It is important to evaluate what factors are exercising control in your marriage: secular agendas, personal fears, or your family heritage. All of these can influence and either encourage or threaten your marital unity. Influence can be a positive or negative factor; it can become a negative factor if the influence fails to encourage biblical attitudes or actions. Influencing factors must encourage the couple to follow the organizational structure God intended for the family unit.

IN-LAWS OR PARENTS

A final threat to marital unity can be in-laws or parents. Many parents are not willing to cooperate with the leaving and cleaving process. Most are motivated out of a genuine love for their child and a desire to maintain the relationship they have enjoyed with their child. However, fear, a desire to maintain control, or a lack of trust in the new partner can significantly hinder their child's success in establishing the new family unit. Parents cause problems by criticizing the new son or daughter-in-law, comparing family practices ("we didn't do it that way"), possessing unrealistic expectations for the attention or time of their child, giving unwanted counsel, or exercising control through the use of money or some other method/mode of influence. Parents should be aware of the potential obstacle they may become for their children if they are unwilling to allow their child to leave and cleave to his/her spouse.

PROTECTION FOR "ONENESS"

Make my joy complete by being
of the same mind, maintaining
the same love, united in spirit,
intent on one purpose.
PHILIPPIANS 2:2 NASB

Couples are able to protect and maintain the "oneness" that God intended for marriage. The first and most obvious step is to know God's Word. "His divine power has given to us all things that pertain to life and godliness, through the knowledge of Him" (2 Peter 1:3). The Wise Woman has the power to develop strong marriage "oneness" if His truths are implemented. It is critical that couples understand the leaving and cleaving process (Genesis 2:18–25 KJV), God's organizational plan for the family (Colossians 3:18–21), and the roles and responsibilities for all family members (Ephesians 5:22–6:4).

COMMUNICATION

Developing oneness in marriage results when couples practice mature love. Mature love is based on communication and commitment. *Communication* is defined as "the giving or exchanging of information or news."[21] The first component of communication is simply taking the time to exchange information and discussing all areas: family calendar, finances, future goals, personal feelings, and parental issues. For many couples, communication breaks down at this basic level because they do not invest the time necessary to discuss and exchange information on fundamental family issues.

Meaningful communication also involves listening. As most communication texts explain, talking is not necessarily productive communication. Productive communication involves listening to the level of understanding. Therefore, learn how to listen by maintaining eye contact, creating a conducive environment for communication (no distractions such as TV or loud noises), asking questions to clarify or gain further insight, and when appropriate, using summary statements to ensure the conversation is accurately understood. Couples need to schedule time to communicate, since it rarely happens spontaneously in the midst of busy routines. A date night with your spouse, reading books together, or the development of a list of topics to discuss provide opportunities for unhurried communication. Whatever the means or method, communication must be intentionally pursued.

Another component of good communication, often not addressed in this context, is the importance of controlling your thoughts (Philippians 4:8). Scripture is filled with instruction about controlling the thoughts; the mind must be renewed (Romans 12:2). Renewing of the mind occurs when the Holy Spirit is allowed to change one's thinking (Psalm 119:11; Colossians 1:18; 3:10). MacArthur explains the renewal of the mind as a "kind of transformation [that] can occur only as the Holy Spirit changes our thinking through consistent study and meditation of Scripture. . . . The renewed mind is one saturated with and controlled by the Word of God."[22] If the mind is not renewed, conversations transpire in the thoughts that can lead to escalated emotions including anger, worry, or guilt. The Wise Woman refuses what Norman Wright calls "inner conversations or self-talk." Wright explains this concept by stating:

> Self-talk is the message you tell yourself, the words you tell yourself about yourself, your spouse, your experiences, the past, the future, God. It is a set of evaluating thoughts about facts and events that happen to you. . . . Your expressions of anger, ways of showing love, how you handle conflict are motivated by conscious and subconscious self-talk . . . most people believe that outside events, other people, and circumstances determine their emotions, behaviors, and verbal responses. Actually however, your thoughts are the source. What you think about these things and about people will determine the emotions you feel and the behaviors and verbal responses you express.[23]

Thoughts are to be controlled; a choice to think on what we know to be true needs to be made (Philippians 4:8). The Wise Woman fills her thoughts with scriptural truths so that her attitudes and actions are controlled by the saturation of the Word of God.

COMMITMENT

Mature love is also based on commitment. *Commitment* is defined as an agreement or a pledge. A commitment implies that one is obligated in some manner. In the case of marriage, one pledges this commitment or obligation in the wedding vows before God and man. Deliberate actions must be taken to ensure the commitment made in the wedding vows is not only maintained but also strengthened over the years.

A simple method for strengthening commitment in a marriage is to "touch" each other daily. Here are some ways the concept of touch can be practiced:

1. *Physical touch.* The most obvious form of touch is the physical component. Physical touch is an important part of any strong marriage. Physical touch should be experienced not only in the form of healthy sexual relationships, but also in the form of daily physical contact such as hand holding, giving hugs, or just sitting close on the couch. The lack of physical touch is often an indicator that there is a problem within the marriage.

2. *Intellectual touch.* Intellectual or mental touch involves cultivating agreement through discussion, study, and decision-making concerning the important issues directly influencing your lives, for example, cultivating intellectual agreement on how to handle the finances or discipline the children. Setting goals for the family and then working together to achieve them can often develop intellectual touch. This helps to build the "oneness" in marriage.

3. *Emotional touch.* Emotional intimacy is developed when marriage partners develop sensitivity to the needs, feelings, and fears of their spouse. This concept is illustrated in 1 Peter 3:7, where husbands are admonished to "dwell with [their wives] with understanding." It suggests that both the husband and wife put the needs of their spouse ahead of their own.

4. *Spiritual touch.* Spiritual touch allows the Word of God to shape ideas, outlooks, attitudes, and actions of the couple as a unit. Human reason should never replace divine instruction (Isaiah 55:8). It is important that couples share Bible study, prayer, local church involvement, and ministry opportunities as a couple.

LOVE FOR IN-LAWS

Finally, couples striving to maintain oneness and unity must establish a plan that will allow them to love their in-laws and include them appropriately in their new family unit. Here are some areas to discuss:

1. The appropriate amount and type of contact.
2. Strategy to handle family holidays and vacations.
3. Identification of parental needs (for example, a mom who calls every day may be very lonely).
4. Methods for actively seeking parental advice and support.
5. Means of communicating love, respect, and concern for parental well-being.

Couples should seek to maintain positive relationships with both sides of the family. It is not uncommon that one will be easier to maintain than the other. For example, one side may live geographically closer. Both partners need to sense a commitment by their spouse to relate to their in-laws. Biblical principles should be practiced in all relationships but are especially important to practice with in-laws in order to maintain healthy parental relationships after marriage. Relational patterns to embrace include the pursuit of peace, forgiveness, kindness, humility, and patience (Matthew 5:9; Romans 12:18; Ephesians 4:31–32; Hebrews 12:14–15).

THE PURPOSES OF MARRIAGE

Wives, be subject to your own husbands,
as to the Lord. For the husband is the head
of the wife, as Christ also is the head
of the church, He Himself being the Savior of the body.
EPHESIANS 5:22–23 NASB

Most women, whether they will readily admit it or not, desire to be married; many young girls have dreamed about the white dress and handsome groom since their earliest childhood.

Even those with career or education goals usually say that someday they would like to be married. As women mature, the childhood dreams may grow into the desire for genuine affection, companionship, security, and the desire to bear children and to nurture a family. Marriage becomes the primary means for accomplishing her heart's desires.

The secular world cultivates these desires by vigorous marketing. The world sets the trends for every detail—the wedding-party apparel, the ceremony order, the cake, and even the etiquette requirements for gifts and bill paying. The tourist industry participates by marketing honeymoon packages! Given the influence of secular input, how should the Wise Woman view the wedding ceremony and the institution of marriage? Wilson says: "Christians need to examine each aspect of the wedding from a Biblical standpoint. . . . Christians more than all people should understand what a wedding is all about . . . we understand covenantal headship and the blessing of marriage and children."[24] What is the purpose of marriage from a biblical perspective? As previously discussed, the marriage relationship was the first human institution established by God (Genesis 2:24). This permanent relationship was complete and whole with one man and one woman becoming one flesh. What were God's intended purposes for marriage? Why is marriage important to God?

THE PRIMARY REASON MARRIAGE IS SIGNIFICANT TO GOD

The primary reason marriage is significant to God is because it is part of His ordained plan to provide the world with a picture of His love for men and women. The marriage relationship is an earthly picture of Christ's love for His church. His love far surpasses any earthly love anyone has given or received because it is perfect, sacrificial, unconditional, and eternal. The picture of marriage reminds the world's people that God loves them perfectly. While married partners do not always demonstrate perfect love to one another, beginning with the marriage covenant they purpose to mature in their understanding of God's love and their ability to demonstrate that love toward their partner. Marriage becomes the primary means for married couples to demonstrate their love for God. Wilson states: "The wedding ceremony is not an end in itself. In fact, marriage is not an end in itself. Marriage is a means of serving and glorifying God. Young women who view marriage as their chief goal are turning the wedding and the married state into an idol. God planned for marriage to be a blessed state of mutual service to Him."[25]

God established marriage as a covenant, not a contract (Malachi 2:14; Proverbs 2:16–17). It is important to understand the difference between these two. Three important differences exist:

1. A *covenant* is based on trust between parties. A *contract* is based on distrust.
2. A *covenant* is based on unlimited responsibility. A *contract* is based on limited liability.
3. A *covenant* cannot be broken if new circumstances occur. A *contract* can be voided by mutual consent.[26]

Therefore, the marriage covenant between a man and a woman is a comprehensive and permanent commitment. This type of marriage covenant was ordained by God to provide believers with a picture of Christ's love and relationship to His church (Ephesians 5:22–33; Revelation 21:2, 9). Research by the *Radio Bible Class* explains marriage as a picture of Christ's relationship to the church by stating:

God's expectation is that husbands and wives will develop an en-during love by keeping their eyes on the "marriage" between Christ and His church (2 Corinthians 11:2). After urging both husbands and wives to see their distinct roles defined by the re-lationship between Christ and the church, the apostle Paul wrote: "For we are members of His body, of His flesh and of His bones. 'For this reason a man shall leave his father and mother and be joined to his wife, and the two shall become one flesh.' This is a great mystery, but I speak concerning Christ and the church" (Ephesians 5:30–32). These expectations of God offer great promise for a marriage. They are expectations that lift us above ourselves, and call from us the kind of love that has its source in God. These expectations form a basis for the covenant that is at the heart of marriage.[27]

The Wise Woman guards her marriage covenant. To mar the picture of Christ and His church by unfaithfulness, divorce, or animosity toward the union distorts the wonderful picture of Christ's abiding and faithful love for His bride, the church. If the Wise Woman embraces the purpose of marriage as mod-eling Christ's relationship to His church, her entire perspec-tive on the marriage relationship will undoubtedly change. She is motivated to live and love as Christ loves His church. She de-sires to respond to her husband's leadership and headship as the bride-church responds to Christ. She willingly submits and gives herself to her husband, thus modeling the church's re-sponse to Christ's headship.

Embracing the concept of modeling the relationship be-tween Christ and the church can result in both partners pur-suing Christlikeness—the marriage relationship stimulates spiritual growth. Marriage becomes a tool to developing Chris-tian character for the Wise Woman. Gary Thomas states:

To spiritually benefit from marriage, we have to be honest. We have to look at our disappointments, own up to our ugly attitudes, and confront our selfishness. We also have to rid ourselves of the notion that the difficulties of marriage can be overcome if we simply pray harder or learn a few simple principles. Most of us have discovered that these "simple steps" work only on a superficial level. Why is this? Because there's a deeper question that needs to be addressed beyond how we can "improve" our marriage: What if God didn't design marriage to be "easier"? What if God had an end in mind that went beyond our happiness, our comfort, and our desire to be infatuated and happy as if the world were a perfect place? What if God designed marriage to make us holy more than to make us happy? . . . Your marriage is more than a sacred covenant with another person, it is a spiritual discipline designed to help you know God better, trust him more fully, and love him more deeply.[28]

There are few life situations that test true Christianity more than the intimacy of the marriage relationship. Due to the close nature of the marriage relationship, sins of selfishness, pride, laziness, and impatience are readily exposed on a daily basis. The apostle Paul vividly describes the natural tendencies of men in 2 Timothy 3:1–13 when he describes sinful men as selfish, arrogant, and unloving. These tendencies are superimposed on the marriage relationship, thus testing Christian character in the areas of sacrificial love, respect, submission, forgiveness, and perseverance. Living together in unity with her husband requires a Woman of Wisdom to embrace biblical means of resolving conflict and demonstrating Christian love. Ralph P. Martin says:

Christian love . . . should have a controlling influence on character and everyday living. Our life with those closest to us in the family circle is subjected to strains and stresses which we can easily brush off in less personal relationships in the outside world. How we act in the intimacy of the home and marriage circle is a true indication of the quality of our love as Christians. In a strange quirk of human behavior we can often injure thoughtlessly those we love the most.[29]

The Wise Woman understands that as she strives to model Christ's relationship to His church she will be required to mature her Christian character. She will subsequently encounter opportunities to demonstrate that character in her marriage relationship, which ultimately allows her to fulfill God's intended purpose for her marriage—the modeling of Christ and His relationship with His bride-church. Both husbands and wives must pursue love as defined in Ephesians 5:25–30 . . . a sacrificial, purifying, and steadfast love.

SECONDARY PURPOSES OR BLESSINGS OF MARRIAGE

Once the Wise Woman embraces God's primary purpose for marriage, she encounters numerous secondary purposes or blessings of a Christ-honoring relationship. Many women have the tendency to pursue these secondary purposes over God's primary purpose. While secondary purposes are good and worthy of pursuit, they should be viewed as blessings resulting from God's primary purpose for marriage—that of modeling Christ's love for his church through the development of Christian character. Secondary purposes for marriage could include:

1. *Companionship.* The affection, love, and true companionship which grow out of a oneness of spirit as each partner models Christ's unconditional love (Amos 3:3).
2. *Enjoyment.* The physical relationship is a reflection of the loyalty and affection shared among marriage partners who have become "one flesh" (Hebrews 13:4).

3. *Fruitfulness*. The blessing of children in a marriage relationship allows that relationship to reproduce itself physically. It is an example of the "oneness" that results in a marriage (Genesis 1:28; 1 Peter 3:7).

4. *Protection*. The husband protects the wife by laying down his life for her (Ephesians 5:25). The wife is to protect the home (Titus 2:4–5) and the parents together protect their children to raise up a godly seed (Malachi 2:15; Psalm 112:1–2).[30]

When secondary purposes for marriage are placed above the primary purpose, discontentment, fearfulness, and disillusionment often result. For example, the woman who has made the primary purpose of marriage fruitfulness will be devastated and unfulfilled if she is unable to bear children of her own. A woman who has made companionship or enjoyment her primary purpose of marriage will desire fulfillment through other relationships or outlets if her husband does not fully meet her every need. The woman who desires security and protection may feel fearful or insecure when finances are constrained and resources limited. Maintaining a godly perspective of the purpose of marriage provides the foundation for a successful marriage relationship. Marriage becomes a spiritual endeavor rather than being dependent on financial status, bearing children, or securing a specific employment. Being able to fulfill God's intended pattern and purpose for marriage should motivate Wise Women to develop Christlike character.

A FINAL THOUGHT . . .

A recent conversation with my husband provides us with an appropriate final thought. He said, "God intended for the marriage relationship to be the hallmark of a Christian home. The love relationship between husband and wife should provide the clearest picture of Christ's perfect love for believers. The model it provides to children, the church, and the world should effectively draw others to the love of Christ. Its ability to model the characteristics of unconditional acceptance, intimacy, forgiveness, and trust makes the marriage relationship a powerful picture of biblical love."

GROWING IN THE ABILITY TO ACKNOWLEDGE THE STRATEGIC POSITION OF THE HOME

1. *Evaluate with your spouse the four threats to "leaving and cleaving"* (ignorance, indecision, influence, *and* in-laws) *to see if there are areas needing change in your marriage. Develop strategies to address the threats.*

2. *For married women, think of ways to practice the four areas of "touch" daily.*

3. *Christians are consistently instructed, "It is more important to be the right person than to find the right person." A marriage must have two complete people to ensure a happy relationship. The lives of Boaz and Ruth give us a biblical example to emulate in courtship and family living. Read the book of Ruth and develop a chart that compares Ruth's personal qualities with that of the Wise Woman of Proverbs 31:10–31. Use a chart like the one below to answer this question.*

RUTH		THE WISE WOMAN	
Verse	Quality	Verse	Quality

4. *A part of marriage preparation is to be successful in
each position the Lord provides one with. Let's look at
Ruth's pattern of behavior to determine why Boaz called
her "a woman of excellence" (Ruth 3:11 NASB). Ruth's pattern of behavior falls into four categories:*

> a. *Her commitment to Naomi*
> b. *Her servant actions*
> c. *Her willingness to wait on God's direction and
> allowing Him to speak through one having au-
> thority over her*
> d. *Her reward*

*Identify examples for each category by listing scriptural
references and describing Ruth's behavior.*

5. *Describe why you think that Boaz called Ruth "a
woman of excellence" (Ruth 3:11 NASB). What personal
goals will you set to allow others to describe you as "a
woman of excellence" (regardless of your current marital
status)?*

The candlelight cast a halo-like effect on the couple as Pastor LaHaye pronounced them husband and wife, offered a tender prayer, and introduced "Mr. and Mrs. —." The guests were then invited to attend the reception in the church's social hall. As a young Christian woman, I was certain that it was simply a matter of time before it would be my turn to be the bride; in fact, I was quite confident that I also knew who would be the groom!

During the reception, Pastor LaHaye caught my eye from across the room; I smiled and continued my conversation, noticing out of the corner of my eye that he appeared to be making his way toward me. Sure enough, he was soon at my side; being a man who wastes no time in stating his purpose, he opened his conversation with, "I prayed about you all the way back from Chicago!" I knew that the purpose of his trip to Chicago was attending the pastors' conference of a well-known speaker who spoke on character issues. My melancholy temperament immediately caused my emotions to plummet as I thought, What is so deficient in my personality that I needed prayer from Chicago to San Diego? *He, sensing my discomfort, immediately followed his statement with, "Oh, you are fine—but I am convinced that we need to train women to be godly women at Christian Heritage College, and* you are just the person to do it!" (He knew that my academic training was in Home Economics and that I was a Home Economics teacher in the San Diego Unified School District.)

Quite frankly, a career change was the last thing on my mind at the moment, so I graciously thanked him and reminded him of my opportunity to be "salt and light" in the public school system. He looked me square in the eye and told me that he would pray for me. As we concluded our conversation, deep in my heart I knew that it had irrevocably changed the course of my life—if I was truly serious about embracing God's plan for me.

As the weeks passed, my "potential groom" asked the "big" question—I responded with an affirmative answer. Though happy externally, nagging doubts assailed me internally. These were magnified when, on a Sunday evening after Pastor LaHaye finished preaching five sermons, my fiancé suggested that we tell him of our engagement. He announced to the pastor, "Pat and I are engaged!" I was ready to ask, "Will you perform the ceremony?" when he bluntly stated, "You have to be kidding me!"—not exactly the affirmation I was seeking from my pastor! We quickly concluded our conversation and my emotions hit rock-bottom.

This time they did not rebound, and after several days my fiancé strongly urged me to make an appointment to talk with Pastor LaHaye. He was a busy man, and I felt my chances of seeing him were slim. As if it were yesterday, I recall sitting in the faculty lounge, dialing the church office and thinking, If I cannot schedule an appointment quickly, I won't go. *When I presented my request to his secretary, her response was, "How about tomorrow afternoon?"*

He was waiting for me at his study door and greeted me with, "Had you not scheduled an appointment with me, I was going to call you." We talked for forty-five minutes, and he affirmed that my hesitancy to marry my fiancé was well-founded. Once the tears were dried, he suggested a "project" to assist me in renewing my mind. That project, as you might have guessed, was to develop a college-level Home Economics program with character development as its core. This time I was more receptive to his suggestion! Almost thirty years have passed since that life-changing conversation; every day has not been perfect, and there are times that I have had to fight Satan's lie that I would have been better off to have consummated that marriage relationship. However, as I matured in my relationship with my loving heavenly Father, I learned that . . .

THREE

THE WISE WOMAN DEVELOPS A HEART OF CONTENTMENT

Let not your heart be troubled; you believe in God,
believe also in Me.
In My Father's house are many mansions;
if it were not so, I would have told you.
I go to prepare a place for you.
And if I go and prepare a place for you,
I will come again and receive you to Myself;
that where I am, there you may be also.

JOHN 14:1–3

Two Wise Woman principles, *trustworthy* and *economical*, contribute to the development of a heart of contentment; the *principle of trustworthy* is evident as our Wise Woman is satisfied with her marital status, while her application of the *principle of economical* is seen in her biblical attitude toward money and material possessions. Drawn from the Greek word *arkeō*, contentment primarily signifies sufficiency or satisfaction. Scripture teaches that godliness with contentment is great gain (Psalm 37:16; 1 Timothy 6:6), God's promises should lead to contentment (Hebrews 13:5), and those who seek contentment from money are never satisfied (Ecclesiastes 5:10). Believers are instructed to exhibit contentment in their callings (1 Corinthians 7:20), with their wages (Luke 3:14), with their possessions (Hebrews 13:5), and with the food and raiment they have (1 Timothy 6:8). Biblically, contentment is exemplified in the lives of

- *Barzillai,* who chose to live out his remaining years in his own home instead of accepting David's offer to reside in Jerusalem as his guest (2 Samuel 19:33–37).
- *The Shunammite Woman,* who did not request anything in return for her care of Elisha (2 Kings 4:13).
- *David,* who focused on God's blessings (Psalm 16:6).
- *Agur,* who sought his sufficiency in the Lord (Proverbs 30:8–9).
- *Paul,* who gained independence from any need for help (Philippians 4:11, 12).

Our Wise Woman develops a heart of contentment by cultivating a welcoming home environment, embracing flexibility and forgiveness, and possessing confidence in God's sovereignty.

CULTIVATING A WELCOMING ENVIRONMENT

You are the salt of the earth; but if the salt has become tasteless,
how can it be made salty again? It is no longer good for anything,
except to be thrown out and trampled under foot by men.
You are the light of the world. A city set on a hill cannot be hidden;
nor does anyone light a lamp and put it under a basket,
but on the lampstand, and it gives light to all who are in the house.
Let your light shine before men in such a way that they may see
your good works, and glorify your Father who is in heaven.
MATTHEW 5:13–16 NASB

The word *welcome* suggests that someone's arrival provides pleasure and is anticipated. Our Wise Woman understands the strategic importance of a welcoming home environment and carefully prepares her home so that those entering it perceive that their arrival is anticipated.

As chapter 2 described, Genesis 2:24 states that the home was the first human institution established by God. In her "Enriched Living" seminars Verna Birkey presents principles that are to characterize the welcoming environment:

- God designed the home to provide the joy, happiness, and satisfaction that every human being longs for and needs.
- The home is the place for each to be supremely happy—whether as a child, a wife, or a husband.
- Apart from your personal relationship to God, there is nothing that should afford you more happiness than your family life.
- For maximum benefit to the individuals, the family life must become more and more what God wants it to be.
- A dwelling place is a place where one looks forward to going. It should be a place of order, but not a showplace. This is important for our emotional and social well-being.
- It's a place where you can bring your friends—a "home base."
- It's where you feel safe and at ease from the conflicts and stress of the world "out there."
- It's a place where you sense you belong because things and people there belong to you.
- It's the place where individual family members acquire an earthly concept of what heaven will be like.
- It should be a place where harmony reigns; some individuals can't wait to get home . . . others can't wait to leave.[1]

A sobering question for the Wise Woman is "How many of these principles describe your home?"

ATTRIBUTES OF THE WELCOMING HOME

Be gracious to me, O God, be gracious to me,
For my soul takes refuge in You;
And in the shadow of Your wings I will take refuge,
Until destruction passes by.
PSALM 57:1 NASB

The Wise Woman's home is a place of refuge. *Refuge,* by definition, means a "shelter or protection from danger, trouble, etc.; anything to which one has recourse for aid, relief or escape."[2] Scripture is filled with illustrations of refuges provided by God; these offer a model for the Wise Woman:

- Numbers 35:6, 11–15 describes the provision made for a place of refuge for those who had done wrong.
- Numbers 35:25–28 teaches that individuals are safe in the place of refuge so long as they stay there.
- Exodus 19:4 and Deuteronomy 32:11 portray God as a bird sheltering the young and fragile with her wings (Psalms 17:8; 36:7; 57:1; 61:4; 63:7; 91:1–4).
- 2 Samuel 22:3 describes a refuge as a stronghold—a secure, lofty retreat that the enemy finds inaccessible. Biblically, the Lord is the refuge of His chosen ones; they are secure from all hostile attacks. Likewise, the welcoming home is a place where those who belong there are safe from the hostility of the world. Excerpts from an article by Steve Goodier, "Three Messages of Strong Families," contain timely truth for our Wise Woman:

At times, families may need some space. They also need togetherness —lots of it. And those of us who live in families realize that our family is far from perfect, even on the best of days. But perfection is not required for a strong family life.

What is required, according to family expert Nick Stinnett (*USA Today,* 1-29-86) are three basics. "When you have a strong family life," he said, "you receive the message that you are loved, that you are cared for, that you are important. The positive intake of love and affection and respect . . . gives you inner resources to deal with life more successfully."

Love, affections and respect—a dynamic trio in any strong family. Where there is love there is a place of safety and security. Where there is affection there is a place of warmth. And where there is respect there is a place where the mind and spirit can flourish.

Not all of us live in family groups. But we probably came from families and there just may be a family in our future.[3]

A simple inspiration is helpful too: Being happy doesn't mean everything's perfect; it means you have decided to see beyond the imperfections.

A foundational principle of Verna Birkey's seminar is that home is to be a "prepared place."[4] Building on the teaching of John 14:2–3, the home is to be the earthly model of the heavenly pattern. Matthew 5:13–16 challenges believers concerning their lives and homes: "A city that is set on a hill cannot be hidden." The welcoming home will provide an environment that fosters growth in many ways:

- Individual growth and expansion of one's thinking abilities (Proverbs 27:17)
- Development of personal abilities (Romans 12:6)
- Assumption of responsibilities (Philippians 2:14)
- Appreciation and respect of all family members (1 Peter 3:8–9)
- Recognition for personal accomplishments (Philippians 2:3)
- Forgiveness of thoughtless actions (Colossians 3:12–13)

- Sympathetic support and understanding during times of failure or discouragement (Ephesians 4:32)
- Correction, admonition, and instruction in righteousness (Proverbs 23:13)
- Listening with concern and understanding (James 3:17)
- The modeling of the Titus 2:3–5 principles

Henri Nouwen offers a description of such a home:

The home, the intimate place, the place of true belonging, is therefore not a place made by human hands. It is fashioned for us by God, who came to pitch his tent among us, invite us to his place, and prepare a room for us in his own house.

Words for "home" are often used in the Old and New Testaments. The Psalms are filled with a yearning to dwell in the house of God, to take refuge under God's wings, and to find protection in God's holy temple; they praise God's holy place, God's wonderful tent, God's firm refuge. We might even say that "to dwell in God's house" summarizes all the aspirations expressed in these inspired prayers. It is therefore highly significant that St. John describes Jesus as the Word of God pitching his tent among us (John 1:14). He not only tells us that Jesus invites him and his brother Andrew to stay in his home (John 1:38–39), but he also shows how Jesus gradually reveals that he himself is the new temple (John 2:19) and the new refuge (Matthew 11:28). This is most fully expressed in the farewell address, where Jesus reveals himself as the new home: "Make your home in me, as I make mine in you" (John 15:4).[5]

The Wise Woman acknowledges that her attitude sets the tone for the home. In the words of Dr. John MacArthur, "If Mama ain't happy, ain't nobody happy!"[6] Proverbs 4:20–27 teaches, "Keep your heart with all diligence, for out of it spring the issues of life." The woman's inner life determines how she acts. Here are some questions the Wise Woman may ask herself as she thinks through how to respond biblically to circumstances:

- "How will I respond to unforeseen circumstances?" (Philippians 4:6–7)
- "Will I trust God or doubt Him?" (Proverbs 3:5–6)
- "Will I trust with increasing grace, patience, and love?" (Proverbs 11:16; Galatians 5:22–26)
- "Will I respond with pride, greed, or bitterness?" (Proverbs 6:16–19; 15:27; Ephesians 4:31; Hebrews 12:14–17)
- "Will I give attention to my words?" (Proverbs 16:24; Ecclesiastes 5:2)
- "Will I keep listening?" (1 Kings 19:11–12)
- "Will I keep God's words before me?" (Psalm 119:11)
- "Will I keep looking straight ahead?" (Genesis 19:12–27)
- "Will I keep His words in the middle of my heart?" (Psalm 37:30–31)
- Will I think about what I am doing?" (Proverbs 12:15; 14:12)
- "Will I remove myself from evil?" (Psalm 34:11–14)

Consistently asking these questions and purposing to respond biblically will assist you—a Wise Woman in progress—in promoting an attitude of contentment in your heart.

MAINTAINING A DILIGENT HEART

Watch over your heart with all diligence,
For from it flow the springs of life.
PROVERBS 4:23 NASB

A diligent heart is maintained by choosing to integrate thoughts that are noble, just, pure, lovely, and of good report (Philippians 4:8–9). *Meditation,* according to *The MacArthur Study Bible,* is "to read with thoughtfulness, to linger over

God's Word."[7] John MacArthur's notes on Psalm 1:2 observe
that the spiritually "happy" woman is characterized by the
"consistent contemplation and internalization of God's Word
for ethical direction and obedience."[8] Reading thoughtfully and
lingering over "The Wise Woman's Meditation Alphabet,"
along with its companion verses, will provide you with spiritual thoughts for keeping your "heart with all diligence."

THE WISE WOMAN'S MEDITATION ALPHABET

A Attitude sets the tone of your home environment. Keep
yours positive—focus on Philippians 4:8–9.

B Beauty . . . maintain careful grooming habits—even
when you don't feel like it. Do consider 1 Peter 3:1–6.

C Cook . . . creative meals within your budget! (Proverbs
31:15).

D Diligent . . . apply enthusiasm to your role as a Home
Manager! Allow Proverbs 4:23 to guide you.

E Everything . . . give thanks for all situations. Consistently
apply 1 Thessalonians 5:15–22.

F Festive Occasions . . . build an album of precious memories in your home by establishing traditions! Implement
the practice of "memorial stones" (Joshua 4:4–7).

G God . . . keep Him as the head of your household to ensure that your home is a welcoming environment! (John
14:3).

H Happy . . . apply Proverbs 3:13. Find wisdom and gain
understanding to acquire consistent happiness.

I Imagination . . . use your God-given gifts (1 Corinthians
12:1–31) to their fullest extent in your home.

J Joyful thoughts . . . look for a blessing in every situation.
Remember there are no problems, just challenges
(Nehemiah 8:10)!

K Kindness . . . treat others in your home as you want to be treated. Strive to model Dorcas's reputation in Acts 9:36.

L   Love as Christ loves. Purpose to memorize and practice 1 Corinthians 13!

M   Manners . . . conduct yourself in such a way that you stimulate others' *best* responses—implement 1 Peter 1:13–16. Consider the truth of Proverbs 11:16 and 22, "A gracious woman attains honor . . . as a ring of gold in a swine's snout, so is a beautiful woman who lacks discretion."

N   Nothing is impossible when we trust God in faith. Meditate upon Hebrews 11:6.

O   Open communication. Speak the truth in love and harbor no bitterness (Ephesians 4:26–32).

P   Plan ahead . . . it saves time, money, and energy. Focus on Proverbs 29:18.

Q   Quiet Time . . . a daily time of fellowship with your Lord. Psalm 119 teaches what God's Word will do for you!

R   Remember the little things that are BIG things to those in your household! Proverbs 31:27 presents the balance of home and ministry.

S   Submission . . . willingly apply the teaching of Ephesians 5:21.

T   Television . . . turn it off! Don't let an appliance consume precious times of fellowship! Apply 2 Corinthians 10:5 to your viewing choices.

U   Unexpected surprises . . . an extra special menu, a fancy dessert, using the good china—all work together to make home a welcoming place. Remember John 14:2.

V   Variety . . . God is the author. Follow His pattern presented in the Genesis account of creation!

W   Welcome others to your home with warmth and expectation! Model Hebrews 11:31!

X (E)Xtra kindness. Learn to give extra attention to those within your home when their spirits need a lift! Recall the truth of Proverbs 25:11 and 1 Timothy 5:8.

Y Your health . . . know your limitations and work within those parameters. Be sure that your family knows them too (1 Corinthians 6:19–20).

Z Zest! Approach each day with a zest for the opportunities that it holds. Ask our Lord daily, "What wonderful things are we going to do today?" Practice Psalm 118:24!

Just as good physical health is the result of implementing sound health practices, so good spiritual health is the result of applying sound spiritual practices. God's Health Plan for the heart of the Wise Woman contains four essential elements:

Weight: A need to eliminate unneeded cares (1 Peter 5: 7–10).
Pulse: The rhythm of one's gratitude (Colossians 3:12–17).
Blood pressure: Reading of anxiety over trust (Psalm 55:22).
Diet: Regular intake and submission to the life-giving thoughts of the Lord (Jeremiah 15:16).

The application of God's Health Plan allows our Wise Woman to mature in a number of godly character qualities:

- Submission to her Lord (Colossians 3:18)
- Submission to her husband (Ephesians 5:22)
- Respect for her husband (1 Peter 3:1–6)
- A commitment to loving her family (Titus 2:4)
- Care for her household (Titus 2:5)
- Self-control, kindness, and purity of heart and mind (Titus 2:5)

The consistent development of these godly character qualities produces visible evidence that our Wise Woman has a heart of contentment. Let's put the eleven principles from chapter 1 into questions that will help to diagnose our level of contentment!

- "Do others affirm my character (am I worth more than fine jewels)?" (Proverbs 31:10)
- "Do I gain the confidence of my husband or others who consistently observe my actions?" (Proverbs 31:11)
- "Do I approach my work eagerly and vigorously?" (Proverbs 31:14, 17)
- "Am I hospitable to my children and others?" (Proverbs 31:15)
- "Do I practice sound money management?" (Proverbs 31:16, 18, 24)
- "Am I willing to share my goods with those who are needy?" (Proverbs 31:20)
- "Do I prepare ahead of time for my family's needs?" (Proverbs 31:21)
- "Am I confident and dignified?" (Proverbs 31:25)
- "Am I a wise and a good teacher?" (Proverbs 31:26)
- "Do I willingly oversee the activities of my household?" (Proverbs 31:27)
- "Have I earned the respect of my family?" (Proverbs 31:28)
- "Do I fear the Lord?" (Proverbs 31:30)

Well, what was your contentment diagnosis? What are the areas that could stand some improvement? Two attributes—*flexibility* and *forgiveness*—will greatly contribute to maintaining a diligent heart.

EMBRACING FLEXIBILITY AND FORGIVENESS

You younger men, likewise, be subject to your elders;
and all of you, clothe yourselves with humility toward one another,
for God is opposed to the proud, but gives grace to the humble.

❧

Therefore, humble yourselves under the mighty hand of God,
that He may exalt you at the proper time.
1 PETER 5:5–6 NASB

Our Wise Woman is steadfast in her faith and commitment to her Lord (1 Corinthians 15:58) and is, at the same time, flexible with His plan for her life (Jeremiah 29:11–13). *Flexible*, by definition, suggests the ability to bend without breaking, a willingness or predisposition to yield; pliable; or adaptable. It is the quality of being able to adjust to change and the capacity to modify our plans in order to leave room for God's plans (1 Peter 5:5–6). *Humility* is the underlying character quality that yields a flexible response.

Humility is "a value that directs persons to stay within their inherited social status, specifically by not presuming on others and avoiding even the appearance of lording over another. Humble persons do not threaten or challenge another's rights, nor do they claim more for themselves than has been duly allotted them in life. They even stay below or behind their right status."[9] Thus, our Wise Woman understands that to achieve flexibility she is to humble herself—she follows her Lord's example in Philippians 2:8–9 and declares herself powerless to defend her status. Such a response, according to Proverbs 3:34 and James 4:10, is praiseworthy before God. A short poem by Lampertus Gedicke (1683–1735) reflects the flexible spirit that the Wise Woman seeks to achieve:

> *Just as God leads me I would go;*
> *I would not ask to choose my way;*
> *Content with what He will bestow,*
> *Assured He will not let me stray.*
> *So as He leads, my path I make,*

And step by step I gladly take,
A child in Him confiding.

The desire to maintain control of a situation frequently causes an inflexible response from the heart of a woman. Eve began the process in Genesis 3 when she stopped and listened to the serpent, and this will continue until our Lord Jesus returns (Revelation 22:20). Here are some principles that will help our Wise Woman gain victory over inappropriate control:

- Recognize that a controlling spirit is sin and purpose to relinquish control (Romans 6:11–13).
- Assume responsibility for possessing a controlling spirit rather than blaming God or others (James 1:13–15).
- Believe that God supplies all needs—He does not need our help! (Philippians 4:19).
- Allow the Word of God to permeate the mind (Colossians 3:16).
- Focus on doing all to God's glory (Colossians 3:17).
- Concentrate on serving others and channeling thoughts, emotions, and energies to accomplish the desires of those in authority (Colossians 3:22).
- Demonstrate a willingness to change direction and plans if unexpected circumstances arise (Philippians 4:6–7).
- Follow the model of biblical women who displayed flexibility: *Sarah* (Genesis 18:1–15; 21:1–13; Hebrews 11:11; 1 Peter 3:6); *Ruth* (Ruth 1–4); *the Jewish Maid* (2 Kings 5:1–5, 14–15; Acts 1:8); *Mary* (Matthew 1:18–25; Luke 1:26–38; 2:6–14, 17–19, 33–35; John 19:25–27); *Elizabeth* (Luke 1:5–20, 24–25, 39–45); and *Anna* (Luke 2:22–27, 36–38).
- Run the race of faith, following the Lord's example (Hebrews 12:1–4).
- Meditate upon the truth taught by "The Teacup"—a

beautiful illustration of the importance of being flexible in the hands of the Master Potter.

THE TEACUP

There was a couple who used to go to England to shop in the beautiful stores. They both liked antiques, pottery, and especially teacups. This was their twenty-fifth wedding anniversary.

One day in this beautiful shop they saw a beautiful teacup. They said, "May we see that? We've never seen one quite so beautiful." As the lady handed it to them, suddenly the teacup spoke. "You don't understand," it said. "I haven't always been a teacup. There was a time when I was red and I was clay. My master took me and rolled me and patted me over and over, and I yelled out, 'Let me alone,' but he only smiled, 'Not yet.'

"Then I was placed on a spinning wheel," the teacup said, "And suddenly I was spun around and around and around. 'Stop it! I'm getting dizzy!' I screamed. But the master only nodded and said, 'Not yet.'

"Then he put me in the oven. I never felt such heat. I wondered why he wanted to burn me, and I yelled and knocked at the door. I could see him through the opening, and I could read his lips as he shook his head, 'Not yet.'

"Finally the door opened, he put me on the shelf, and I began to cool. 'There, that's better,' I said. And he brushed and painted me all over. The fumes were horrible. I thought I would gag. 'Stop it, stop it!' I cried. He only nodded, 'Not yet.'

"Then suddenly he put me back in the oven, not like the first one. This was twice as hot and I knew I would suffocate. I begged. I screamed. I cried. All the time I could see him through the opening, nodding his head and saying, 'Not yet.'

"Then I knew there wasn't any hope. I would never make it. I was ready to give up. But the door opened and he took me out and placed me on the shelf. One hour later he handed me a mirror and said, 'Look at yourself.' And I did. I said, 'That's not me; that couldn't be me. It's beautiful. I'm beautiful.'

"'I want you to remember, then,' he said, 'I know it hurts to be rolled and patted, but if I had left you alone, you'd have dried up. I know it made you dizzy to spin around on the wheel, but if I had stopped, you would have crumbled. I knew it hurt and was hot and disagreeable in the oven, but if I hadn't put you there, you would have cracked. I know the fumes were bad when I brushed and painted you all over, but if I hadn't done that, you never would have hardened; you wouldn't have had any color in your life. And if I hadn't put you back in the second oven, you wouldn't have survived for very long because the hardness would not have held. Now you are a finished product. You are what I had in mind when I first began you.'"

God knows what He's doing for all of us. He is the potter, and we are His clay. He will mold us and make us, so that we may be made into a flawless piece of work to fulfill His good, pleasing, and perfect will (Isaiah 45:9).

—Author Unknown

Forgiveness is an action that demonstrates the Wise Woman's ability to be flexible and contributes to a heart of contentment.

Forgiveness [is] a term denoted in the Old Testament by words that mean "send away," "cover," "remove," and "wipe away." In the New Testament "send away" is used most often; forgiveness is also communicated by words which mean "loose" (Luke 6:37), "be gracious to" (Luke 7:43; 2 Corinthians 2:7), and "pass over" (Romans 3:25). The Bible records human sinfulness, God's eagerness to forgive, and frequent calls by the prophets, Jesus and Jesus' followers for repentance from sin and return to God.[10]

The Scriptures paint a magnificent word portrait of God's forgiveness. Nehemiah 9:17 portrays God as being "ready to pardon, gracious and merciful, slow to anger, abundant in kindness." Exodus 34:6–7 compares God's response to the penitent and impenitent sinner. The psalmist offers the imagery that "as far as the east is from the west, so far has he removed our transgressions from us" (Psalm 103:12). Isaiah paints God as casting all of the prophet's sins behind his back (Isaiah 38:17) and as blotting out the people's transgressions (Isaiah 43:25). The vivid language of Jeremiah 31:34 and Micah 7:19 emphasizes the completeness of God's forgiveness. When He forgives, men's sins are dealt with thoroughly. God remembers them no more!

Our Wise Woman will seek to incorporate God's gracious response and her Lord's model (Luke 23:34) into her own biblical method for forgiving others, as well as seeking others' forgiveness. Scriptural principles that contribute to the formulation of a "forgiveness formula" include:

- Nehemiah 9:17—our God is a God of forgiveness
- Psalm 86:5—all who call on the Lord will be forgiven
- Matthew 18:22—forgiveness is to be unlimited
- Mark 11:25–26—forgiveness can be unilateral and unconditional
- Luke 17:4—forgiveness should be granted unendingly
- Luke 23:34—Christ set the example of forgiveness
- Colossians 3:13—I am to forgive as Christ has forgiven me

The Scripture used to create the Wise Woman's "forgiveness formula" confronts her with the immeasurable forgiveness she receives from God. That forgiveness is to overflow into the lives of those who wrong her. She focuses on the importance of forgiving others from her heart and the need to work toward reconciliation whenever possible (Matthew 5:23–24). She acknowledges that it is not God's plan for her to seek revenge—He reserves that for Himself (Hebrews 10:30); He assists her in refusing to develop a bitter spirit toward those who have wronged her

(Hebrews 12:14–16). Jesus said to His disciples, "Take heed to yourselves. If your brother sins against you, rebuke him; and if he repents, forgive him. And if he sins against you seven times in a day, and seven times in a day returns to you, saying, 'I repent,' you shall forgive him" (Luke 17:3–4). Since God commands us to forgive others, refusing to do so is an act of direct disobedience against Him.

Equally important to forgiving others is the Wise Woman's acknowledgment that at times she will need to seek the forgiveness of those she has wronged. Adam and Eve (Genesis 3:9–12) demonstrate the unbiblical response to sin—blame someone else! It is her responsibility to assume personal responsibility for her part in the transgression (James 5:16), seek the Lord's forgiveness (1 John 1:9), and pursue reconciliation (Matthew 5:23–24). Phrasing such as, "I was wrong when I *(fill in the offense)*. Will you forgive me?" allows her to accept personal responsibility without casting blame on the offended person. Such a response demonstrates her humility and fear of her Lord (Proverbs 8:13).

DEVELOPING A HEART OF CONTENTMENT

Not that I speak from want, for I have learned to be content
in whatever circumstances I am. I know how to get along with
humble means, and I also know how to live in prosperity;
in any and every circumstance I have learned
the secret of being filled and going hungry,
both of having abundance and suffering need.
PHILIPPIANS 4:11–12 NASB

Developing a heart of contentment can be challenging in the midst of difficult life circumstances. *Contentment* is defined as "having an ease of mind or satisfaction."[11] Contentment, from a biblical perspective, is much more than mere satisfaction with life. For the Christian woman, the dictionary definition of *contentment* merely reflects the outward manifestation of her deep inner convictions. The Wise Woman develops contentment in the midst of difficult circumstances by embracing three key truths found in Scripture: *God's sovereignty, God's goodness,* and *God's work.*

CONFIDENCE IN GOD'S SOVEREIGNTY

Also we have obtained as inheritance, having been predestined according to His purpose who works all things after the counsel of His will. (Ephesians 1:11 NASB)

First, she embraces the knowledge that God is sovereign and is in control of all life's circumstances (1 Chronicles 29:11; Isaiah 55:8–9; 1 Corinthians 2:7; Ephesians 1:5, 11). God's sovereignty implies that "God is the supreme ruler and authority, that He ordains whatever comes to pass, and that His divine purpose is always accomplished."[12] God's sovereignty is demonstrated first in the believer's salvation (Ephesians 1:5–11). Believers are predestined or "marked with a boundary beforehand"[13] to enter into a relationship with Jesus Christ, God's Son.

God's sovereignty does not, however, cease with salvation; rather, God works *all* things according to His sovereign will (Ephesians 1:11). This means that God has sovereignly ordered the blessings, the joys, and the rewards of everyday life—a job, a safe home, a spouse, the birth of a child, the fulfillment of ministry. God's sovereignty also includes the trials, fears, and difficulties of one's life—the death of a spouse, the loss of a job, the pain of a terminal illness. God Himself sovereignly ordains all things. Arthur Pink says that embracing the concept of God's sovereignty is the fundamental difference between the man of faith and the man of unbelief. He explains this concept further:

The unbeliever is "of the world," judges everything by worldly standards, views life from the standpoint of time and sense, and weighs everything in the balances of his own carnal understanding. But the man of faith brings in God, looks at everything from His standpoint, estimates values by spiritual standards, and views life in the light of eternity. Doing this, he receives whatever comes as from the hand of God. Doing this, his heart is calm in the midst of storm. Doing this, he rejoices in hope of the glory of God.[14]

Will we ever understand all of the circumstances that God allows to enter into our lives? Scripture answers this question directly by stating that God's judgments are "unsearchable" and "His ways past finding out" (Romans 11:33). Elizabeth George explains this concept by saying:

> God's judgments flow from His holy wisdom and infinite knowledge, and these judgments reveal His plans for the universe, the human race, and each of us individually. Through His judgments, God works out His will in the universe He formed. As human beings, you and I do well to remember the events in our lives are the results of God's judgments. We are therefore to accept in faith that the events—those of a very personal nature as well as those greater events, which, although somewhat removed, impact us personally—are accomplishing something in His plan for us and for His world. Even when from our perspective, it seems that something has gone unnoticed by God; we are to acknowledge that He is at work and in control of our universe and our life.[15]

We will never fully comprehend God's ways, plans, or purposes. We must walk by faith, trusting in the fact that God is accomplishing His perfect, sovereign plan. Paul Enns summarizes this concept by saying, "God's wisdom and knowledge cannot be comprehended. God has consulted no one and no one has advised Him. But because God knows all things He controls and guides all events for His honor and for our good (Psalm 104:24; Proverbs 3:19)."[16] The Woman of Wisdom is able to accept with peaceful confidence the circumstances of her life because of her unshakable trust in God's sovereign plan for her life.

GOD'S GOODNESS

How great is Your goodness, which You have stored up for those who fear You, which You have wrought for those who take refuge in You, before the sons of men! (Psalm 31:19 NASB)

The second truth a Woman of Wisdom embraces when developing contentment is the knowledge that God's character is good, regardless of life circumstances (Psalms 52:1; 119:68; Nahum 1:7; 1 John 1:5). God is not a "good" God only when good things are happening in one's life and a "bad" God when bad things are in one's life. Scripture is clear that God's goodness is the essence of His being. It is part of His divine nature. First John 1:5 states, "God is light and in Him is no darkness at all." Psalm 52:1 teaches, "The goodness of God endures continually," while Psalm 119:68 states, "You are good, and do good." Since God's goodness is based on His character, it is not dependent in any way on life circumstances. Thomas Manton explains God's goodness in this manner: "He is originally good, good of Himself, which nothing else is; for all creatures are good only by participation and communication from God. . . . He is eternally and immutably good, for He cannot be less good than He is; as there can be no addition made to Him, so no subtraction from Him."[17]

God's goodness is not dependent upon the events or circumstances. Rather, God is always, unchangeably a good God, though in the midst of difficult circumstances this is often hard to reconcile. However, we can see God's goodness even in the most difficult life events. For example, God's goodness to us can be seen in His forgiveness of our sin. We deserve nothing more than hell. However, out of God's great compassion and goodness to each one of us He sent His only Son to pay the price for the sin of the world, which includes our own individual sin (John 3:16–18; 1 Timothy 2:5–6; 1 John 2:2).

When life events seem their worst, this truth will remain one constant reminder of God's goodness. He has forgiven us of our sins and made it possible for us to cry, "'Abba, Father!' Therefore you are no longer a slave but a son, and if a son, then an heir of God through Christ" (Galatians 4:6–7). Arthur Pink says, "Because God's goodness endures forever, we ought never to be discouraged."[18] Nahum 1:7 says, "The Lord is good, a stronghold in the day of trouble; and He knows those who trust in Him." Thus, the Wise Woman can be content with life due to the fact that she serves a good God. She can say, with C. H. Spurgeon, "We must never tolerate an instant's unbelief as to the goodness of the Lord; whatever else may be questioned, this is absolutely certain, that Jehovah is good; His dispensations may vary, but His nature is always the same."[19]

GOD'S WORK

Who can speak of the mighty deeds of the Lord, or can show forth all His praise? (Psalm 106:2 NASB)

Finally, not only does a Wise Woman embrace God's sovereignty and goodness in her life, but she also believes that God is lovingly completing a work in her life, even in the midst of troublesome life circumstances (Psalm 104:24; Proverbs 3:19; Romans 8:28–29). God is completing a specific work, which will fulfill His plan and purpose for her life. "It is God who works in you both to will and to do for His good pleasure" (Philippians 2:13).

God has also given us the promise of Romans 8:28, which states, "And we know that all things work together for good to those who love God, to those who are the called according to

His purpose." "In His providence [or sovereignty, as we discussed earlier], God orchestrates every event in life" for our earthly and eternal good.[20] There are no surprises or unplanned events in our lives. All things, whether good or bad, are a part of God's work in our lives. He is using each circumstance, each person, each experience, to mold us and shape us into the person He would have us to be. Philippians 1:6 reminds us, "Being confident of this very thing, that He who has begun a good work in you will complete it until the day of Jesus Christ." The good work begun was our salvation. The completion is the secure promise of spending eternity with our heavenly Father. From the moment of our salvation until the moment that work is completed by our joining Him in heaven, He is intentionally at work in our lives. He is molding us, shaping us, and pruning us through all of life's circumstances, good and bad. The Wise Woman accepts *with contentment* the unique work God is completing in her life.

Developing contentment is not passively giving up, but rather a confident patience to see a circumstance resolved in God's perfect timing. This confidence comes from the biblical truths that God is sovereign, God is good, and God is completing His work. Don't waste precious time or energy worrying about or questioning God's work in your life. Invest your time and energy in sacrificing and meeting the needs of others. Develop your own gifts and abilities in the midst of unresolved life circumstances, such as singleness, infertility, or widowhood. The Woman of Wisdom cultivates the *principle of contentment* in her life.

PRACTICING THE PRINCIPLE OF CONTENTMENT

Make sure that your character is free from the love of money,
being content with what you have; for He Himself has said,
"I will never desert you, nor will I ever forsake you."
HEBREWS 13:5 NASB

WAIT WITH JOY (PSALMS 5:11; 28:7; 1 PETER 1:16)

Each day is a new opportunity to rejoice in the fact that we have confidence in God's sovereignty, goodness, and control in our lives. Purpose in your heart to rejoice: "I *will* rejoice today!" Memorize and meditate on Scripture that will help you maintain a joyful heart. For example, James 1:2 says, "Count it all joy when you fall into various trials." We are responsible for our attitudes toward the trials in our lives. Cynthia Heald explains this concept in this way:

> My attitude toward experiencing trials determines whether or not I truly believe that it is a joy to go through them. If I consider them unwelcome burdens, I will chafe at them in resentment and miss any opportunity to experience the joy that God offers in the midst of them. Essentially, trials should make us more dependent upon the Lord by helping us realize that we cannot live life in our own strength. As we depend upon and draw strength from God, we grow in endurance, the ability to continue in the same state without perishing; to suffer without resistance or compromise; to bear without opposition or sinking under pressure.[21]

MAXIMIZE THE TIME AND DEVELOP YOUR SKILLS (1 CORINTHIANS 12:7–11; EPHESIANS 5:16; COLOSSIANS 4:5)

While you wait to see how the Lord will work out His will in your life, be a good steward of your time, resources, and energy. We all have different gifts and abilities. We should be faithful to develop these gifts and abilities for the benefit of the body of Christ. Develop a new skill or become involved in a ministry meeting the needs of others. For example, return to school to complete a college degree or just take classes in areas of interest, such as art or computers; take music lessons, read books that stimulate your mind, or travel to see other parts of the world. There are many meaningful and productive activities to participate in while enduring difficult life circumstances with unresolved outcomes.

PURSUE PEOPLE (JOHN 15:12; ROMANS 12:10; PHILIPPIANS 2:4)

Invest yourself in the lives of others. How can you practically love others? Can you volunteer for a crisis pregnancy center or offer to mentor the young women of your church? Get involved in the lives of others so that you are not solely consumed by the events of your own life. Focusing on and meeting the needs of others will refresh your heart and help you maintain a proper perspective on the difficulties you are facing.

STUDY GOD'S WORD TO RENEW YOUR MIND (ROMANS 12:2; EPHESIANS 4:23–24)

Be intentional about your spiritual walk with God. Just as you develop an exercise routine for physical fitness, you should develop a "spiritual exercise" routine for growth and maturity. Begin with a regular time in the Word and praying daily for your needs and the needs of others. Support your personal study of God's Word with faithful attendance at a local church that communicates God's truths with accuracy and conviction. Other ideas for renewing your mind would include selecting specific topics for in-depth study (pride, stewardship, characters of the

Bible). Listen to cassette tapes or read books on your selected areas of interest. Join a Bible study or fellowship group from your church or disciple a younger woman. Begin teaching a Sunday school class. There are numerous activities that will help you develop your knowledge and understanding of God's Word.

PURSUE A DISCIPLESHIP OR MENTOR RELATIONSHIP (TITUS 2:3–5)

Pray for the Lord to bring an older woman into your life who can help you in these ways:

- Model for you a mature spiritual walk with God
- Hold you accountable for your attitudes and actions
- "Stir up love and good works" (Hebrews 10:24) in your life

Pray for a woman to mentor you who has proven to be faithful in modeling the Titus 2:3–5 concepts. Martha Peace suggests finding an older woman who can disciple you in three areas—doctrine, character, and ministry.[22] Discipleship and mentor relationships are discussed in more depth in chapter 10 of this book.

A FINAL THOUGHT . . .

I have a friend whose young son was recently diagnosed with cancer. It has challenged me to evaluate how I would respond if one of my own children were to be stricken with a life-threatening illness. My friend is a remarkable example of how believers can have a peaceful confidence in God's sovereignty, goodness, and work in our lives—even in seemingly devastating circumstances. Her response to her son's illness has been, "If this is God's best for me, God's plan to mold my character,

God's will for my family, why would I want to change anything?" I pray that you and I will respond in the same manner
when we are faced with difficult life circumstances.

GROWING IN THE ABILITY
TO DEVELOP A HEART
OF CONTENTMENT

1. Write a description of your home. What would be your family's reaction to the statement, "Some individuals can't wait to get home . . . others can't wait to leave"? Establish goals that will cultivate a welcoming environment in your home.

2. Study the book of Psalms and use a chart format to record the references to the Lord's being a source of refuge. Personalize the references by setting goals for your own home.

THE LORD IS . . .	
Scripture Reference and Content	**Personal Application To My Home**
Psalm 18:2: "The Lord is my rock and my fortress and my deliverer; my God, my strength, in whom I will trust." He is a shield to all those who put their trust in Him.	I will choose to create a trustworthy environment in my home. I will trust in the Lord and not my own understanding to make this a reality.

3. Using the Wise Woman's Meditation Alphabet, prepare meditation cards that direct your mind toward having a welcoming heart for those within your home. Place the cards in a prominent location. Record on the back of the cards specific incidents where you nurtured others. Daily meditate upon both the verses and the incidents of application.

4. *Develop your own Wise Woman's Meditation Alphabet that focuses on your specific needs.*

5. *Study the lives of biblical examples of women who displayed flexibility:* Sarah *(Genesis 18:1–15; 21:1–13; Hebrews 11:11; 1 Peter 3:6);* Ruth *(Ruth 1–4);* the Jewish Maid *(2 Kings 5:1–5, 14–15; Acts 1:8);* Mary *(Matthew 1:18–25; Luke 1:26–38; 2:6–14, 17–19, 33–35; John 19:25–27);* Elizabeth *(Luke 1:5–20, 24–25, 39–45); and* Anna *(Luke 2:22–27, 36–38). Record principles from their lives that will assist you in developing a heart of contentment.*

The commitment to managing the home with excellence is not necessarily viewed as a high priority among Christian women. This was illustrated to me one day while waiting for my husband at his office. A mutual friend dropped by to see him, and since my husband was tied up in a meeting we began to talk as we waited for him to return. The conversation quickly turned to the recent change that had occurred in my life, the transition from full-time teacher to full-time mommy. As we talked, it became apparent to me that she did not understand why I would choose to quit work and stay at home. After all, I had just completed my doctorate in education, and wasn't it a waste of my education to stay at home? She then asked the questions that most stay-at-home moms have heard at one time or another, "What do you do all day?" and "Isn't it very boring to be at home all day long?"

Her questions prompted me to think, what DO I do all day? I thought about just a few of my week's activities: I cleaned the house, paid the bills, grocery shopped, ran errands, prepared meals, did the laundry, and cared for the needs of my baby (which at the time of this discussion meant feeding him six times a day!). Each day seemed very full and never once had I been BORED! Exhausted—yes; sometimes overwhelmed—yes; but NEVER bored! There always seemed to be projects to work on and things to accomplish at home; I still used every skill I learned going through graduate school. I had to problem solve, manage my time, and make decisions on a daily basis. My place of full-time employment had simply changed. While the conversation with our friend made me feel at first as though I had to justify why I was staying at home, it later saddened me to think that often in the Christian community women do not understand it takes skill and excellence as . . .

FOUR

THE WISE WOMAN MANAGES HER HOME

By wisdom a house is built,
And by understanding it is established.

PROVERBS 24:3 NASB

Historically, Home Management was viewed as essential to family life. The National Conference on Family Life held in 1948 stated, "Management in the home is part of the fabric of living. Its threads are interwoven because decisions for the use of resources are made, whether the family is at work or play." Educators typically define Home Management as the way families use their resources to achieve family goals. Theoretically, Home Management involves a manager making decisions to allocate family resources, including time, money, or energy to reflect the family goals and priorities. This theory statement makes management sound like a simple process by which all family goals can be easily achieved. Management, however, is very complex, since we all have limited resources and competing goals. Also, there are uncontrollable circumstances or demands that interfere with the management process.

How then does the Wise Woman manage her home effectively? There are three components to consider: First, the Wise Woman *embraces a biblical motivation*. Second, she *understands the biblical mandate for Home Management*. Finally, she *implements effective methods for Household Management*.

EMBRACING A BIBLICAL
MOTIVATION FOR HOME MANAGEMENT
But prove yourselves doers of the word,
and not merely hearers who delude themselves.
JAMES 1:22 NASB

Effective Home Management generally includes accomplishing goals, meeting family needs, and managing resources efficiently. The incentive for effective management for contemporary society is frequently for self-gratification and/or control. Elizabeth B. Goldsmith clearly illustrates this point by stating, "Management is the process of using what one has to get what one wants."[1] As well, contemporary society thinks that management allows women "to feel in control of their lives" resulting in an increased sense of well-being.[2]

The Wise Woman, however, has a very different motivation or incentive for effective management. She desires to manage in order to be a faithful steward of her God-given resources (Matthew 25:21). Viewing herself as a steward of God's resources indicates that she acknowledges God is the owner of her resources; she is simply the manager. Since the Wise Woman understands her role, she is not motivated by control or self-gratification; her motivation is one of pleasing God through faithful management.

Second, the Wise Woman is motivated to manage effectively out of obedience—obedience to the commands and principles of God's Word. James 1:22 admonishes believers to be doers of the Word, not simply hearers. The following portion of the chapter discusses the clear scriptural mandate for women to manage their homes effectively.

The Wise Woman learns to manage her home so that she will be found to be a faithful steward of the resources (time, energy, money) God has entrusted to her. She seeks to become a successful Home Manager in obedience to the priorities God has called her to accomplish.

UNDERSTANDING THE BIBLICAL MANDATE FOR HOME MANAGEMENT

*She looks well to the ways of her household, and does not
eat the bread of idleness.* (Proverbs 31:27 NASB)

The Wise Woman understands that Scripture teaches that her primary domain is her home. She bears much responsibility in the management and organization of her home and family. Three primary passages set the tone for the mandate for management and indicate the extent of her responsibility: Proverbs 31:10–31; Titus 2:3–5; and 1 Timothy 5:14. Let's review the key principles found in each of these passages.

PROVERBS 31:27

Proverbs 31:27 states: "She watches over the ways of her household, and does not eat the bread of idleness." She is a competent manager in a variety of areas. Proverbs 31 provides a clear picture of the areas women should endeavor to manage in their households:

1. *Managing food*—she knew where to travel to secure quality food (Proverbs 31:14).
2. *Managing clothing*—she knew how to identify quality materials for clothing (Proverbs 31:13, 19).
3. *Managing time*—she rose early and stayed up late to ensure her family's needs were met (Proverbs 31:15).
4. *Managing business*—she knew how to conduct business outside the home that profited her home (Proverbs 31:16, 24).
5. *Managing physical energy*—she was strong because she knew how to work hard and utilize her strength (Proverbs 31:17).
6. *Managing production of goods*—she was an entrepreneur who knew how to produce quality goods (Proverbs 31:18).
7. *Managing people*—she knew how to plan for the needs of people (husband, children, servants, the poor, merchants) (Proverbs 31:15–18, 20–24).

The Proverbs 31 woman was a skilled manager in a variety of areas. It may be necessary for the Wise Woman to obtain specific training in areas in which she lacks proficiency. She may choose to take a class, read books, or learn from an older woman. She must make it her priority to be an effective manager of her home. Martha Peace states:

Unless providentially hindered by God, it is the wife's responsibility to be a worker at home and maintain an orderly and organized home. It does not mean that her husband and children cannot help, but she sets the tone. Chaos and disorder create tension and contention. It drains her of the needed energy to work on her relationship with her husband and children. A wife should make it her business to find out how to keep an orderly and clean home and stay organized with her grocery shopping and meals. There are many good books on the market or in the library that are very helpful, and if this area in her life is out of control, she should seek the resources to change.[3]

TITUS 2:3–5

Younger women may also learn how to be workers at home from older women as indicated in Titus 2:3–5. The term "workers at home" in Titus 2:5 (NASB) is the Greek word *oikouros*. This is a compound word, which comes from two root words: *oikos*, meaning "a dwelling, a home, or a household," and *ergon*, which means, "to work or be employed." It suggests that women should seek to manage a home with excellence. John MacArthur explains *ergon* in this manner:

> *Ergon* does not simply refer to labor in general; it often refers to a particular job or employment. It is the word Jesus used when He said, "My food is to do the will of Him who sent Me, and to accomplish His work" (John 4:34). Our Lord focused His entire life on fulfilling God's will. In a similar fashion, a wife is to focus her life on the home. God has designed the family to be her sphere of responsibility. That does not mean she should spend twenty-four hours a day there, however; the woman in Proverbs 31 left her home when she needed to buy a field or when she needed supplies, yet even those trips benefited her family. She poured her life into her family—she woke up early and went to bed late for the sake of those in it.[4]

Titus 2:5 reveals that women are to love their families and manage their households with excellence so that "the word of God may not be blasphemed"—as Wise Women practice godly conduct in their homes they are obedient to God's Word.

1 TIMOTHY 5:14

First Timothy 5:14 builds on this concept by stating, "I desire that the younger widows marry, bear children, manage the house, give no opportunity to the adversary to speak reproachfully." The term "manage the house" is also a Greek term, which implies all aspects of household administration. It is not simply the raising or care of children. It is all aspects of Home Management. What will management look like for the Wise Woman?

- *She is a skilled worker* (Proverbs 31:10–31; Titus 2:3–5). A Wise Woman will understand the components of her domain—she does not just manage, she manages with excellence.
- *She is industrious* (Proverbs 6:6; 20:13; Philippians 2:3). A Wise Woman is a hard worker. She is not lazy and develops the self-discipline needed to fulfill her obligations. She applies the principle of considering others more important than herself.
- *She is orderly and well managed* (1 Corinthians 14:40). A Wise Woman takes the time to be organized. She implements the principle of doing everything "decently and in order," as the King James Version puts it. She learns how to plan, establish goals, and make decisions that reflect her priorities.
- *She anticipates her family's needs* (Proverbs 31:27). A Wise Woman practically meets the needs of her family in all areas of family life, including scheduling, meal planning, household maintenance, and finance.
- *She manages her time well* (Psalm 90:12; Ephesians 5:16). A Wise Woman has determined her priorities. She takes the time to plan. She is disciplined but not driven.
- *She works as unto the Lord* (Colossians 3:23). A Wise Woman possesses character that complements her skills. Her motivation for management is to please God, not man.
- *She sets a godly tone in her home* (Psalm 28:7; Proverbs 31:21). A Wise Woman reflects that the "law of kindness" is on her tongue. Her words, tone of voice, and deeds all work together to maintain a godly atmosphere in her

home. She is confident in the future because of her faith in God and reflects joy in the Lord (Nehemiah 8:10).

Proverbs 14:1 states, "The wise woman builds her house, but the foolish pulls it down with her hands." A key ingredient determining whether women build or tear down their houses is how they choose to manage their households. The Wise Woman will not only understand what Home Management is, but will develop, with proficiency, the skills needed to manage her household in a biblical manner. The home is the domain where the married woman fulfills God's design for herself.

The concept of being a homemaker is very unpopular in contemporary society. It is frequently viewed as demeaning, inferior, and limiting. Contemporary society's view, however, is not God's. Homemaking is a divine assignment from God and should be embraced with enthusiasm and skill. Dorothy Patterson describes the value of homemaking in this way:

Homemaking—being a full-time wife and mother—is not a destructive drought of usefulness but an overflowing oasis of opportunity; it is not a dreary cell to contain one's talents and skills but a brilliant catalyst to channel creativity and energies into meaningful work; it is not a rope for binding one's productivity in the marketplace, but reins for guiding one's posterity in the home; it is not oppressive restraint of intellectual prowess for the community, but a release of wise instruction to your own household; it is not the bitter assignment of inferiority to your person, but the bright assurance of the ingenuity of God's plan for complementarity of the sexes, especially as worked out in God's plan for marriage; it is neither limitation of gifts available nor stinginess in distributing the benefits of those gifts, but rather the multiplication of a mother's legacy to the generations to come and the generous bestowal of all God meant a mother to give to those He entrusted to her care.[5]

THE PRINCIPLE OF PRUDENCE

I, wisdom, dwell with prudence, and I find knowledge and discretion. (Proverbs 8:12 NASB)

The goals of biblical management emphasize provision, organization, and anticipation of family needs. These goals are combined with the principles of hard work, diligence, and meeting the needs of others. *Wisdom* can be defined as the application of knowledge to daily living. It is discussed at length in the book of Proverbs and is often associated with several other character traits, including *prudence*. Prudence is a rather "Victorian"-sounding trait that is not frequently used in contemporary vocabulary. It is, however, a very applicable concept to the area of Home Management—to be a wise manager, one must be a prudent manager. Prudence, as it relates to Home Management:

- practices wise thought before acting, which results in good judgment.
- displays good management and economy.
- emphasizes cautious good sense and giving thought to one's actions and their consequences.
- manifests foresight, meaning careful thought in planning and acting.
- dictates care in the use of natural resources.
- emphasizes the ability to see what is likely to happen and prepare for it accordingly.

Samuel Smiles summarizes the importance of prudence as it relates to Home Management in *Happy Homes*, published in 1888: "Prudence is another important household qualification. Prudence comes from cultivated judgment; it means practical wisdom. It has reference to fitness, to propriety. It judges of the right thing to be done, and of the right way of doing it. It calculates the means, order, time, and method of doing. Prudence learns much from experience, quickened by knowledge.[6] His thoughts are as relevant for the twenty-first century as they were for families in 1888.

From a biblical perspective, the Wise Woman is a prudent Home Manager when she applies the attributes of prudence to her character as well as her management skills. The character traits identified in the book of Proverbs suggest that the Prudent Woman:

- is a Wise Woman (Proverbs 8:11–14; 16:21).
- has understanding of her own ways (Proverbs 14:8, 15).
- acquires knowledge (Proverbs 18:15; 13:16; 14:18).
- identifies sin and keeps away from it (Proverbs 22:3).
- is teachable (Proverbs 15:5; 13:18).
- is not ostentatious (Proverbs 12:23).
- is preserved by her discretion (Proverbs 2:11).

Therefore, the Wise Woman, who reflects the practice of prudence in her Home Management, is careful to plan, able to anticipate family needs, sensible, teachable, and able to discern the consequences of her decisions.

IMPLEMENTING EFFECTIVE METHODS OF HOUSEHOLD MANAGEMENT

Whatever you do, do your work heartily,
as for the Lord rather than for men.
COLOSSIANS 3:23 NASB

Once the Wise Woman has a proper motivation for management and understands the biblical mandate for making Home Management a priority, she is ready to begin implementing management techniques. Effective Home Management involves many practical aspects, including *planning and organization, goal setting,* and *decision making.* All aspects must be addressed in order to be a successful Home Manager.

THE PRINCIPLES OF PLANNING AND ORGANIZATION

Commit your works to the Lord, and your plans will be established. The Lord has made everything for its own purpose, even the wicked for the day of evil. (Proverbs 16:3–4 NASB)

The first practical aspect of management is developing the ability to plan and organize the household. Planning is simply deciding in advance what, why, and how things will be done. It implies there was thought before undertaking the project, task, or action. Organization suggests that the parts were arranged in an orderly manner. Planning and organization are dependent on one another; in other words, to be an organized woman, one must be a woman who knows how to plan. Planning involves anticipating family needs and then deciding in advance how those needs will be met. The key concept in planning is deciding in advance. For example, your family needs to be fed daily; typically this will require three meals a day. The planning phase of management decides in advance when the food will be purchased, how the food will be prepared, and what food will be served. In other words, the planning occurs before the family is sitting down at the dinner table! Organization, on the other hand, requires that the Home Manager understands what she is planning for. If the woman is not organized, her planning will be ineffective.

Planning combined with organization assists the Home Manager in making wise decisions to meet demands or needs within the family.

1. TAKE TIME TO PLAN

Many women fail to manage effectively because they do not take time to plan or to plan adequately for the needs of their family. As the saying goes (paraphrased!), "Many women plan to fail, because they fail to plan." The time invested in the planning process is worth the sacrifice and effort. Practical examples of taking the time to plan might include making a weekly menu plan before grocery shopping to ensure there is adequate food in the house or keeping a family calendar of events to prevent scheduling conflicts. Planning should become a habitual part of household management.

2. ORGANIZE YOURSELF BEFORE ORGANIZING YOUR FAMILY

Generally, if the woman is unorganized, her family will be unorganized. The Wise Woman sets the organizational tone for her family. Emily Barnes suggests four organizational tools:

- A "to do" list
- A calendar
- A telephone/address source list
- A simple filing system[7]

3. ANTICIPATE FAMILY NEEDS[8]

Planning looks ahead to anticipate the wide variety of family needs. Proverbs 31:21 provides an excellent model of a woman who anticipated her family's needs—she was not afraid of the winter because she foresaw the clothing needs of her family. As our Wise Woman implements this model, her household needs in a variety of areas, including clothing, transportation, food, finances, and cleaning, are met. Project further than one week and predict: Do supplies need to be purchased for a project? Do appointments need to be made? A Wise Woman anticipates needs and plans in advance the methods and means for meeting these obligations.

4. PLAN REALISTICALLY

Women frequently become discouraged when they attempt to plan, because of unrealistic expectations. Unrealistic expectations result from one of two reasons:

- The plan is far too complex to implement.
- There is inadequate information to develop an effective plan.

Either reason can lead to failure in planning. The Wise Woman learns how to develop a balanced plan that realistically meets the needs of her family.

5. DEVELOP A PERSONAL PLANNING STYLE

Some women try to use methods of planning that do not complement their natural personalities or giftedness. In other words, what works for one woman may not work for another. Some women will be very goal-oriented and detailed in their planning, whereas others will be more directional or flexible. The Wise Woman develops a method of planning that complements her personality. For example, some women will do the same task on the same day of the week (i.e., every Monday is laundry, every Wednesday is grocery shopping). Others will decide at the beginning of each week what day they will accomplish the required tasks (i.e., some weeks laundry is done on Mondays, others on Wednesday). Each is an effective example of planning to meet needs.

6. ORGANIZE

Organization implies that multiple parts have been arranged to form a whole unit. The Home Manager develops methods of planning in four broad categories:

- *Individual family calendars*—keep track of school, work, church, and extracurricular activities for each family member.
- *Financial records*—develop an orderly method for paying the bills, maintaining the finances, and implementation of a simple filing system (see chapter 6).
- *Meals and menus*—develop a method of weekly menu planning, organizing grocery shopping, and food preparation requirements (see chapter 7).
- *Household cleaning*—develop a weekly, monthly, and yearly schedule for household cleaning and general maintenance.

Once the general areas of organization are addressed, each Home Manager will need to identify unique needs of her family. For example, the home-school mom will have to plan and organize schooling needs. Women with small children may need to develop lists with pertinent emergency medical and contact information on it. Whatever the needs are, the Wise Woman anticipates those needs, organizes the parts, and develops a plan for her household.

ORGANIZING HOUSEHOLD CLEANING

In all labor there is profit, but mere talk leads only to poverty. (Proverbs 14:23 NASB)

Household cleaning is one of the major areas of Home Management to organize. While most of us enjoy the product of cleaning—a fresh, neat, and tidy house—few of us enjoy the actual process of cleaning. Cleaning can be hard work! Unfortunately, there is no way to avoid the responsibility of cleaning. There are many benefits to a clean home; for example, homes that are clean have fewer health problems and accidents. A recent study by the University of Michigan even said that the "cleanliness of the home children grow up in predicts their ed-ucational attainment and earnings more than twenty-five years later. Parents who keep their homes clean may be more orga-nized and efficient than others, and these characteristics may carry over to other aspects of their lives, such as parenting. As a result, children raised in clean homes may be more successful in school and at work."[9]

Beyond the visible benefits of cleaning, the Wise Woman un-derstands that keeping a neat and orderly house is part of the practical out-working of Titus 2:3–5 where women are com-manded to be keepers of the home. Cleaning, therefore, be-comes a divine assignment from God. Cleaning is a ministry to our family and an act of service to God. Proper care of our belongings should be viewed as a part of biblical stewardship. Since keeping an orderly and clean household is an important priority for the Wise Woman, we need to take the time to dis-cuss how to organize cleaning. The best way to handle clean-ing is to organize it. Cleaning is only difficult when it is *not* completed on a regular basis. When regular attention is given to cleaning, it is relatively easy to maintain an orderly and clean home. Here are a few practical points to consider:

1. KNOW HOW TO CLEAN

Many women fail to keep a clean and orderly home because they simply do not know how to clean or what needs to be ac-complished. There are many good resources that can help. If you have never learned "how" to clean, you must begin here. Two excellent resources may be helpful:

- A video entitled *Is There Life After Housework*[10] (demon-strates how to clean)
- *Cleaning 101*[11] (tells how to clean and explains cleaning products)

You may also find it helpful to ask a friend who has an orderly home for practical advice on how to clean and keep things organized.

2. Develop a cleaning schedule

Once you know what needs to be done to keep a clean home, you need to develop a schedule that allows you to keep up with all the tasks. I suggest that you develop daily, weekly, quarterly, and annual schedules for cleaning. Use the blank spaces on your monthly calendar to write in the quarterly and seasonal cleaning tasks as a reminder. The daily and weekly tasks should become part of your routine so that once you are in the habit of completing the tasks you shouldn't need reminders. Use the sample cleaning schedule found at the end of this chapter and modify it to fit your needs.

3. Get the necessary supplies and equipment

Being unprepared with the needed supplies and equipment can cause time to be wasted in two ways. First, you will spend longer cleaning because you are trying to manually clean rather than allow the chemicals to clean, and, second, you will waste time trying to collect the needed supplies. A helpful suggestion is to put basic cleaning supplies in a caddie so that you can carry it around the house while you clean (get two if you have a two-story house). This saves time and allows you to have everything you need within reach. It is also easier to see when it is time to restock a supply. Remember—you do not need specialized cleaners for every job. Only stock the basics. These would include a spray bottle with water and dish detergent (used for about 75 percent of household cleaning), a disinfectant cleaner (for toilets and other areas needing disinfecting), a window cleaner, a dusting cleaner, and the appropriate floor cleaners (determined by the type of flooring in your home).

4. DECIDE THE ORDER FOR YOUR CLEANING JOBS

Cleaning goes a lot faster when you establish a routine for your daily and weekly tasks. Fretting over the question of "Do I dust or vacuum first?" every time you clean wastes precious time and energy! Determine in advance how you will complete your household tasks. (To answer the dusting or vacuuming question—it is generally advised that you dust first so that the vacuum will pick up the debris that has fallen onto the floor. This is, of course, assuming that your vacuum is functioning correctly and not generating dust itself!)

5. SET A TIME LIMIT

Researchers on the organization of work often refer to a principle called "Parkinson's Law," which states, "Work expands so as to fill the time available for its completion."[12] If you do not set time limits for your cleaning jobs, they will consume your entire day. Watch the clock and make sure you are spending only the needed time for each task. Setting time limits will help keep you motivated also.

6. READ THE LABELS AND USE CLEANING PRODUCTS ACCORDING TO THE DIRECTIONS

Using the appropriate product and following the given directions will help protect your belongings from chemical harm. It will also help protect you from physical damage. For example, you should *never* mix cleaning products. For example, mixing bleach and ammonia, two common cleaning agents, produces a toxic and deadly gas.

7. Avoid false starts and always finish what you start

When you do not have the time or proper cleaning materials to complete the task, it is generally better to wait until you have enough time to complete the job. Starting and stopping consumes too much time. Don't allow yourself to get sidetracked by phone calls, the television, or other controllable interruptions. It is also important to finish what you start. Don't leave jobs halfway completed—for example, washing the dishes but not putting them away. Leaving the dishes until the next day simply adds to the cleanup time on the following day.

8. Be disciplined and diligent

As mentioned earlier, house cleaning is only difficult when it is *not* completed. It is much easier to clean on a regular basis. Avoid the "pile-ups" that produce the stressful kind of cleaning. For example, not cleaning the shower doors allows buildup, which is difficult to remove, or not completing the filing for your finances on a regular basis is stressful when you sit down to organize the bills.

9. Make good use of people-power

When it is appropriate, delegate household cleaning chores to family members. Wise Women will oversee and organize the household cleaning, but they do not have to be the sole family member actually doing the cleaning. Children learn valuable character traits when required to participate in caring for their home. Likewise, husbands can demonstrate servant leadership by helping out around the house.

10. DOVETAIL

The time invested in cleaning can be profitable in other ways by applying the management principle of dovetailing—listen to music, sermons, or books on tape while cleaning. Memorizing and meditating upon Scripture is also a great cleaning activity.

THE PRINCIPLE OF GOAL SETTING: REFLECTING PRIORITIES

May He grant you your heart's desire and fulfill all your counsel! (Psalm 20:4 NASB)

The second practical aspect of management is the ability to set goals that reflect individual priorities. Setting goals can be very beneficial to the Wise Woman in helping her to accomplish tasks, holding her accountable to commitments, and/or providing criteria for evaluation of accomplishments. Priorities, on the other hand, help her to determine what activity is most important to pursue.

Here is a simple definition of a goal: "What you are striving to attain or achieve."[13] Goals are defined by type and time. Types or categories of goals include intellectual, spiritual, academic, financial, social, family, physical, or career goals. Women should consider establishing goals in each of these areas as well as other areas that are pertinent to their lives. Once the type of goal is determined, goals can be further defined by the timeline of the goal; for example, there are short-, intermediate-, and long-range goals. Viewing goals through time assists in breaking them down into smaller, more manageable parts. Short-range goals should help facilitate intermediate goals, which in turn assist in accomplishing long-range goals.

Examples of how the short-, intermediate-, and long-range goals work together to accomplish the overall goal are listed in Table 4.1. The table also illustrates viewing goals by type.

	Short-Range Goals	Intermediate-Range Goals	Long-Range Goals
TABLE 4.1 **TIME LINES AND TYPES OF GOALS**			
Type—Physical	Research fitness program options	Implement exercise routine	Become physically fit
Type—Spiritual	Memorize verses on prayer	Study book of James	Improve prayer life
Type—Financial	Pay off credit card debts	Develop a savings program	Purchase a home
Type—Academic	Complete class assignments	Pass each semester course	Graduate from college

Goals require the completion of specific steps for successful accomplishment. Step development is the planning phase of goal establishment. As previously discussed, planning is simply deciding in advance the actions to be taken. Many women possess good intentions in relation to establishing goals; however, they frequently struggle in their ability to accomplish them. Many factors contribute to the failure to accomplish their goals: lack of skill, lack of planning, unexpected events, conflict in goals, and/or availability of resources. Doug Sherman and William Hendricks suggest a practical model using the acronym of S-M-A-C for goal setting that may help remove some of the hindrances to goal accomplishment. Here are their suggestions:

- Goals should be *specific*. Many goals fail due to the lack of detail. They are too broad and general. Therefore, you are most likely to accomplish a goal if it is clearly defined.

- Goals should be *measurable*. A goal needs to be measurable in order to determine if it has been accomplished. When appropriate, defining the goal quantitatively may help in being measurable.
- Goals should be *achievable*. Sometimes goals fail because they are unrealistic. Remembering we all have limited time, energy, and resources is critical to establishing successful goals.
- Goals should be *compatible*. Goals must be compatible with all current obligations and responsibilities represented in your life. This becomes a good criterion for establishing goals in the first place. You may not be able to start working on a goal due to your existing obligations.[14]

Understanding how to define goals is the simple part of the process. Goal setting becomes complicated because of competing demands on time, energy, and resources (such as money). The second phase of goal setting is the establishment of priorities. The concept of priorities suggests activities or goals hold different levels of importance to the goal setter. Priorities force a choice as to how time, energy, and resources will be utilized. Furthermore, priorities reveal an individual's value system since they reveal where time, energy, and resources are invested.

What are priorities for the Wise Woman? First, from a spiritual perspective, there are only two priorities for all believers. Jesus articulated them in Matthew 22:37–39. "'You shall love the Lord your God with all your heart, with all your soul, and with all your mind.' This is the first and great commandment. And the second is like it: 'You shall love your neighbor as yourself.'" All aspects of a Christian woman's life should support and promote loving God and loving others.

Second, from a management perspective, priorities are generally developed from our individual responsibilities. This means that no two women will have exactly the same priorities in life because no two women will have exactly the same obligations. How then do women identify and establish with wisdom specific priorities to be manifested in their lives? The place to begin when establishing personal priorities is to write a life mission statement. Companies and corporations, to indicate their primary purpose for existing, use mission statements.

Similarly, the Wise Woman takes the time to summarize what is her primary purpose in life. Her mission statement becomes a general direction from which she establishes goals. Once the goals are established, she will be able to make decisions on a daily basis to support them and thus accomplish her mission statement. An example of a mission statement would be:

> I want to be found faithful to be a teacher of good things; to model with excellence to younger women how to love their husbands and children; to be self-controlled, to be pure, busy at home, kind, and submissive to my husband. This will be accomplished first by giving my time and energy to loving God with all my heart (Matthew 22:37); second, by protecting my family and home through prudent management and sincere love (Proverbs 8:11–14); and finally, by continuing to grow in the grace and knowledge of our Lord and Savior Jesus Christ (2 Peter 3:18).

Though her mission statement and goals are outlined, she may still be challenged from a practical perspective to know how to spend her time, energy, and resources in order to accomplish the identified goals and mission statement. Donna Otto sheds light on this area by observing that priorities are those things, activities, or responsibilities that only the Wise Woman herself can take care of.[15] Here is an application of this model:

- (For all believers) I alone am responsible for my relationship with God.

- (For wives) I alone can be wife to my husband.
- (For mothers) I alone can be mother to my children.
- (For married women) I alone am responsible for managing my household.
- (For daughters) I alone can care for my aging parent.
- (For the employee) I alone can complete a work obligation.
- (For the student) I alone can complete this assignment for my class.

Priorities are those obligations for which only the Wise Woman assumes responsibility. These are the areas in which she must invest her limited time, energy, and resources. Priorities will vary for each woman depending on her life circumstances and even season of life (for example, the different seasons of life require different priorities for the new mom compared to the grandmother).

Finally, when discussing priorities it is important to address the concept of ordering your priorities. Typically, when identifying priorities for the believer, authors will have a linear approach to ordering priorities; for example, priorities for the Christian woman may be ranked in order of importance:

God
Husband
Children
Home
Church
Career
Community

It is often assumed once a list of priorities is established, the time spent on each priority will correlate with the rank order of the priority—for example, in this system, the majority of the Wise Woman's time will be spent on spiritual endeavors, followed by time with her husband. Many women become exasperated with this concept of priorities because in the reality of their daily lives they may spend only an hour in endeavors they define as spiritual, several hours with their spouse, and most of the day consumed with child-care or household maintenance. The linear model can leave the woman feeling that she is not maintaining her life priorities properly.

A more practical approach to priorities may be viewing life as a "comprehensive unified whole."[16] This concept suggests that God has called women to fulfill multiple responsibilities and roles (wife, mother, daughter, homemaker, community servant). Therefore, she should avoid compartmentalizing her life into the spiritual and secular. Thus, she avoids measuring the success of maintaining priorities solely by the amount of time given to them on a daily basis. Some days more time will be spent with her husband, some days more time with her ministry obligations, while other days more time on household chores. This does not mean that she has neglected her priorities. Maintaining priorities means fulfilling all the obligations that God has uniquely and specifically called the Wise Woman to accomplish —priorities that are reflected in her mission statement, goals, and ultimately how her time is spent.

THE PRINCIPLE OF DECISION MAKING: WISDOM APPLIED

He who gives attention to the word will find good, and
blessed is he who trusts in the Lord. (Proverbs 16:20 NASB)

The third practical aspect of management is the ability to make wise, prudent, and discreet decisions based on the wisdom of God's Word. The eleven principles from Proverbs 31 discussed in chapter 1 of this book provide a model to follow for building our homes with wisdom—virtuous, trustworthy, energetic, physically fit, economical, unselfish, honorable, lovable, prepared, prudent, and God-fearing. And what is true wisdom? Proverbs 9:10 teaches that *true wisdom is the understanding of God's holy Word and the ability to apply that Word in your life.* Wisdom is not merely knowledge but rather the ability to apply that information with understanding to daily life circumstances.

Applying wisdom to daily life circumstances requires prudence and discretion (Proverbs 8:12; 16:21; 18:15). Proverbs 18:15 states, "The heart of the prudent acquires knowledge." *Prudence,* a word not often used in today's conversations, can be defined as careful (or wise) thought before acting or planning. Good judgment or good management characterizes a prudent person. Discretion complements prudence. Discretion implies good judgment and carefulness in actions. The ability to exercise discretion comes from the Wise Woman's dedication to the pursuit of wisdom through the knowledge of God's Word. Often an outcome of gaining an understanding of God's Word is a well-managed home.

Appropriate decision making is the foundation of successful management. In order to be a successful manager you must be able to make appropriate decisions. The decisions a woman makes on a daily basis will reflect her wisdom, prudence, and discretion. Decision making implies the selection of and commitment to a course of action—and, obviously, for decision making to occur there must be a choice among alternatives or multiple options for a solution. Without alternatives or options, there is no need for a decision. A decision suggests that a choice was made among the possible alternatives. An alternative is one of a set of strategies. Each strategy is capable of fulfilling a common objective in some degree, but each results in somewhat different consequences. Each alternative has a different set of characteristics that sets it apart from the other alternatives. For example, a student selecting his/her college might be accepted into three colleges. Each of the three alternatives would fulfill a common objective, in this case a college education, but each would result in a slightly different type of education based on the school size, location, and mission of the school.

Everyone makes decisions on a routine basis. Some decisions are small and insignificant, whereas others are complex and have lasting consequences. Regardless of the type, size, or importance of the decision, the woman who is building her home with wisdom will implement biblical decision-making procedures. What does this mean? It means she will be able to discern the best or most appropriate alternative through the application of biblical principles.

Biblical decision making assumes that the decision maker has a right relationship with God (2 Corinthians 5:14–21) and is pursuing a lifestyle that honors God (Philippians 1:21; 3:10–14). It assumes she is willing, on a daily basis, to humbly submit her life circumstances to God's will (Matthew 6:25–34; Philippians 4:6–9). Biblical decision making assumes that she will pray for wisdom and understanding to apply God's revealed Word in every circumstance requiring her to make a choice, select an alternative, or exercise her judgment (Proverbs 3:5–6; James 1:5).

With these assumptions stated, how do we make good decisions and what does biblical decision making look like? Let's look at a ten-step model for making decisions. The model can be applied to any decision a woman might face.

DECISION-MAKING MODEL

Instead, you ought to say, "If the Lord wills,
we will live and also do this or that."
JAMES 4:15 NASB

STEP ONE—PRAY FOR WISDOM AND THE ABILITY TO APPLY KNOWLEDGE IN THE DECISION-MAKING PROCESS.

As discussed earlier, biblical decision making assumes the decision maker is humbly dependent on God. Scripture tells us that when we lack wisdom we should ask God for wisdom (James 1:5). Scripture says that God gives wisdom "liberally" if we will only ask. God desires to help us make biblical decisions and is very generous in giving wisdom.

STEP TWO—LIST ALL POSSIBLE ALTERNATIVES OR SOLUTIONS.

The second step in the decision-making process requires us to identify all possible alternatives. This is not the time for eliminating ideas. It is the time for creativity. Take out a piece of paper and write down all ideas, regardless of how ridiculous they may seem at the moment.

STEP THREE—GATHER THE INFORMATION NEEDED TO MAKE THE CHOICE AMONG THE ALTERNATIVES.

Once you have listed all the possible alternatives for the decision under consideration, collect additional information before you can select one alternative. Look at the list you made in step two and write down what information is needed. Identify how you will collect the answers to the questions you may have generated. For example, if you are trying to decide how to pay for a college education, a school loan may have been one of the alternatives you listed in step two. Step three would be to contact the appropriate agencies and request the needed information, forms, or procedures. You need to collect accurate information from reliable sources. Information can come from books, journal and newspaper articles, government or state agencies, and people you know. Friends or colleagues who have faced the same decision are often a good source of information.

STEP FOUR—SEARCH THE SCRIPTURES FOR DIRECT AND INDIRECT PRINCIPLES THAT APPLY.

While you are collecting the needed information related to your alternatives, it is imperative that you take time to search out the Scriptures. Scripture has a bearing on all decisions (2 Timothy 3:16–17). Psalm 119:24 says that God's Word can be our counselor. It is the believer's responsibility to search out the Scripture for principles that apply to the decision under consideration.

There are two categories to consider when searching out the Scripture. First, identify the direct principles or statements contained in Scripture that apply to your decision. Direct principles would include all the "thou shalt" or "thou shalt not" statements found in Scripture; for example, stealing would not be an alternative for meeting a financial need because Scripture commands us not to steal. Second, look for indirect principles that apply—statements in Scripture that address the need for believers to be good stewards may be an influencing factor in deciding to set up a family budget. There is not a statement in Scripture saying, "Thou shalt have a budget"; however, a budget is a useful tool for implementing principles of stewardship found throughout Scripture.

STEP FIVE—PRAY ABOUT EACH ALTERNATIVE AND SEEK GODLY COUNSEL.

Once you have the required information for each alternative, you must again turn to the Lord for wisdom and discernment. Specifically pray about each alternative; in addition to prayer, there is wisdom in seeking the counsel of others. We can learn much from those who are older and more experienced— Proverbs 15:22 tells us that "without counsel, plans go awry, but in the multitude of counselors they are established." Seek a variety of counselors, including parents, pastors, teachers, or mentors. It should be noted here that the purpose of seeking counsel is not to find someone who validates your decision. If we look long enough, we will always be able to find someone who agrees with our choices, even when they are poor ones! The purpose of seeking counsel is to gain further insight into applicable biblical principles and/or to learn from the practical experiences of an older individual before a decision has been made.

STEP SIX—EVALUATE AND LIMIT THE ALTERNATIVES.

Based on the principles found in God's Word, the information collected, and the counsel received, you should now be able to eliminate several of the alternatives listed. Weed out any alternative that contradicts Scripture (either directly or indirectly). The remaining alternatives may all be amoral (neither good nor bad), so you will have to continue to ask yourself questions to eliminate some of the alternatives. You might ask, for example, "What would be the consequences of implementing this alternative, and can I live with that?" or, "How will this alternative impact the people in my life (spouse, children, parents)?" You should narrow your alternatives to two or three choices.

STEP SEVEN—CHOOSE THE BEST ALTERNATIVE OR DELAY THE DECISION.

Now it is time to commit to a course of action—remember our definition of a decision? *A decision implies you have selected and committed to a course of action.* There are times however, where you still may not feel the freedom to make a choice among the alternatives identified. It is at this point that you should delay making your final decision. Your heart should not condemn your decision (Romans 14:23; 1 John 3:21). Perhaps you need to collect more information or seek additional counsel; God's peace in your heart should be a confirming factor that the right decision has been made (Philippians 4:7).

STEP EIGHT—PRAY ABOUT YOUR DECISION AND ACT UPON YOUR CHOICE.

Once a decision is made, specifically pray and commit your course of action to the Lord. You must then implement the alternative you have selected as your course of action—a decision is not really made until you act upon your choice. This is the step where you put together the necessary resources so that the decision can become a reality.

STEP NINE—EVALUATE AND TAKE RESPONSIBILITY FOR YOUR DECISION.

Once a decision is made, a good manager takes time to evaluate its outcome. It is important that you take time to consider the ramifications—whether planned or unexpected—of your decision. We must take responsibility for the consequences of the decisions we make. Sometimes it will be necessary to make adjustments based on the consequences of our decision. This leads us to the final step of the decision-making process.

STEP TEN—MONITOR THE RESULTS AND MAKE ADJUSTMENTS AS NEEDED.

Even when a "good" decision is made, you still must take responsibility to monitor the results and make adjustments as necessary. This may mean that you have to retrace your steps in the decision-making process by collecting more information or seeking new counsel based on the result of your decision. Decision making is an ongoing process. The difference between making decisions and just "letting things happen" is that decision making involves recognition that past and present decisions have an impact on those you will make in the future.

Sometimes action is taken without using the formal decision-making process. This may occur when a routine or habit has been established. Recognizing that a decision needs to be made is a critical part of the decision-making process. Decision making plays a crucial role in the management of all resources.

A discussion of the decision-making process would be incomplete without acknowledging that God is sovereign over all. Psalm 115:3 says that God does what He pleases. He is not confined to the alternatives we have defined for our decision. God's ways are not our ways (Isaiah 55:8–9; Romans 11:33). We must be willing throughout the decision-making process to yield our will, our alternatives, our decision, to the Sovereign Lord who rules the world. James 4:13–16 reminds us that every decision we make should be made with the attitude of "If the Lord wills, we shall live and do this or that." We must pursue the decision-making process with humility, acknowledging that "a man's heart plans his way, but the Lord directs his steps" (Proverbs 16:9). The woman who applies wisdom with understanding, prudence, and discretion to the decision-making process, will truly be a happy woman. As Proverbs 3:13 states, "Happy is the man who finds wisdom, and the man who gains understanding."

A FINAL THOUGHT . . .

A significant area of responsibility for women is the management of their home. Proverbs 31:27 says, "She looks well to the ways of her household, and does not eat the bread of idleness" (NASB). To manage a household with excellence requires diligence, hard work, and training. Older women are encouraged to help the younger women learn how to successfully manage their homes (Titus 2:3–5). While the world often does not value the sacrifice of women who choose to work at home, Scripture is clear; a Wise Woman is one who "builds her house" (Proverbs 14:1; 24:3). Part of building your home is to practice careful management, effective planning, and wise decision making. It is a privilege to be given the responsibility of caring for the daily needs of a family and home.

TABLE 4.2
SAMPLE CLEANING SCHEDULE

	Bedroom	Bathroom	Living Room and Family Room	Kitchen and Dining Room	Laundry
Daily	Make beds Put away clothes Straighten dresser	Wipe out wash basin Change soiled towels Empty trash can Check toilet (clean if needed)	Dispose of papers Straighten pillows, magazines, and other accessories	Wash dishes Run dishwasher Clean countertops Clean sink Empty garbage Sweep or mop floor	Empty pockets Check clothing for tears or stains Put dirty clothes in the hamper Air out washable items Hang up clothes
Weekly	Change bed linens Dust furniture Care for floors (e.g., vacuum) Empty trash cans	Wash floor Clean toilet Clean bathtub Scrub sinks Clean toothbrush holder (and other fixtures) Clean mirrors	Vacuum Dust furniture Care for floors Empty trash cans Dust lamps	Dispose of left-over food Clean range thoroughly Wipe out refrigerator Care for floor Clean trash cans	Sort clothes Mend clothes before washing Pretreat stains Hand wash as needed Iron as needed Fold/hang clothes Take non-washables to the dry cleaner
Quarterly (i.e., January, April, July, and October)	Organize closets Turn mattresses Wash mattress pads Wash walls and baseboards Clean under furniture Wash windows, blinds, and shutters	Wash throw rugs, toilet cover, and shower curtains Wash walls and baseboards Wash windows, blinds, and shutters Wash curtains	Vacuum furniture and lamp shades Wash walls and baseboards Clean TV or computer screens Wash windows/blinds and shutters	Clean oven and microwave Move and clean under furniture Wax floor Wash walls and baseboards Wash windows/blinds	Wash sweaters/ jackets Discard or give away clothes not worn
Annually (Seasonal)	Wash blankets Wash comforters Wash curtains Clean screens/ storm windows	Clean closets or cabinets Replace worn towels Clean windows	Shampoo rugs and upholstered furniture Clean windows Wash curtains	Defrost and clean refrigerator/freezer Clean out cabinets Clean windows Wash curtains	Wash and store out-of-season clothes Wash curtains, throw rugs, pillows, and other washable home furnishings

GROWING IN
THE ABILITY TO
MANAGE YOUR HOME

1. Write your own personal mission statement that reflects your priorities. Use several key Scriptures for its foundation (see "Goal Setting to Reflect Priorities" in this chapter).

2. Establish three goals that will help you put your mission statement into practice. Break the goals into three steps—short, intermediate, and long-term (see "Goal Setting to Reflect Priorities" in this chapter).

3. Establish a daily, weekly, quarterly, and annual (seasonal) cleaning schedule. Use the "Sample Cleaning Schedule" located at the end of the chapter to get started.

4. Expand your knowledge of how to clean by purchasing the cleaning video by Don Aslett (see endnotes) or by visiting the Soap and Detergent Web site (www.SDAhq.org).

5. Apply the "Decision-Making Model" presented in this chapter to an upcoming decision. Develop a Scripture list that identifies the direct and indirect principles that apply to your decision.

$\mathcal{A}$s I stood before my senior students and explained the assignment that would allow them to practice the Titus 2 principle by entertaining the younger women in the department, their body language told me they were less than excited. It wasn't that they lacked servants' hearts or didn't embrace the principle of hospitality—it was just that they already thought they were busy enough without this responsibility; to their credit, they did not try to talk me out of the assignment. Our Lord sovereignly placed eleven VERY different people in the class! At the beginning of the course we spent time establishing a sense of family among the ten students. As part of this effort, I used chapter one of Edith' Schaeffer's classic book What Is a Family? The principles that would serve as guidelines for how the class was to be conducted looked great on paper—now, however, it was time to turn theory into practice.

I reminded my "older women" that while I was concerned about the quality of the event, I was most concerned that they demonstrate a spirit of graciousness throughout its planning, preparation, serving, and cleanup; the truth of Proverbs 15:17 (NRSV), "Better is a dinner of vegetables where love is than a fattened ox and hatred with it," was our motivating verse.

They chose a dinner party for their entertainment type and elaborated on the principles learned from What Is a Family? for their theme. There were many opportunities to implement the principles as group members faced personal challenges in the midst of the planning and preparation process. Finally, the long-awaited evening arrived and was tenderly executed. Their guests lingered long (always the sign of a good party), the students stretched their cleanup time, seemingly savoring their final moments together, and remained after the lab was "spic and span" to take pictures. As we recounted the blessings of the evening the following Monday, we were reminded that . . .

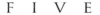

THE WISE WOMAN CREATES A GRACIOUS HOME

A gracious woman attains honor.
PROVERBS 11:16 NASB

The gracious home bears the attributes of the welcoming home described in chapter 3 and is embellished with good taste, comfort, courtesy, respect, and gratitude. *Gracious* is defined as being kindly disposed or showing favor and mercy to someone, usually by a person of superior position and power.[1] Scriptural instances portray Potiphar dealing graciously with Joseph (Genesis 39:4), Ruth finding favor in the eyes of Boaz (Ruth 2:10), and King Ahasuerus' gracious treatment to Esther (Esther 2:17; 5:2). Biblically, our heavenly Father sets the standard for graciousness toward human beings, as stated in the ancient liturgical formula: "The Lord, the Lord God, a God merciful and gracious, slow to anger, and abounding in steadfast love and faithfulness" (Exodus 34:6 NRSV). Psalm 86:15 portrays God as "full of compassion, and gracious, longsuffering and abundant in mercy and truth." Psalm 103:8 declares, "The Lord is merciful and gracious, slow to anger, and abounding in mercy" while Psalm 145:8 affirms, "The Lord is gracious and full of compassion, slow to anger and great in mercy."

Seeking to practice graciousness in her home, our Wise Woman draws upon the *principles of trustworthy, energetic, unselfish, prepared, lovable, prudent,* and *God-fearing* to nurture an environment that mirrors courtesy, respect, and gratitude. She keeps focused on the knowledge that it takes both time and energy to create a gracious home—however, the memories that result are well worth the effort!

GROWING IN GRACIOUSNESS

As a ring of gold in a swine's snout
So is a beautiful woman who lacks discretion.
PROVERBS 11:22 NASB

Etiquette is a formal word for simple kindness. A behavior used to display courtesy, etiquette is blatantly absent in twenty-first-century Christian culture. A woman's manners are a mirror in which she reveals her character. The apostle Paul states in 1 Corinthians 9:19, 22, "For though I am free from all men, I have made myself a servant to all, that I might win the more. . . . I have become all things to all men, that I might by all means save some." Regrettably, Christians are frequently the greatest offenders in failing to demonstrate common courtesy. Our Wise Woman, though not inflexible in her behavior, displays courtesy by abiding by standard etiquette protocol.

RESPONDING GRACIOUSLY TO INVITATIONS

Treat others the same way
you want them to treat you.
LUKE 6:31 NASB

Receiving an invitation is a special privilege; failing to respond to it within the allotted time period is an ungracious action that demonstrates a lack of discretion. Proverbs 11:22 provides a poignant description of such a woman: "As a ring of gold in a swine's snout, so is a beautiful woman who lacks discretion" (NASB). Here are some ways our Wise Woman displays a gracious attitude in her social interactions.

SHE RESPONDS TO ANY INVITATION NO LATER THAN THE DATE INDICATED.

Often the letters RSVP (French, *répondez, s'il vous plaît*), meaning, "The favor of a reply is requested," appear on the invitation. Use the response card, if one is included, to fulfill the RSVP request. A note declining the invitation is appropriate for a formal occasion if a response card is not enclosed. Purchase quality stationery for such notes and use a blue or black pen. A phone call is an adequate RSVP for an informal occasion. It is inappropriate to ask the hostess if you may bring additional guests.

SHE ARRIVES FOR THE FUNCTION FASHIONABLY ON TIME.

The standard rule is no earlier than and no more than fifteen minutes after the function begins. Punctuality demonstrates consideration of the host and hostess, attention to detail, and your interest in the social event. Hosts and hostesses appreciate being able to start entertaining guests on time.

SHE HANDLES INTRODUCTIONS WARMLY.

Our Wise Woman is aware that she never has a second chance to make a good first impression. Thus, she remembers that younger people are introduced to older people and people of all ages are introduced to people in authority. She may shake hands when she is introduced to a man or a woman and has a choice to sit or stand when introduced. She should not use first names unless invited to do so.

SHE SELECTS A SUITABLE HOSTESS GIFT.

She knows that a small gift when she is entertained in a person's home for a meal or when staying overnight is a gracious, and necessary, action. The gift reflects her appreciation for her hostess's kindness.

SHE ACKNOWLEDGES HER STATUS AS A GUEST.

When invited to someone's home she is in a position of honor. Whether for a meal or for an overnight stay, she must be considerate of the family and fit into their schedule. Here are some important reminders:

- Be punctual, but not early.
- Cancel *only* if there is an emergency.
- Don't "double book" yourself—commit yourself to the entire occasion.
- Offer to help the hostess.
- Make it a point to speak with the other guests.
- Do not attend if you are ill!
- Wear appropriate, modest attire—if you are unsure, ask the hostess.

- Don't be the first or last to leave.
- *Always* verbally express your enjoyment of the occasion to your hostess before departing.
- Call your hostess the following day to tell her you enjoyed the evening and write a thank-you note *immediately!*
- Fit in with the family's standard of orderliness or exceed it.
- Maintain your living area in an orderly manner.
- Make your bed, unless it is departure day or you are instructed not to.
- Remove personal items from the bathroom after each use unless it is reserved for your private use.
- Keep the bathroom clean.
- Refrain from using the phone without permission.
- Treat the house and all things in it with great respect.
- Make your schedule fit into your host's and hostess's schedule.
- Blend in with the family.
- Be sensitive about not using all the hot water, listening to the television or music too loudly, or asking for too many items that you forgot.
- Display a willingness to help.

SHE DRESSES ACCORDING TO THE OCCASION.

Dressing appropriately is one of the sure signs of etiquette success; it is preferable to be understated rather than overstated anytime. If in doubt, ask the hostess the appropriate attire for the occasion. When attending with a male escort, our Wise Woman focuses on complementing, not competing with him. Modesty is her first criterion in clothing selection. She remembers the clothing design principle that states, "The eye stops where the line stops" and that her clothing is a label for her character!

SHE EXHIBITS GRACIOUS POSTURE.

Gracious posture requires the woman to sit with her knees together or legs crossed. She is to sit up straight, shoulders back, and head high; she avoids slouching.

SHE PRACTICES POLITE TABLE MANNERS.

Table etiquette, or the proper way of handling yourself during a meal, could mean the difference in one's ministry or career! Our Wise Woman knows that practice makes perfect. Adhering to correct etiquette at home ensures that it will soon become a natural behavior. She is aware that there is not a place in the world where courtesy is as necessary as in the home. Our Wise Woman chooses to master polite table manners by:

- Observing her hostess and taking cues from her.
- Waiting for the hostess to be seated before taking a seat.
- Allowing the gentleman to seat the lady to his right. He pulls out her chair for her, and she waits for him to seat her. Once seated, he then takes his seat beside her.
- Observing the hostess when placing the napkin. She may place her napkin in her lap before the blessing or wait until after to do so. It may be unfolded or left folded in half with the fold against the body. The napkin is placed on the seat if she leaves the table during the meal. At the end of the meal, it is placed to the right of the plate. It does not need to be refolded and should *not* be wadded up.

SHE HANDLES SILVERWARE WITH PRECISION.

- Regardless of how many implements are on the table, always start from the outside of the setting and move toward the inside. Silverware placed at the top of the plate is used.

- *Never* place used silver back on the linens.
- If in doubt as to which piece of silverware to use, watch the hostess.
- Refrain from grasping either knife or fork in a sort of clenched fist.
- When pausing during eating, leave the fork and knife in a crossed position in the center of the plate. A trained waiter will know that you are signaling him not to remove your plate.
- When you are through eating, indicate this by placing the fork and knife on the side of the plate, side by side, at an angle. On a clock this would be 10:20, with the tips of the knife and fork at ten, the ends of the handles at four. This lets the waiter know that your plate may be removed.

SHE CONFIDENTLY MANEUVERS FORMAL DINNERS.

Our Wise Woman follows basic etiquette protocol by

- sitting according to the instructions of her hostess.
- tasting her food before adding salt or pepper.
- closing her mouth while chewing.
- not creating noise with her silverware.
- sitting up straight in her chair.
- matching her eating pace with that of the other guests— not too slow and not too fast.
- taking a small serving of all foods.
- demonstrating graciousness with her words and actions.
- being polite and patient with the other guests.
- watching her hostess for cues.
- planning to enjoy herself!

A formal dinner may include beverages that violate the Wise Woman's standards. Etiquette and Christian graciousness motivate her to unobtrusively refrain from partaking of the beverages to avoid drawing attention to her or embarrassing her hostess. Understanding the order of the formal table setting allows her to proceed with confidence. The white wineglass is placed to the far right, followed by the red wineglass and the water glass. The champagne goblet is in the rear. Decline beverages by simply turning the vessel upside down.

In addition to discussing thanksgiving, Elisabeth Elliot also shared with her *Gateway to Joy* radio audience on July 8, 1999, the importance of courtesy in the Christian culture:

> Talking with a group of seminary students, I mentioned that the common rules of courtesy are often overlooked nowadays, especially by those who grew up in the past two decades, an era in which all conventions and traditions were suspect. Mere convention came to mean pure hypocrisy. If a thing was labeled traditional, it had to be discarded as no longer relevant, meaningful or even intelligent. If a man had the temerity to hold a door open for the woman, he was sometimes labeled sexist.
>
> My brother Tom, who was a professor in a Christian college, once had the temerity to hold open a door for a girl student, a girl who was wearing blue jeans, a sweatshirt and a backpack. She had what they used to call "wafflestompers" on her feet. She spun around angrily and said to him, "Did you hold that door open because I'm a lady?" Tom's answer was, "No, I did it because I'm a gentleman."
>
> My point in bringing up the subject of courtesy was simply that it is a small way of demonstrating that deep principle, central to our Christian faith: My life for yours. That was the message that Jesus gave us from the cross, wasn't it? My life for yours. I asked my class if any of the husbands in that room made a habit of helping their wives into their chairs at the table, even when company was not present.
>
> A week later one of the men stopped me in the seminary hall.

"I just want to tell you that my behavior toward my wife has been altered since last week's lecture. You know what? It's changed my attitude toward her, as well as hers toward me. It's really been revelatory. Just wanted to say thanks." I was immensely cheered. It's always cheering to know somebody has had ears to hear and has actually done something about what he heard.[2]

Our Wise Woman understands that without good manners, she will fall off the ladder of success!

SPEAKING GRACIOUSLY

A man has joy in an apt answer,
And how delightful is a timely word!
PROVERBS 15:23 NASB

The *principle of prudence,* presented in chapter 1, describes our Wise Woman's speech as exhibiting good judgment and discretion (Colossians 4:6). Elizabeth George, writing in *A Woman's High Calling,* poses a significant question:

Suppose you were in the presence of a woman who was thinking about God and enjoying sweet communion with Him as her thoughts ascended to His throne in prayer, who was continually absorbed in some portion of God's Holy Word, who was perhaps humming a hymn of praise to God. If you began to talk to one another, what do you imagine would come out of her mouth?

I think you can safely answer something like this: You would hear words of blessing, words filled with graciousness and sweetness from such a woman. Tumbling forth from her lips would be soothing, healing words of comfort or uplifting encouragement, whichever would be appropriate. Certainly you would witness words of mercy, concern, and compassion.

And, so, you would find her to be like the woman of Proverbs 31:26—"She opens her mouth with wisdom and on her tongue is the law of kindness." Our description would not be complete without adding such adjectives as courteous, respectful, and honoring.[3]

Portions of God's Holy Word that could contribute to words filled with blessing, graciousness, and sweetness when memorized and meditated upon include:

- Proverbs 10:19–20—"When there are many words, transgression is unavoidable, but he who restrains his lips is wise. The tongue of the righteous is as choice silver, the heart of the wicked is worth little" (NASB).
- Proverbs 15:1—"A gentle answer turns away wrath, but a harsh word stirs up anger" (NASB).
- Proverbs 16:24—"Pleasant words are a honeycomb, sweet to the soul and healing to the bones" (NASB).
- Proverbs 17:27—"He who restrains his words has knowledge, and he who has a cool spirit is a man of understanding" (NASB).
- Proverbs 29:20—"Do you see a man who is hasty in his words? There is more hope for a fool than for him" (NASB).
- Proverbs 25:11—"Like apples of gold in settings of silver is a word spoken in right circumstances" (NASB).
- Psalm 19:14—"Let the words of my mouth and the meditation of my heart be acceptable in Your sight, O Lord, my rock and my Redeemer" (NASB).

The bit of poetry entitled "Only One Childhood," by Linda Ellis, puts into perspective the devastating message frequently communicated to loved ones when we choose to be ungracious with our speech.

Only One Childhood

I stopped to watch my little girl
Busy playing in her room.

In one hand was a plastic phone;
In the other a toy broom.

I listened as she was speaking
To her make-believe little friend
And I'll never forget the words she said,
Even though it was pretend.

She said, "Suzie's in the corner
Cuz she's not been very good.
She didn't listen to a word I said
Or do the things she should."

In the corner I saw her baby doll
All dressed in lace and pink.
It was obvious she'd been put there
To sit alone and think.

My daughter continued her "conversation,"
As I sat down on the floor.
She said, "I'm all fed up, I just don't know
What to do with her anymore.

"She whines whenever I have to work
And wants to play games, too;
And never lets me do the things
That I just have to do.

"She tries to help me with the dishes,
But her arms just cannot reach
And she doesn't know how to fold the towels
And I don't have time to teach.

"I have a lot of work to do
And a big house to keep clean.
I don't have time to sit and play—
Don't you know what I mean?"

And that day I thought a lot about
Making some changes in my life;
As I listened to her innocent words
That cut me like a knife.

I hadn't been paying enough attention
To what I hold most dear.
I'd been caught up in responsibilities
That increased throughout the year.

But now my attitude has changed
Because, in my heart, I realize
I've seen the world in a different light
Through my little darling's eyes.

So, let the cobwebs have the corners
And the dust bunnies rule the floor,
I'm not going to worry about
Keeping up with them anymore.

I'm going to fill the house with memories
Of a child and her mother
For God grants us only ONE childhood,
And we will never get another.[4]

Our Wise Woman chooses to use these guidelines for her speech:

- *Always* show your appreciation for the efforts of others.
- Say affirming comments about the food or the occasion; if you can't, then say nothing at all.
- *Don't* dominate the conversation.
- *Don't* be too silent.
- Refrain from "taboo topics," such as salary or net worth, commissions or promotions, politics and religion, age, weight, and any personal areas.

"The Tale of the Frogs" reminds the Wise Woman of the power she wields each time she uses her tongue!

THE TALE OF THE FROGS

A group of frogs were traveling through the woods, and two of them fell into a deep pit. All the other frogs gathered around the pit. When they saw how deep the pit was, they told the two frogs that they were as good as dead. The two frogs ignored the comments and tried to jump out of the pit with all of their might. The group of frogs kept telling them to stop because they were as good as dead.

Finally, one of the frogs took heed to what the other frogs were saying and gave up. He fell down and died. The second frog continued to jump as hard as he could. Once again, the crowd of frogs yelled at him to stop the pain and just die. He jumped even harder and finally made it out. You see this frog was deaf, unable to hear what the others were saying. He thought they were encouraging him the entire time.

There is the power of life and death in the tongue. An encouraging word to someone who is down can lift him up and help him make it through the day. A destructive word to someone who is down can be what it takes to kill him. Be careful of what you say. Speak life to those who cross your path. The power of words . . . an encouraging word can go such a long way. May your words be a blessing to someone today.

—Author Unknown

DISPLAYING GRATITUDE

In everything give thanks;
for this is God's will for you in Christ Jesus.
1 THESSALONIANS 5:18 NASB

The English word *gratitude* is derived from the same word that gives us *grace*. Our Wise Woman acknowledges that gratitude and grace are Siamese twins. Since Christian women daily experience the grace of God, and if they are looking for ways to acknowledge that God's grace is at work in their lives and the lives of others, then they have many reasons to express gratitude. Many Christian women complain more frequently than they express gratitude—and they don't appear to realize what devastating effects their complaining has on their spiritual lives. Though they may temporarily feel better emotionally for having transferred their negative thoughts to others, the spiritual toll that the emotional release renders is often devastating.

❦ ❦ ❦

I can personally attest to the negative impact that a complaining spirit has on one's life; before our Lord drew me into His family, my attitude was so negative that when I awoke each morning my first reaction was, "I wonder what terrible thing is going to happen to me today." I was always a prophet of my own doom—by nightfall I always had several items to add to my list of "Poor Pat Protests." Unfortunately, I carried my negative, complaining spirit into my new life as a Christian. Then one day my pastor began to preach about "walking in the spirit" (see Galatians 5:16), and I learned that my negative, complaining spirit was SIN rather than the discerning spirit I attributed to it. I also learned that the best antidote for a complaining spirit is a thankful spirit, and that is something I needed to cultivate daily. He challenged his congregation to make a list of the things we were thankful for and when we were tempted to complain, instead choose to meditate on all of God's gifts to us. I accepted his challenge, purchased a pretty journal that invited me to write in it, and began by writing Psalm 103 on the first page. Daily I recorded only God's blessings to me— and I found my attitude gradually changing. I have filled multiple journals, and at least one entry a week records my heavenly Father's blessings to me; now when I feel a tendency to revert back to my habit of "Poor Pat Protests" I spend time reviewing my journals and find that by the conclusion of my reading session my "protests" have turned to "praise"!

> *We can give thanks in everything*
> *And say, "Your will be done."*
> *For God's at work in everything*
> *To make us like His Son.*[5]

❦ ❦ ❦

Giving thanks for everything seems like an oxymoron. Twenty-first-century society tells us that this is an unrealistic expectation. However, the Bible directs us to give thanks for everything (1 Thessalonians 5:18). Our Wise Woman confronts the discrepancy between earthly wisdom and biblical wisdom and chooses to embrace biblical wisdom (James 3:17).

Real gratitude expands the ministry opportunities of our Wise Woman. The more thankful she is, the more she is aware of her many blessings. If she only offers praise and thanksgiving when things go her way, she develops tunnel vision. If she is grateful for all that her heavenly Father brings into her life, then her horizons are expanded and her ability to sincerely offer praise, regardless of the circumstances, increases!

I can speak with conviction about this spiritual principle. Many circumstances in my life (being abandoned as an infant, being orphaned by my adoptive parents in my early twenties, being single, to name a few) initially appeared to be insurmountable obstacles; however, as I chose to believe that my Lord is a sun and shield; that He gives grace and glory; and that there is no good thing that He will withhold from me if I am walking uprightly (Psalm 84:11), I realized that all I need to do is take care of the walking uprightly part (that includes being grateful for all things), and He will do the rest! Looking in retrospect at the seemingly devastating circumstances, I can now see how my loving, heavenly Father used each as a vehicle to minister to others as well as to shape my character.

The September 16 selection of *Joy and Strength* contains a piece of prose written by Priscilla Maurice (1810–54) that clearly describes this thought:

Begin with thanking Him for some little thing, and then go on, day by day, adding to your subjects of praise: thus you will find their numbers grow wonderfully; and, in the same proportion, will your subjects of murmuring and complaining diminish, until you see in everything some cause for thanksgiving. If you cannot begin with anything positive, begin with something negative. If your whole lot seems only filled with causes for discontent, at any rate there is some trial that has *not* been appointed you; and you may thank God for its being withheld from you. It is certain that the more you try to praise, the more you will see how your path and your lying down are beset with mercies, and that the God of love is ever watching to do you good.[6]

In the same *Gateway to Joy* radio broadcast mentioned earlier in this chapter, Elisabeth Elliot talked about a book, *New Every Morning,* written by her father, Philip E. Howard Jr. A piece in that book, "An Exercise in Thanksgiving," provides a glimpse of his character.

Blessings taken for granted are often forgotten, yet our Heavenly Father daily loadeth us with benefits. Think of some of the common things which are nevertheless wonderful:

- the intricate delicate mechanism of the lungs steadily and silently taking in fresh air 18 to 20 times a minute,
- the untiring heart pumping great quantities of clean blood through the labyrinth of blood vessels,
- the constant body temperature normally varying less than one degree,
- the atmospheric temperature (varying widely, it is true, but never so much as to destroy human and animal life),
- the orderly succession of day and night, spring, summer, autumn and winter, so that with few exceptions man can make his plans accordingly,
- the great variety of foods from the farm, the field, the forest and the sea, to suit our differing desires and physical needs,

- the beauties of each day, the morning star and growing light of sunrise, the white clouds of afternoon, the soft tints of a peaceful sunset and the glory of the starry heavens,
- the symphony of early morning bird songs, ranging from the unmusical trill of the chirping sparrow to the lilting ecstasy of the goldfinch and the calm, bell-like tones of the wood and hermit thrushes,
- the refreshment that sleep brings,
- the simple joys of home—the children's laughter and whimsical remarks, happy times around the table, the love and understanding of husband and wife, and the harmony of voices raised together in praise to God. . . .

All these and many others come from the beautiful hand of Him who redeemeth thy life from destruction, who crowneth thee with lovingkindness and tender mercies, who satisfieth thy mouth with good things, so that thy youth is renewed like the eagle's" [Psalm 103 KJV].[7]

A study of Christian biographies reveals that God's "giants" were people who knew how to praise the Lord in the midst of suffering. God used their lives to impact others because they knew how to give thanks—even in difficulties. Are you the type of Christian woman whose prayer list is filled with personal wants, while your praise list stays the same or shrinks? Or are you choosing to be a Wise Woman who offers praise and thanksgiving daily? Your response to these questions determines your level of spiritual maturity. If you are increasing in your knowledge of the Word, then you have many reasons to thank our Lord. If you are seeking to serve others (Mark 10:45), then you will have new motivation to praise the Lord. If you are looking for ways to bear the burdens of others (Galatians 6:2), then your praise for what *God* is doing should increase. Praise should touch every area of your life. If it is your heart's desire to mature into a Wise Woman, then you will praise more and complain less!

The primary obstacle to praise is pride, and it is most often revealed through an attitude of criticism. We will not always get the best or have people serve us in the way we think we deserve; in fact, the Lord may reprove us by giving us the opposite of what we expect. Pride not only goes before a fall (Proverbs 16:18), it also goes before a lot of disappointments. Our heavenly Father wants us to strive for spiritual maturity; pride and selfishness hinder the process. As Wise Women in Progress, we will want to remember that the *first* of the seven things that are an abomination to our Lord is a "proud look," or "haughty eyes" (NASB) (Proverbs 6:16–19).

It is vital to acknowledge that it is not easy to look up and say, "Thank you, Lord," when circumstances are challenging; however, it is a necessary reaction and one that demonstrates that our Wise Woman is exercising her will rather than her emotions. While our Lord may not change the circumstances, praise will affect what the circumstances do to her. Remember, the psalmist directs his writings to the will, not the emotions!

The unsaved world is accustomed to hearing people complain; they really don't know what to do with people who are joyfully praising the Lord! The Philippian jailer (Acts 16:25–29) was not brought to Christ by the earthquake—that made him want to commit suicide! It was because Paul and Silas praised the Lord—under difficult circumstances—that the man heard the gospel and knew that there was a way of salvation. It is a sober realization that a complaining Christian woman will be a pitiful witness for her faith; in reality, she is too much like the world to have much effect on it.

The story of the ten lepers highlights the fact that we are prone to accept blessing without saying, "Thank You." Too often Christian women are like the nine lepers who were healed of a disease that labeled them as outcasts of society; they wanted the gift of healing but failed to give thanks to the Lord Jesus (Luke 17:11–19) once it was bestowed. Paul provides a severe warning in 2 Timothy 3:1–7 to believers who fail to offer thanks.

Just as we delight in hearing others express gratitude to us, so God finds great delight in hearing His children say, "Thank You." He inspired the psalmist to write, "It is good to give thanks to the Lord" (Psalm 92:1); since saying, "Thank You," pleases God and encourages others, Wise Women will do it often!

If we were thankful for everything
The way God tells us to be,
What a wonderful change in our living
We would be able to see!
—Author Unknown

A FINAL THOUGHT . . .

We know that we cannot force others to practice graciousness; however, we can model behavior that challenges them to integrate graciousness into their lives. As Wise Women, when we "model what we mandate," others will see a visual example, a lifestyle that allows them to "attain honor," and that reflects the heart of their heavenly Father (Psalm 145:8)!

GROWING IN THE
ABILITY TO CREATE
A GRACIOUS HOME

1. Develop a plan to cultivate gracious table manners in your home.

2. Cultivate a thought life that could contribute to words filled with graciousness and sweetness.

> *a. Write out Proverbs 10:19–20, Proverbs 15:1, Proverbs 16:24, Proverbs 17:27, Proverbs 29:20, Proverbs 25:11, and Psalm 19:14 on attractive cards.*
> *b. Memorize and meditate upon each of the verses.*
> *c. As the verses are used to promote words filled with graciousness and sweetness, write examples of their fruit on the back.*
> *d. When meditating, focus on both the verse and the examples.*
> *e. Add additional memorization and meditation verses as proficiency with those listed above are mastered.*

3. Purchase a blank journal that is aesthetically pleasing.

> *a. Inscribe the first page with a statement similar to "Remembrances of God's benefits displayed to <u>insert your name and the date</u>."*

b. *Write out Psalm 103:2–5 and Philippians 1:6 on the second page.*

c. *Record weekly God's blessings to you.*

d. *Review monthly the journal's contents.*

4. *Study the lives of individuals who manifested thankful spirits in the midst of tribulation. Daniel, David, Paul, Hannah, Anna, Mary, and Elizabeth are examples to stimulate your thoughts. Develop principles that will assist you in "giving thanks in all things."*

5. *Locate missionaries that you can communicate with and share their burdens. Record in your journal praise for what God is doing.*

Every time my husband returns from a trip overseas, I am struck by the significant differences in the lifestyles of Americans compared to many other cultures around the world. It happened again recently when he returned from teaching in Russia. As I looked through his pictures and listened to the stories about his students, I was reminded of how many conveniences I enjoy on a daily basis—I have my own car to shuttle my family around town and can afford the gas to run it. I have a large refrigerator that will store a week's worth of groceries and a nearby supermarket stocked full of thousands of products from which to choose. I have a computer in my home with the capability of Internet access. I have a closet full of clothes for every season. The list of conveniences could go on and on.

In contrast to my life are people from various parts of the world who work twelve to fourteen hours a day just to earn enough for one day's food; who own the clothes on their back and no others; who will never own a car, refrigerator, or computer; and who have little choice in how they spend their time, money, or energy because they must use all their resources merely to survive another day. The recurring question each time I am confronted with the affluence of my culture is why, when I am living in a society full of modern conveniences, is life so complex? Why is it so difficult to decide how to spend my time or money? The answer I think is fairly simple. It is because more conveniences result in the need for more choices; more choices result in making life more complex. Since life is complex it requires a real understanding of biblical stewardship. The contrast of my American lifestyle to other cultures around the world reminds me that . . .

THE WISE WOMAN PRACTICES STEWARDSHIP

Not that I speak from want,
for I have learned to be content in whatever circumstances I am.
I know how to get along with humble means,
and I also know how to live in prosperity;
in any and every circumstance I have learned
the secret of being filled and going hungry,
both of having abundance and suffering need.

PHILIPPIANS 4:11–12 NASB

The Wise Woman, as we have seen in previous chapters, is called to manage prudently. She is motivated out of a desire to be a faithful and obedient steward. In addition to managing her home with wisdom, she is challenged to practice stewardship in several additional areas of her life. A steward, remember, is simply a manager of someone else's property. It is usually easy to see how the concept of stewardship applies to management of our money or other material possessions. It is a little more difficult, however, to remember that we are stewards of *everything* God has given us—our time, energy, education, abilities, family, and even our life experiences. Wise

Women will strive to be faithful stewards (or managers) in all areas of their lives. It is important to recognize we are stewards in all areas so that we strive to manage with excellence (in order to be found faithful) and so that we practice the principle of *contentment,* as Paul reminds us in Philippians 4:11–12. Although there are many areas women will be called upon to manage with excellence, there are three primary areas that women typically find challenging to manage: finances, time, and work (or ministry obligations). Let's take a look at these three areas to identify some principles that will help us become better stewards of the resources God has given us.

PRINCIPLES OF FINANCIAL MANAGEMENT

Better is the little of the righteous
Than the abundance of many wicked.
PSALM 37:16 NASB

The principle of *contentment* developed in chapter 3 must be reviewed before identifying basic financial management concepts. *Contentment* is defined as "ease of mind; being pleased; or satisfied."[1] Contentment as it relates to finances, therefore, infers that one is at ease, pleased, and satisfied; how many women can say that about their finances? Unfortunately, not many of us; that is the reason the principles of financial management are so critical. These principles allow women to manage the financial resources God has given them so that they can become faithful and obedient stewards, which in turn allows them to experience financial contentment. This motivation is significantly different from motivation in the secular world. Most people in the secular world are motivated to manage their finances out of a desire to maximize their wealth, find life-satisfaction, and reach a state of financial security.[2] Stewardship and obedience that result in financial contentment motivate the Wise Woman.

In Philippians 4:11–13 Paul states, "Not that I speak from want, for I have learned to be content in whatever circumstances I am. I know how to get along with humble means, and I also know how to live in prosperity; in any and every circumstance I have learned the secret of being filled and going hungry, both of having abundance and suffering need. I can do all things through Him who strengthens me" (NASB). Notice that Paul said, "I have *learned*" to be content; Larry Burkett says:

> In the areas of finances, contentment does not mean complacency. Complacency means that I have a problem and I suffer through it with a good attitude; but contentment means I know that I'm in the center of God's will. I change the things I can. The things I cannot change I am willing to accept and be content with because I know the One who is in control. The secret to a happy life is learning how to deal with both the good times and the bad and, like the apostle Paul, knowing how to be content with either.[3]

Contentment is something women must learn. Developing contentment begins with a proper understanding of finances from a biblical perspective. There are ten basic biblical financial principles for the Wise Woman to implement:

1. *How money is handled impacts our relationship with God.* The parable of the talents illustrates that money must be handled appropriately so that the Wise Woman is a faithful steward and thus enters into the "joy of [our] Lord" (Matthew 25:21).
2. *God is owner of everything.* When the Wise Woman acknowledges God's ownership, "every spending decision becomes a spiritual decision"[4] (Leviticus 25:32; 1 Chronicles 29:11–12; Psalms 24:1; 50:10–12).
3. *Financial contentment must be learned.* Contentment results

when God is acknowledged as the owner and controller of everything (Psalm 135:6; Isaiah 45:6–7; Romans 8:28).

4. *God requires faithful financial stewardship.* A steward is one who manages another's property. Regardless of how much the Lord provides, all are called to manage faithfully (Matthew 25:14–15; 1 Corinthians 4:2).

5. *God promises to provide for the Wise Woman's needs.* Needs are the basic elements required to sustain our lives (for example, food and clothing). God does not promise to provide our wants (Matthew 6:25–34).

6. *God expects the Wise Woman to work hard and with integrity and honesty.* The Wise Woman represents Christ in all her financial dealings. She is to work as unto the Lord. Dishonest dealings in any area of her finances violate the primary command to love God and love our neighbors as ourselves (Leviticus 19:11; Proverbs 12:22; Proverbs 20:7; Matthew 22:37–39; Colossians 3:23–24).

7. *The Wise Woman is to be a cheerful giver.* The Wise Woman is to be a generous giver, not giving grudgingly or out of necessity (Proverbs 3:9; Acts 20:35; 2 Corinthians 8:1–5; 9:7).

8. *Debt represents slavery.* Debt limits the Wise Woman's ability to give, save, and invest. It threatens contentment and consumes her time because "the borrower becomes the lender's slave" until the debt is paid in full. Debt limits her ability to serve God because she is no longer completely free to follow Him (Proverbs 22:7 NASB).

9. *A portion of all financial resources is to be saved and invested.* As the principle of *prepared* teaches, controlling expenses and saving allows the Wise Woman to be prepared for unexpected circumstances. Saving and investing are tools that can be used to provide for the family's needs (Proverbs 13:22; Proverbs 21:5, 20; Proverbs 30:24–25; 1 Timothy 5:8).

10. *Children are to be discipled in financial management.* Training children should include teaching them about financial responsibility. The best way to teach children about financial stewardship is to model for them biblical financial principles (Deuteronomy 6:6–7; Proverbs 22:6; Luke 6:40).

Clearly, God is concerned with how money is managed; more than two thousand verses in the Bible relate to money management. Scripture clearly outlines God's expectations for handling material resources.

DEVELOPING FINANCIAL MANAGEMENT SKILLS

His master said to him,
"Well done, good and faithful slave;
you were faithful with a few things,
I will put you in charge of many things,
enter into the joy of your master."
MATTHEW 25:21 NASB

Once the Wise Woman understands God's expectation of financial management, she is ready to implement five steps that will assist her in developing the skills needed to become a wise money manager:

STEP ONE: ACQUIRE THE NEEDED FINANCIAL KNOWLEDGE.

Specific and concentrated study is needed to gain knowledge regarding personal financial management. Enrolling in finance classes, reading books, and seeking counsel from experienced financial planners are helpful. Each woman must identify her specific financial deficiencies and then pursue the needed education.

STEP TWO: DEVELOP SKILLS IN THE USE OF FINANCIAL TOOLS.

As a part of knowledge acquisition, develop skills that include the ability to use financial planning tools, such as developing a budget, choosing insurance, selecting investments, and/or using credit. There are tools to master for each category of financial planning.

STEP THREE: ESTABLISH FINANCIAL GOALS.

Good financial management allows the Wise Woman to distinguish between wants and needs. Financial management will help her meet financial goals. Financial goals should be set in areas such as saving, giving, investment, and retirement. Additionally, she can set goals for identifying spending and debt limits.

STEP FOUR: EXAMINE THE INFLUENCES ON FINANCIAL BEHAVIOR.

Many factors—both internal and external—influence financial behavior. A Wise Woman understands the factors that impact her financial behavior and is willing to make the needed changes to improve her financial management skills. Personality, family background and habits, education level, age, and cultural issues are examples of factors influencing financial behavior.

STEP FIVE: ESTABLISH A PLAN.

The Wise Woman develops a plan for the areas of financial management:

- *Budgeting*—She controls spending in order to accomplish financial goals.
- *Money management*—She develops cash, credit, and savings plans.
- *Life and Asset Protection*—She purchases appropriate insurance.
- *Investment choices*—She invests for the future and for special needs of the day.
- *Retirement and estate planning*—She plans for her retirement and looks ahead to the estate she will leave her heirs.

BASIC BUDGETING PRINCIPLES

Know well the condition of your flocks,
And pay attention to your herds;
For riches are not forever,
Nor does a crown endure to all generations.
PROVERBS 27:23–24 NASB

A Wise Woman who desires to manage her finances should begin by establishing a budget. A budget helps organize, monitor, and control spending and savings; as well, it is a document or set of documents used to record projected and actual income and expenses over a specific period of time. Generally a budget is established annually and maintained on a monthly basis. Budgets are the key to accomplishing most financial goals. Therefore, financial goals should be established prior to establishing a budget. Budgets should be viewed as a tool to assist in financial management. A budget is not a punishment or a restriction. There is great freedom in spending when a budget is established because the Wise Woman understands the flow of her financial resources. (A sample budget is provided at the end of this chapter.) The basic steps to establishing a budget include the following:

STEP ONE: LIST ALL AVAILABLE INCOME (GROSS AND NET).

Examples of income include salary income, wage income, rent income, interest income, investment income, and tax refunds.

- *Gross Income* is the total income amount before deductions.
- *Net Income* is the amount of income after taxes and all other standard deductions have been taken out; budgets are developed on net income amounts. Women who tithe regularly may also want to subtract their tithe. Once tithe, taxes, and standard deductions are subtracted, you have your net income.

STEP TWO: LIST ALL EXPENDITURES (FIXED AND VARIABLE EXPENDITURES).

- *Fixed Expenditures* are those expenses that remain the same amount every month. For example, a house payment (if it is a fixed mortgage) or rent, car payments, insurance premiums, loan payments, or savings. (See "Sample Budget Form" at the end of this chapter for more examples.)
- *Variable Expenditures* are those expenses that change monthly (you pay them every month like fixed expenses, but the actual amount differs). Examples might include a house payment (if it is a variable mortgage), food, clothing, medical costs, auto repairs, and entertainment. (See "Sample Budget Form" at the end of this chapter for more examples.)

STEP THREE: COMPARE INCOME VERSUS EXPENSES.

Income must be compared to expenses and then the needed adjustments made to balance the budget. Use past records to estimate expenses. There are only two possibilities when comparing income to expenses:

- *Surplus—income exceeds expenses.* Decisions must be made as to how the surplus will be utilized.
- *Deficit—expenses exceed income.* Decisions must be made as to how to cut expenses and/or generate more income.

STEP FOUR: MONITOR AND EVALUATE.

Once the budget is balanced in Step Three, it is critical that continuous monitoring takes place to ensure the budget remains balanced. Adjustments will need to be made as circumstances change. Monitoring and evaluating include the following:

- *Record Keeping*—A simple filing and recording system should be set up. Records that will be needed in order to monitor the success of your budget will include salary or wage reports, monthly bills or expenses, tax records, insurance policies, employment benefits, investment reports, and any other personal financial documents (such as wills, living trusts, or an inventory of personal property).
- *Recording*—Each month enter the actual amount of bills and actual income. Reconcile the budget. If there is a surplus during a particular month, decide whether or not to save it or apply it to paying off a bill early (decide what to do with surplus in advance).
- *Evaluation*—Make adjustments to the budget on an annual or semiannual basis. This will help to ensure the budget is an accurate reflection of income and expenses. Compare actual spending with projected spending. Look for patterns of overspending, analyze how you can adjust your budget, and consider how you will handle unexpected expenses. Additionally, it is recommended that

you fix the maximum level of spending in advance and not just keep readjusting it as income increases. This will allow for the Wise Woman to increase savings, investments, and retirement plans.

Developing a budget plan should not take more than three to four hours to initially set it up and thirty minutes a week to maintain. If it takes longer, it is probably more complicated than it needs to be. It will take seven to nine months for the budget plan to work efficiently. During this initial phase, careful monitoring and adjustments need to be made so it is an accurate document.

The two most common budgeting challenges are not using the budget after it is established and developing a budget that is so complicated you are unable to maintain it. Setting up a convenient work area for record keeping and bill paying helps keep finances orderly. Each household has a uniquely developed budget based on its individual circumstances. However, some standard percentage guidelines are helpful when initially establishing a budget. Larry Burkett suggests the following categories and average projected guidelines when establishing budgets:

GROSS INCOME:
1. Giving—10–20%
2. Taxes—15–32%

NET SPENDABLE INCOME:
1. Housing—30–38% (the average is about 34%)
2. Food—15%
3. Automobiles—15%
4. Debts—5%
5. Insurance—5%
6. Recreation/Entertainment—5%
7. Clothing—5%

8. Savings—5%
9. Medical/Dental Expenses—5%
10. Miscellaneous Household Expenses—5%
11. School/Child-care Expenses—10% (reduce the other
    categories to accommodate this expense)[5]

PRINCIPLES FOR PARTNERING ON FINANCES

The plans of the diligent lead surely to advantage,
But everyone who is hasty comes surely to poverty.
PROVERBS 21:5 NASB

Married women are involved with the family finances under
the leadership and authority of their husbands. Each couple
will need to determine how they will handle the practical out-
working of financial planning, including bill paying, maintaining
the filing system, budget maintenance, and accomplishing financial goals. There is no "right way" or "wrong way" when
it comes to these decisions as long as the issue of leadership and
responsibility is maintained. Ultimately, husbands are responsible, regardless of who writes the checks. Here are a few principles that may help married women as they work together with
their husbands to manage the finances:

1. ASSUME MUTUAL RESPONSIBILITY.

The husband and wife must be committed to biblically handling the finances. Both must participate in accomplishing the
financial goals established as a team that view financial resources as "ours," not "his" or "hers." It is not uncommon that
one partner will have more experience or training in the area
of finances. In order for couples to work together in this area,
they may need to take a class together or participate in a Bible
study focused on financial management so that they can share
common information and principles for their family finances.

2. ENCOURAGE GIFTEDNESS AND ABILITY.

A common question among married couples is "Who should handle the money?" The issue of leadership and responsibility is already established in Scripture—the husband is the head of the household in all things. However, the practical application of writing checks or maintaining files may be delegated to the wife, especially if she is gifted in the area of financial management. A wife can have a significant ministry to her husband by handling the finances with prudence. If a wife becomes the bill payer, however, the husband needs to actively participate by asking, on a regular basis, about the state of the finances. Wives are to consult their husbands before making independent financial decisions, always acknowledging his responsibility and authority for the finances.

3. RECOGNIZE THE DIFFERENCE BETWEEN GENEROSITY AND IRRESPONSIBILITY.

Sacrificial giving must be balanced with stewardship and the command to provide for the needs of the family. Couples should decide together their philosophy of giving. A family who manages its finances well will be free to give generously.

4. COLLABORATE ON BUDGETING.

Both partners must participate in the development phase and the implementation phase in order for a monthly budget to succeed. Each should be intimately aware of the categories of their budget and how much can be spent.

5. COMMUNICATE WITH RESPECT.

Finances can cause tension in a marriage relationship, especially when finances are tight or there are differing management views. Therefore, it is critical that couples communicate with respect. Criticizing, blaming, or attacking are common responses when financial challenges arise. Effective communication requires both speaking and listening—and listening should come first.

6. UNDERSTAND THE TRUE NATURE OF SUBMISSION.

There are numerous ways to define *submission*. One definition is "strength under authority." The wife who submits to her husband is not in a position of weakness but rather has chosen to defer to another's authority. The wise husband will invite his wife's counsel in all areas, including finances.

7. APPRECIATE THE DIFFERENCES BETWEEN MEN AND WOMEN.

Men and women will potentially respond very differently to finances. For example, men may tend to be more comfortable taking risks, whereas women tend to need security. These differences will manifest themselves in the area of finances. Most families will benefit by acknowledging these differences and seek a balanced approach to financial planning.

8. ACKNOWLEDGE EACH PARTNER'S FAMILY MODEL.

Both partners will bring habits or patterns of financial management into their marriage relationship based on what they saw modeled in their homes. Sometimes this is not a negative factor; often, however, each partner has a different experience with finances. How the differences have impacted them must be acknowledged before a balanced approach to their finances can be achieved.

9. DEFINE THE DIFFERENCE BETWEEN BIBLICAL "FAITH" AND IRRESPONSIBILITY.

Trusting in God's sovereign control as well as taking responsibility to plan in the area of the finances are both seen in Scripture. The parable of the talents illustrates that God expects us to make wise decisions (Matthew 25:14); the goal in finances is balanced stewardship.

10. SCHEDULE SEMIANNUAL *FUN* BUDGET AND FINANCIAL PLANNING SUMMITS.

Couples need to take time semiannually (or at least annually) to have a formal time of discussing and planning for their finances. This is the time to establish the next year's budget, to identify financial goals, and to evaluate how they are handling their finances. It is recommended that couples get away from their children and make this experience a fun, enjoyable time of communication and encouragement.

PRINCIPLES OF TIME MANAGEMENT

So teach us to number our days,
that we may present to You
a heart of wisdom.
PSALM 90:12 NASB

The Wise Woman is challenged to manage her time as well as her finances. Since time is a limited resource, it requires that intentional decisions be made about how it is used or spent; God expects us to live in light of the fact that our time is limited. Romans 14:12 says, "So then each of us shall give account of himself to God," while Ephesians 5:15–16 teaches, "Therefore be careful how you walk, not as unwise men, but as wise, making the most of your time, because the days are evil" (NASB).

Life is very short in the eternal perspective. The difficulty in time management is not the *lack* of time, but *how* we spend our time. So before addressing time organization principles, it is important for the Wise Woman to understand the context for time management. As previously discussed, she must have first determined her life priorities. Once her life priorities are determined, she can write a mission statement that reflects those priorities. Determining short-term, intermediate, and long-term goals that will make her mission statement functional follows this step. Once these steps are accomplished, she is ready to determine a daily or weekly schedule that will allow for reaching her goals, fulfilling her mission statement, and maintaining her life priorities. (See chapter 4 for further details on these steps.)

The first step in effective time management is to take time to plan! A little planning saves a lot of time. It also keeps the Wise Woman moving in the direction she established for her life, based on her goals and priorities. Planning should occur in the following areas:

- *A yearly calendar*—list all the main events that must be planned around. This includes birthdays, anniversaries, family vacations, work, travel, etc.
- *A monthly calendar*—at the beginning of each month, review the obligations that are unique to that month, including holidays, school commitments, doctor appointments, etc.
- *Weekly and daily plans*—establish a weekly schedule. Use calendars, Day-Timers, Palm Pilots, or even a simple "to do" list. Block unavailable times first (i.e., sleep, eat, exercise, devotions) and then fill in the rest of each day or week. Weekly schedules should be flexible since no two weeks are identical. The principle of planning your week is that you do plan each week, not that tasks are accomplished on exactly the same day.

PRINCIPLES OF SCHEDULING

The mind of man plans his way,
But the Lord directs his steps.
PROVERBS 16:9 NASB

There are numerous ways to schedule time. The purpose of this section is not to identify what tasks to complete each hour of the day, but rather to provide principles for making decisions relating to how time is spent. Every Wise Woman has different responsibilities and obligations, and each must determine her life priorities. As Charles Hummel says:

> When we stop to evaluate, we realize that our dilemma goes deeper than shortage of time; it is basically the problem of priorities. Hard work does not hurt us. We all know what it is to go full speed for long hours, totally involved in an important task. The resulting weariness is matched by a sense of achievement and joy. Not hard work, but doubt and misgiving produce anxiety as we review a month or year and become oppressed by the pile of unfinished tasks.[6]

Planning will help Wise Women use their time effectively. A few principles of scheduling include the following:

1. BEGIN EACH DAY BY SPENDING TIME WITH THE LORD.

Spending time committing her day to the Lord before beginning the day impacts how she views the time she has that day. Most women are comfortable giving God themselves, their possessions, and even the people in their lives. However, they sometimes are reluctant to give God their time. Therefore, unfinished tasks, interruptions, or deviations from their planned day become frustrating. Elizabeth George clearly illustrates this concept:

After giving God everything, I give God Plan A for the day. Giving God my schedule for the day means laying before Him all of the projects I want to get done. Committing my plans to God through prayer helps me fight a better battle against impulsiveness and laziness. It also helps me to be more sensitive to His leading me to do something other than what I have planned—which brings me to the third point of my prayers. I give God Plan B for the day. Wanting my plan to be His plan for me, I commit my day, my goals, and my energies to Him. Although I have a plan, I want God's will for my life. I therefore hold my plan loosely and stand ready to defer to what He would have me doing during the course of the day.[7]

Remembering God is sovereign means that "interruptions" to her day are divinely sent by God. She must be flexible and willing to alter her day's plans when called upon; by committing her day to the Lord she begins with a biblical mind-set.

2. Write everything down.

Develop a usable system for organizing the daily system. For some women, this will be simple "to do" lists, while others will enjoy more modern technologies. Whatever the method, the Wise Woman needs a system (such as a Day-Timer) that allows her to see things as a whole.

- Write everything down in order, so that a realistic view of your commitments is seen. (Don't rely on memory!)
- View the daily schedule in light of "family" schedules or other obligations (i.e., children's school commitments or ministry obligations).
- Remind yourself of upcoming events that will draw on your time (such as holidays or family events).

3. LEARN TO WAIT BEFORE COMMITTING.

The Wise Woman develops the habit of graciously not committing to a responsibility when she is first approached. An example of responding graciously might be to say, "Thank you so much for considering me for this opportunity. I would like to spend time praying about this opportunity, check my calendar, and seek the counsel of my husband. May I respond to your invitation by the end of the week?" Develop the habit of waiting to commit to an obligation until you have allowed yourself to think about it thoroughly.

- Pray about the commitment.
- Consult your calendar.
- Seek counsel (from your spouse or another authority in your life).

4. LEARN TO SAY NO.

Saying no is often difficult. The Wise Woman evaluates why she has difficulty doing this. Is it because of pride (I am the only one who can do it), because I am a people pleaser (if I don't do this they will not like me), because I will feel like a failure (if I don't fulfill every opportunity given to me I have failed)? Some women simply feel "unspiritual" if they are not involved in every opportunity life provides. That is not a realistic view of time. Women cannot do everything and should graciously say no when it is appropriate. As well, women should evaluate *why* they cannot say no.

5. REMEMBER THE THREE "D's."

Three key principles will help you maximize time:

- *Dovetail*—Dovetailing is the concept of completing two tasks at once. For example, you can listen to a sermon tape while ironing, visit with a friend while having lunch, or fold the laundry while talking on the telephone. There are many ways you can dovetail your time.
- *Delegate*—Some responsibilities do not need to be accomplished by the individual. For example, the Wise Woman can solicit help from her children with home obligations or enlist help from other women in accomplishing a ministry task. Although she may still need to give oversight and take responsibility that the task is fulfilled, she may not have to actually accomplish the work herself.
- *Delete*—There are many commitments women should not be involved in simply because they are not a priority for their time. Remember, as previously discussed in planning, priorities are those things that only the Wise Woman herself can accomplish. Eliminate any obligations that are not priorities (however, one word of caution—you may have overcommitted yourself and need to fulfill your obligations before eliminating the responsibility).

6. BE DISCIPLINED, BUT DON'T DRIVE YOURSELF.

Ask God to daily provide discipline; self-control is a fruit of the Spirit (Galatians 5:22–23). Be careful not to do more than you can do in the right spirit, and don't jeopardize your health or contentment. Your family is dependent on you, and if you overcommit, you will not be able to fulfill your primary responsibilities related to your family and home.

7. AVOID FALSE STARTS.

Make sure you have realistically allowed enough time to accomplish each task. This includes being realistic about commuting time as well as allowing for normal interruptions (i.e., telephone calls, children's needs, or crowded stores). It is better to allow extra time; a second task can always be started if time is available. By allowing realistic time segments, the Wise Woman will avoid the stress of feeling under pressure to accomplish the task. Her goal is to finish each task that she starts. Charles Swindoll says, "Some folks feverishly work right up to the deadline on every assignment or project they undertake. Time management allows room for ease and humor, much needed oil to soothe the friction created by motion."[8]

8. DON'T MISS THE PEOPLE FOR THE PLAN.

People always take priority over the plan. People will not always "fit into" a plan, but they always should be the priority. This reiterates the importance of committing the day to the Lord. He has sovereignly placed people in the Wise Woman's life. People will always have needs, needs that the Lord may be asking you to meet. The two most basic commands in Scripture are to love God and to love your neighbor (Matthew 22:37–40; see Leviticus 19:18; Deuteronomy 6:5).

9. WATCH OUT FOR TIME WASTERS.

A final thought regarding time management—watch out for the time wasters! There are many things in life that can challenge or waste our time; some things are uncontrollable and part of God's sovereign plan for our day. The Wise Woman should develop a plan to help eliminate or minimize the intrusions time wasters create. Sharon Carr suggests that one must first learn to recognize what wastes time before a solution for each challenge is formulated.[9] She further suggests that time robbers fall into four categories:

1. *Procrastination*—indecision and putting things off.
2. *Disorganization*—lack of planning or improper planning.
3. *Spinning Wheels*—lack of priorities or goals.
4. *Forgetfulness*—not writing things down or mind clutter.[10]

The Wise Woman strives for balance in her standards and in how much time she commits to fulfilling her obligations. Finally, Donna Partow suggests that another time waster is "stewing," meaning that much of our time is wasted on worry, anger, or bitterness.[11] All these emotions waste our time. She encourages women to pray about the obstacles they face and to choose to live by faith and trust in God's provision (Philippians 4:6–7). Regardless of the time robber, the Wise Woman recognizes what wastes her time and then devises a plan that eliminates or minimizes the wasting of it.

In addition to practicing stewardship with our finances and time, Women of Wisdom will practice stewardship with their individual gifts and abilities. If we consider the example of the Proverbs 31 woman, we see that in addition to meeting the needs of her family, she was involved in business transactions and ministered to the needy in her community. Proverbs 31:16 states, "She considers a field and buys it; from her earnings she plants a vineyard" (NASB). Furthermore, Proverbs 31:24 states, "She makes linen garments and sells them, and supplies belts to the tradesmen" (NASB). The Proverbs 31 woman was a successful entrepreneur who knew how to conduct business and reinvest her earnings. In addition to working for profit, we see in Proverbs 31:20 she also was involved in ministry to the poor and needy. She used her gifts and abilities to meet the needs of others. Likewise, women today may also have the opportunity to work for profit or to work for ministry purposes.

Work can be simply defined as the physical or mental effort put into an activity. *Work* may or may not be for paid employment. For example, we often say that cleaning the house is work or that repairing a car is work. Wise Women will see that they are called to be stewards of all work opportunities, whether paid employment or unpaid volunteer work. They are stewards of the physical or mental efforts they put into activities apart from their family and home responsibilities. Work opportunities allow women to exercise their individual gifts and abilities in expanded ways outside their homes.

WOMEN AND WORK

How blessed is the man who finds wisdom,
And the man who gains understanding.
For her profit is better than the profit of silver
And her gain better than fine gold.
She is more precious than jewels;
And nothing you desire compares with her.
PROVERBS 3:13–15 NASB

Developing a biblical perspective on women and work is a difficult and often emotional question to answer due to current worldviews and intense personal opinions. There are, however, several biblical principles that help define the parameters for women and work. Principles which, when properly applied, allow women to maintain the priority of their home and experience a great deal of freedom to pursue ministry opportunities, serve their community, and/or supplement the family income. It is important to note that both ministry opportunities, such as teaching a women's Bible study, and professional employment, remove the woman from the home. Therefore, the same principles apply when women are discerning how to spend their time after the needs of their family and home have been met.

Any activity that removes the woman from the home should be evaluated in light of biblical principles that help her maintain her primary focus, her family and home. It is as sad to see a woman immersed in women's ministry at her local church as it is to see the woman who is consumed by a career; both situations may cause her to neglect her family and home. Many Christians, however, often have a greater tolerance for ministry activities outside the home. All too often Christians spiritualize certain activities and condemn others. Principles related to women and work should be applied to *any* activity that removes the woman from her home, whether that activity is paid employment, volunteer work in her local community, or a ministry in her local church. How does a woman determine if she should take on obligations outside the home? There are five principles that can be applied to help answer this question.

PRINCIPLE ONE: WORK SHOULD NEVER COMPROMISE GOD'S DESIGN FOR THE FAMILY AND THEREFORE SHOULD NEVER COMPROMISE THE WOMAN'S ABILITY TO MEET THE NEEDS OF HER FAMILY AND HOME.

The Wise Woman will implement that knowledge of God's design for the family into practical daily living (Proverbs 31; 1 Peter 3:1–2). There are three areas in which she will be able to fulfill her role. First, she is a helper to her husband (Genesis 2:18–24). Wives should seek to apply their gifts and abilities to assist their husbands in all areas. Second, a wife's domain is her home. She is to be a "worker at home" (Titus 2:3–5). The home is her primary responsibility and focus. Domestic duties are a part of this responsibility, but it is much more than just keeping a clean home. It also means creating a place of refuge and rest for her husband, children, and friends. It means managing the household to assure peace and organization within the home. Third, a woman's highest calling is to raise godly children who will lead future generations (Proverbs 22:6). True motherhood is for a woman to work sacrificially at the God-given command to love her children. It may mean pouring her life into her children, thus setting aside her own pursuits, desires, and goals for the benefit of her family. It means making her home a training ground for the hearts of her children. A woman must be able to help her husband, keep her home, and train her children before taking on additional responsibilities outside the home, whether it is ministry or employment.

PRINCIPLE TWO: WOMEN WHO WORK OUTSIDE THE HOME NEED TO SECURE THE SUPPORT AND BLESSING OF THEIR HUSBANDS.

As we have previously discussed, God gives specific instructions for each member of the family unit (Ephesians 5:18–6:4). The father is to lead, love, provide, train, not provoke, and disciple his family. The mother is to submit, love, train, and disciple. The children are to obey their parents. Women have a specific role to fulfill and must fulfill this role before taking on other obligations. The Bible does not command or forbid women to work outside the home. The Bible does, however, command a wife to be and do many things within the home. Submission is a high priority for the Christian woman. If she does not secure the blessing of her husband to leave her home for employment, she has already violated a biblical principle, which is to submit to and love her husband.

PRINCIPLE THREE: THE DECISION TO WORK IS NOT BASED ON THE WOMAN'S ABILITY TO PERFORM THE JOB.

A woman may be very qualified to perform a job outside the home but may choose not to take the position for numerous reasons. For example, when a woman leaves the home and places herself under the authority of another individual (i.e., an employer) she may be put in a position of conflicting authorities (i.e., her husband and her employer). Not all employment opportunities will allow women to maintain the priority of her family and home. Therefore, even though she may be qualified for a position, she may choose to decline the position or take another job in order to maintain her priorities. Another alternative may be to work part-time rather than full-time in order to fulfill her home obligations. Women will need to prayerfully evaluate their ability to manage family and home obligations as each unique circumstance arises. Several practical questions will help women evaluate whether or not an employment opportunity is feasible:

- "What are my motives for taking on an outside employment opportunity (do they violate biblical principles, for example, materialism being more important than spirituality)?"
- "Am I willing to make lifestyle adjustments rather than work outside the home in order to have the option of staying at home?"
- "Can I meet the needs of my husband in addition to this work opportunity?"
- "Can I thoroughly and with excellence care for my home in addition to this work opportunity?"
- "Can I train and teach my children in addition to this work opportunity?"
- "Can I submit to this employer's authority without violating my husband's authority?"
- "Do I have the support and blessing of my husband to pursue this work opportunity?"
- "Can my home and family responsibilities (e.g., sick children) take priority over work obligations?"
- "Can my heart be at home and manage the pressures of work concurrently?"
- "Am I applying the same criteria to work and ministry opportunities?"

PRINCIPLE FOUR: THERE ARE REASONS AND SEASONS
FOR A WOMAN TO WORK OUTSIDE THE HOME.

Once women fulfill their biblical role and responsibilities, there is a great deal of freedom to pursue outside interests. The Proverbs 31 woman gives us an example of this model. She engaged in business outside the home, but it is clear that the needs of her family were met and that her business pursuits benefited her family (Proverbs 31:16, 18–20). A woman may leave her home for ministry or employment and not violate the biblical principles due to a variety of circumstances:

- *The need to support herself.* Many women are single, widowed, or have a husband with a partial or full disability. She may need to work outside the home temporarily or permanently.
- *The desire to fill her extra time while her children are at school or after her grown children leave home.* For example, she may choose to volunteer at her child's school one day a week.
- *The need to supplement the family income.* She may have an ill or disabled husband, or the family may have other extraordinary expenses connected with the children or grandparents.
- *The desire to exercise her spiritual giftedness.* She may choose to teach a Bible study class for women or Sunday school class.
- *The desire to be a steward of her education.* Many women who marry older will have completed college and graduate education and would enjoy the opportunity to continue to use their degrees. Women who desire to maintain their teaching credentials may choose to tutor in order to maintain their professional credentials.
- *The opportunity to participate in community service as*

a light to her community. Food pantries and other social services organizations need and welcome volunteers.

Working outside the home may be required during various stages of life. John MacArthur, in a sermon on 1 Timothy 2:9–15, states:

> A woman's responsibility is in the home. Her duty and opportunity to impact the world lie right there. She does this by raising a Godly generation. What if she can go and help a couple of hours a day to help at school or to serve the kingdom? The answer is . . . if it does not impact or take away from your home responsibilities and you and your husband take it to the Lord and examine your motives, it is OK. If it enhances and enriches the life in the home then it is between you and your husband and the Lord. If you understand God's plan and you work out with your husband how the specifics will work in your home it is not sinning.[12]

PRINCIPLE FIVE: WOMEN WHO DESIRE TO STAY AT HOME MUST PLAN AHEAD.

Many women desire to stay at home as a full-time wife and mom but do not take the practical steps needed to ensure they have the freedom to live on their husband's income. Therefore, women who desire to be at home must plan appropriately. These are a few practical suggestions for couples planning to have the wife stay at home:

- Eliminate debt immediately.
- Live a modest lifestyle and begin to save consistently (do not spend all that you earn).
- Establish a budget and stick to it.
- Build a cash reserve for emergencies (e.g., the loss of the husband's job).

- Live off one income from the start (don't get used to having two incomes).
- Identify community resources that will help lower expenses (e.g., libraries, economical grocery shopping alternatives, and free community programs).
- Develop a support network of family and friends (e.g., swap babysitting with a friend instead of paying for a sitter).

PRINCIPLE SIX: DEVELOP ENTREPRENEURIAL SKILLS.

Women who desire to stay at home may choose to operate a home-based business. However, the same criteria for working outside the home should be applied to entrepreneurial opportunities. Anything that potentially compromises the priority of meeting the needs of family and home should be carefully evaluated. The following section will discuss in more detail the fundamentals of entrepreneurship.

FUNDAMENTALS OF ENTREPRENEURSHIP

She makes linen garments and sells them,
And supplies belts to the tradesmen.
PROVERBS 31:24 NASB

Women all over the world are marketing their skills from their homes. Women have home-based businesses as accountants, education consultants, child-care providers, interior designers, seamstresses, and speech therapists—to name a few! There are many reasons why women start a home-based business. While the scope of this chapter does not allow for a detailed discussion of every aspect of entrepreneurship, there are several fundamental considerations for women to think through before starting a home-based business. Let's consider three aspects of entrepreneurship: (1) The motivation for starting a home-based business, (2) factors to consider when making the decision to start a home-based business, and (3) keys to success in a home-based business.

First, while the motivation for starting a home-based business is a very personal decision, there are several common reasons why women desire to start a home-based business.

AVAILABILITY TO ONE'S CHILDREN AND MORE FAMILY TIME

The most common reason women choose to work from the home is to be able to be at home with their children. Women who work at home avoid the cost of day care, maintenance of a professional wardrobe, and commuting expenses. Women who work at home are able to put their family before their career. They are able to maintain the flexibility needed to meet their family's needs on a daily basis (e.g., being at home with a sick child). By working at home women also do not spend as much time "on work"; for example, they eliminate the morning and evening commute. This one factor alone gives them more family time.

SUPPLEMENTING THE FAMILY'S INCOME

Many families find it extremely challenging to live on one income. Therefore, many women choose to work from the home. While the long-term goal for most stay-at-home moms is to live on one income, there may be seasons of financial strain when extra income is needed. Some families committed to ministry pursuits also find it helpful if the wife supplements the family income. Other families are able to live on one income and use the supplemental income for additional savings or the "extras," such as lessons for the children or family vacations. Whatever the need, many women are able to work from the home to supplement the family's income.

THE ABILITY TO SET ONE'S OWN HOURS AND ENJOY GREATER FLEXIBILITY

Women who work from the home are often able to be "their own boss" and set their own hours. They are able to set a work schedule that is compatible with the daily family schedule and yearly calendar. If, for example, a child has soccer practice on Thursday afternoon, Mom is able to quit early to provide the shuttle services. Women can avoid working during their children's school holidays. Some women even choose to get up early before their family's day begins to accomplish their work hours, thus completely avoiding conflicts with family schedules. Working at home can be a more efficient use of time with fewer interruptions.

PERSONAL ENJOYMENT

Yes! Many women simply enjoy working. They enjoy the artistic expression, mental stimulation, sense of accomplishment, and social interaction that running a home-based business provides.[13] In addition to personal enjoyment, many women find that running a home-based business allows them to continue to be involved with their professional career—a career that many began prior to marriage and children. Teachers, nurses, and business professionals alike invest many years of training in their education. Many view working as a stewardship issue of their education and abilities. Additionally, women enjoy keeping current and maintaining their professional certifications.

MINISTRY OPPORTUNITIES

While a woman's primary sphere of influence is in her home, home-based business provides an opportunity for women to expand their sphere of influence. Donna Partow states, "The most effective way of influencing people for the gospel is by interacting naturally, in the course of our daily lives. As your home-based business gets underway, you will have many opportunities to demonstrate a Christian lifestyle to an ever-widening circle of business associates."[14]

Once women determine their motivation for desiring to start a home-based business, they must consider carefully the factors that will impact their success or failure in their endeavor. Lindsey O'Connor suggests eight questions for women to consider when making the decision whether or not to start a home-based business:

1. Do I feel the Lord's direction to do this?
2. What is my calling and where are my passions?
3. What would I enjoy doing and what are my gifts, talents, and experiences?
4. Does my spouse agree with my decision?
5. Would my family be supportive?
6. Am I suited for working at home?
7. Is there a market for what I want to do?
8. Have I researched my topic?[15]

Finally, Larry Burkett suggests several key ingredients for helping women reach their home-based business goals:

• Choose a business you really enjoy.
• Conduct thorough research before you begin.
• If you are going to invest your valuable time and energy, it should be on something you enjoy and that will ultimately be profitable.[16]

Additionally, Mr. Burkett reminds his readers that there are numerous character issues involved in running a home-based business, including persistence, self-discipline, and flexibility. He challenges women to work like professionals even though they are working from their homes (e.g., in appearance, office routines, and phone manners). In other words, take your home-based business seriously! A final suggestion for those considering beginning a home-based business—get the needed training and/or education; for example, it is extremely helpful to take a class on running a small business.

A home-based business will take much time, effort, and hard work. It will not succeed overnight. Running a home-based business will challenge your management skills as you seek to maintain your primary priority of caring for the needs of your family and home. It will force you to develop your character in the areas of time management, diligence, and patience. While a home-based business is definitely not a good choice for everyone, for some women it will be an excellent means of supplementing their family income, maintaining their professional involvement, and/or providing a creative outlet.

A FINAL THOUGHT . . .

We all have complex lives that require us to make careful choices about how we use our finances, time, and individual abilities. Our primary motivation for practicing biblical stewardship should be so that we are found to be faithful and obedient managers of the resources God has given to us (Matthew 25:14–15). The practical skills we have discussed in this chapter —budgeting, scheduling your time, or entrepreneurship—will only help you be a successful steward if the motivation of your heart is correct—to be found faithful with all of our God-given resources.

TABLE 6.1
SAMPLE FOUR-STEP BUDGET FORM

Step One: Estimate Available Income

Estimated Income per Month:

Salary	_____	TOTALS
Interest Income	_____	
Dividends	_____	
Rents	_____	
Stipends	_____	
Other	_____	

TOTAL GROSS INCOME: _____

Minus—Tithe (_____) and Taxes (_____) = *NET SPENDABLE INCOME:* _____

Step Two: List all Fixed and Flexible Expenses

Fixed Expenses:

Rent or Mortgage	_____	Life Insurance	_____	Credit Card (1)	_____
Housing Insurance	_____	Health Insurance	_____	Credit Card (2)	_____
Property Taxes	_____	Property Insurance	_____	Auto Loan	_____
Sanitation	_____	Automobile Insurance	_____	Student Loan	_____
Emergency Fund	_____	Disability Insurance	_____	Other Loans	_____
Goals	_____	Education: Tuition	_____	Auto—License	_____
Savings/Investments	_____	Education: Room/Board	_____	Auto—Gas/Oil	_____
Gifts	_____	Allowances	_____	Other (fixed):	_____

TOTAL FIXED EXPENSES: _____

Flexible Expenses:

Gas (Housing)	_____	Medications/Prescriptions	_____	Clothing (adults)	_____
Electricity	_____	Food (at home)	_____	Clothing (kids)	_____
Water	_____	Food (away from home)	_____	Beauty/Barber	_____
Telephone	_____	Auto: Repairs	_____	Laundry/Cleaning	_____
Doctor Visits	_____	Entertainment/Recreation	_____	Childcare	_____
Dentist Visits	_____	Household Maintenance	_____	Other (flexible)	_____

TOTAL FLEXIBLE EXPENSES: _____

Step Three: Compare Income and Expenses

Net Spendable Income	_____
Less Fixed Expenses	_____
Less Flexible Expenses	_____

TOTAL (Deficit/Surplus) _____

1. A *balanced* budget requires careful monitoring to prevent overspending in *any* category.
2. Decide *in advance* how you will handle a budget *surplus* (e.g., pay off debt, put toward savings, etc.).
3. Budget *deficits* require expenses to be cut and/or more income to be generated (begin by reviewing the flexible expense categories—are there areas you can cut and/or control the amount allocated?).

Step Four: Monitor and Evaluate Budget

1. Set up your workspace and filing system. Decide when and who will pay the bills each month.
2. Reconcile the budget each month (see the Budget Balance Sheet).
3. Annually review your budget and analyze your spending habits. Review and establish financial goals.
4. As income increases do not increase spending, but rather increase giving, savings, and investments.

TABLE 6.2
BUDGET BALANCE SHEET—FIXED EXPENSES
(MONTHLY)

Date/Month of Budget Balance Sheet: _____

FIXED EXPENSES	Amount Estimated	Amount Spent	Difference (plus/minus)
Rent or Mortgage			
Housing Insurance			
Property Taxes			
Sanitation			
Emergency Fund			
Goals			
Savings/Investments			
Gifts			
Life Insurance			
Health Insurance			
Property Insurance			
Automobile Insurance			
Disability Insurance			
Education: Tuition			
Education: Room/Board			
Allowances			
Credit Card (1)			
Credit Card (2)			
Auto Loan			
Student Loan			
Auto—License			
Auto—Gas/Oil			
Other:			

TOTAL FIXED EXPENSES FOR THE MONTH = $ Surplus OR Deficit

Add Fixed and Flexible expenses, subtract from Net Spendable Income to determine if budget balanced each month.

TABLE 6.3
BUDGET BALANCE SHEET—FLEXIBLE EXPENSES
(MONTHLY)

Date/Month of Budget Balance Sheet: _____

FLEXIBLE EXPENSES	Amount Estimated	Amount Spent	Difference (plus/minus)
Gas (Housing)			
Electricity			
Water			
Telephone			
Doctor Visits			
Dentist Visits			
Medications/Prescriptions			
Food (at home)			
Food (away from home)			
Auto: Repairs			
Entertainment/Recreation			
Household Maintenance			
Clothing (adults)			
Clothing (children)			
Beauty/Barber			
Laundry/Cleaning			
Childcare/Babysitters			
Other: Flexible			
Auto Loan			
Student Loan			
Auto—License			
Auto—Gas/Oil			
Other:			

TOTAL FLEXIBLE EXPENSES FOR THE MONTH = $ Surplus OR Deficit

Add Fixed and Flexible expenses, subtract from Net Spendable Income to determine if budget balanced each month.

GROWING IN
PRACTICING
STEWARDSHIP

1.   *Develop a usable budget. Use the forms at the end of this chapter to help you establish your budget. If you are currently using a budget, take some time to review it to make sure it is accurate. (A note to married women—be sure to work together with your husband when making decisions about your finances.)*

2.   *Use the following Scriptures to help identify your attitudes toward money: Psalms 37:16; 50:10–12; 135:6; Proverbs 12:22; 13:22; 20:7; 22:7; 30:24–25; Matthew 25:21; 1 Corinthians 4:2; 2 Corinthians 8:1–5; Philippians 4:11–13. After reviewing the Scriptures, evaluate your strengths and weaknesses in the area of money management.*

3.   *Read 1 Timothy 6:6–10. What conclusions can we draw about our attitudes toward money?*

4.   *Develop a personal time-management system. Take the time to get organized! Collect the resources you need to help you be successful in the area of time management— for example, do you need to purchase a calendar or some kind of Day-Timer?*

5.   *Identify the skills you possess that you might be able to turn into a home-based business. What do you enjoy doing? Once you have generated this list, answer the eight*

questions in the chapter that help you evaluate whether or not you are a good candidate for operating a home-based business. If so, conduct further research.

I grew up in a home where hospitality was modeled. Regularly we had friends over for dinner, hosted missionaries on furlough, and provided the meeting place for weekly church activities. I could look back and say that we participated in these things out of "obligation" or Christian duty, but I do not think that would be an accurate observation. I think what was modeled for me was my parents' commitment to the principle found in 1 Peter 4:9, which says, "Be hospitable to one another without grumbling." You see, it would have been easy for them not to practice hospitality because my mother had (and still has) the crippling and painful disease of rheumatoid arthritis; she has had the disease since she was twenty-six years old. Daily she experiences severe pain, extreme fatigue, and physical exhaustion; the amount of pain is associated with the amount of activity and rest she has in her daily schedule (in other words, the more she does, the more she hurts). She had a "good excuse" not to practice hospitality, yet my parents chose to exercise hospitality regularly because it was a biblical priority, despite the pain Mom would experience. My mother describes it as "a trade-off," meaning she is willing to "hurt" tomorrow in order to participate in today's opportunities. This is a valuable life lesson for me and clearly illustrates biblical hospitality; my mother's example teaches me that biblical hospitality considers the needs of others above personal needs and that . . .

SEVEN

THE WISE WOMAN PRACTICES BIBLICAL HOSPITALITY

Contributing to the needs of the saints,
practicing hospitality.

ROMANS 12:13 NASB

Hospitable is defined as given to generous or cordial reception of guests, promising a generous or cordial welcome, offering a pleasant or sustaining environment.[1] *Hospitality* is the art of creating a generous, cordial, pleasant, or sustaining environment. I believe most Christian women desire this type of environment for their homes and hope to be characterized as hospitable women.

However, for the Christian woman, becoming a hospitable woman requires more than just developing the needed skills in entertaining, food preparation, or home management (although, as we will see, developing those skills will free you up to focus on people as your priority). For hospitality to be executed with love and graciousness, a Wise Woman understands God's definition of hospitality. The Greek word *philoxenia* used in the New Testament for hospitality literally means "love of strangers."[2] The word has two parts—*philos*, meaning "loving," and *xenos*, meaning "a stranger or a guest." We see an example of hospitality used in Romans 12:13 (NASB), where the phrase "practicing hospitality" is included in the listing of character traits for a Christian.

A second example is seen in Hebrews 13:2 (NIV) and reminds us, "Do not forget to *entertain* strangers, for by so doing some people have entertained angels without knowing it" (italics added). The word *entertain* in Hebrews 13:2 can be translated as "to show love to" and emphasizes the importance of not forgetting to be hospitable to strangers or guests.[3] It is used several times in Scripture.

The Greek word for *hospitable* is *philoxenos;* being "hospitable" is a requirement for church overseers (1 Timothy 3:2), a requirement for elders (Titus 1:8), and a command for all Christians to practice (1 Peter 4:9). An application for our Wise Woman would find her demonstrating love for strangers or guests in her home by meeting their specific needs.

Our modern-day Christian approach to hospitality generally does not include the "stranger"; synonyms for *stranger* include *foreigner, immigrant, visitor,* or *newcomer* and communicate the idea of a person with whom you are unacquainted. It also includes someone who is a guest in your house. Typically, we entertain family and friends whom we already know and love. An important lesson presented in Scripture is that biblical hospitality is not dependent on preestablished relationships. Hospitality is a command to be implemented with all people, whether they are friends or strangers.

If biblical hospitality is *loving strangers and meeting the needs of others,* who are the "others" and what kind of "needs" can we meet? How do we show our love to others? Scripture gives us several examples of people who exercised and received hospitality. These examples give us categories of people to love and include:

- Fellow believers (Romans 12:13; 1 Timothy 3:2; 5:9–10; Hebrews 13:2)
- Widows and orphans (1 Timothy 5:1–16)
- Unbelievers (Luke 5:29; Acts 5:42)
- The poor and needy (Luke 14:12–14)
- Missionaries or Christian workers (Matthew 10:9–11; Luke 10:7–16; Acts 16:15)
- Foreigners or travelers (Genesis 18:1–22)

A further look at biblical examples of hospitality illustrates the various "needs" that can be met:

- *Preparing food* (Genesis 24:15–21; 1 Kings 17:9–16; Matthew 14:15–21; Acts 2:46; 20:11)
- *Providing housing/lodging* (2 Kings 4:8–17)
- *Giving physical protection or safety* (Joshua 2:1–15)
- *Sharing material possessions* (Acts 2:44; Romans 12:13–20; James 2:15–16; 1 John 3:17)
- *Offering a place to rest* (Genesis 18:1–22; Mark 14:3–8; Luke 7:36–47; John 12:1–8)
- *Extending love and encouragement* (Romans 12:10–13; 1 Thessalonians 4:9–10)
- *Sharing the gospel* (Acts 10:24; 20:20; 3 John 7, 8)
- *Giving spiritual teaching or encouragement* (Romans 16:5; Colossians 4:15)

Biblical hospitality seeks to meet the needs of others. My students in a class entitled Meal Management have illustrated this definition of hospitality to me over the years. The course, as the name suggests, focuses on teaching skills related to menu planning, entertaining, and food preparation. In addition to the practical skills, we discuss biblical hospitality. I begin this discussion by asking the students to describe for me what made them feel welcomed when they were the recipients of someone's hospitality. The students respond with answers such as, "They treated me like a family member," "Their home was a comfortable place where I could rest," or, "I enjoyed learning from the hostess and participating in her family." The descriptions of what made them feel welcomed never mention things like the size of the home, the type of home decor, or even the homemade food. They always describe a comfortable, gracious environment that met a personal need (providing food, rest, fellowship, or counsel). They always focus on the love that is communicated to them as guests. This illustrates true hospitality. Hospitality, as seen in Scripture, focuses on *meeting the needs of others*.

Biblical hospitality can be exercised to *all* people and has as its goal to meet *all* needs. It is important to remember that practicing hospitality is not an option for believers but, rather, a command (Romans 12:13; Hebrews 13:1–2). Synonyms for *command* include *call, mandate,* or *directive.* The Wise Woman will actively participate in hospitality out of obedience to the Word of God and view hospitality as a Christian responsibility that is a practical out-working of her faith.

THE ATTITUDE OF HOSPITALITY

Each one must do just as he has purposed in his heart,
not grudgingly or under compulsion,
for God loves a cheerful giver.
2 CORINTHIANS 9:7 NASB

"Be hospitable to one another without grumbling" (1 Peter 4:9) teaches us the right attitude required for biblical hospitality. Grumbling includes complaining, murmuring, whining, or protesting. The opposite of grumbling or complaining is cheerfulness, enthusiasm, or gladness. Alexander Strauch describes the attitude needed for hospitality in this way:

> The opposite of complaining is gladness—the willingness to cheerfully accept the inconvenience, labor, and cost of hospitality. Hospitality is a form of giving, and "God loves a cheerful giver" (2 Corinthians 9:7 NASB). So let us ask God to give us a cheerful spirit as we practice hospitality.
>
> Certainly the ministry (and corresponding inconveniences) of hospitality can easily rattle our grumbling bones. Hospitality demands old-fashioned work. It may be costly and is often inconvenient. It is time-consuming. It places a strain on the family. Sometimes guests abuse their Christian brothers' and sisters' hospitality. And during times of persecution, hospitality can even be dangerous.
>
> Hospitality, therefore, is a concrete, down-to-earth test of our fervent love for God and His people. Love can be an abstract, indistinct idea; hospitality is specific and tangible. We seldom complain about loving others too much, but we do complain about the inconveniences of hospitality. Hospitality is love in action. Hospitality is the flesh and muscle on the bones of love. Through caring acts of hospitality, the reality of our love is tested.[4]

Biblical hospitality requires the Wise Woman to make an intentional commitment to sacrificing time, energy, and resources. Exercising biblical hospitality can require her to overcome challenges in one or more areas of her life.

THE CHALLENGES OF HOSPITALITY

And my God will supply all your needs
according to His riches in glory in Christ Jesus.
PHILIPPIANS 4:19 NASB

Fulfilling the mandate to exercise hospitality can be intimidating and challenging. I recently had a conversation with a young wife who stated that she doesn't really enjoy practicing hospitality. She went on to say that she "stresses out" so much over things like preparing the food and cleaning her house that she does not experience joy while entertaining people in her home. Her response is a common one, due to the many different challenges associated with hospitality, which threaten our enthusiasm and cheerfulness and tempt us to grumble and complain. Perhaps you can relate to one of the following examples of challenges associated with hospitality:

Lack of
- Experience (which usually results in a lack of confidence)
- Time
- Physical energy or other physical limitations
- Space, equipment, or material resources (for example, furniture or dishes)
- Money (or limited resources from a budget perspective)
- Support from family (for example, from your spouse)
- Skill in food preparation, menu planning, or home management
- Flexibility or skill in responding to unexpected events

However, these challenges are just that—"challenges." They are the individual constraints we all must work within to practice hospitality, and they should not prevent us from practicing hospitality. Pat often says, "We have no problems, only challenges!" This is particularly true when we apply this saying to hospitality. All of the "lack of" challenges are simply areas women need to learn how to manage in order to exercise hospitality with cheerfulness. For example, lack of experience requires practice, lack of time requires planning, lack of money requires creativity, and lack of skill requires training. All challenges are merely constraints, but none should prevent us from participating in hospitality opportunities.

Developing practical skills in the areas of menu planning, food preparation, and organizational management can change many of the "lack of" challenges. Once a woman embraces a biblical attitude, she then can develop the needed practical skills to help her practice hospitality with ease and comfort. Since many opportunities for women to exercise hospitality are related to food, I have provided four simple meal-management goals that will help you develop your confidence and begin to enjoy the process of entertaining.

MEAL-MANAGEMENT GOALS

Whether, then, you eat or drink or
whatever you do, do all to the glory of God.
1 CORINTHIANS 10:31 NASB

Developing your hospitality skills in the area of meal management does not have to be an overwhelming thought. Successful meal management can be accomplished by focusing on four basic goals—achieving nutritional adequacy, matching meals to the food budget, matching meals to the available time, and preparing meals your guests and family members want and like.

MEAL-MANAGEMENT GOAL ONE: ACHIEVING NUTRITIONAL ADEQUACY

Nutrition is the most basic goal for meal management. Good nutrition is needed for children to grow and develop; likewise, adults need good nutrition to maintain a healthy body. A Wise Woman knows how to prepare well-balanced meals to meet this need of her family and guests. *The Food Guide Pyramid* is a simple tool developed by the U.S. Department of Agriculture Center for Nutrition Policy that can be used to evaluate the nutritional adequacy of menus. Table 7.1, "Servings of Foods to Be Consumed Per Day to Ensure a Balanced Diet," is developed from *The*

Food Guide Pyramid. The smaller number of servings is for children and smaller women, whereas the large number of servings are for men (for more detailed information contact the Federal Citizen Information Center online at www.pueblo.gsa.gov, search for topics: food, then *The Food Guide Pyramid*).

TABLE 7.1 SERVINGS OF FOODS TO BE CONSUMED PER DAY TO ENSURE A BALANCED DIET		
Food Group	Adult Servings	Children Servings (2–6 years old)
Bread, Cereal, Rice, and Pasta Group	6–11 Servings	6 Servings
Vegetable Group	3–5 Servings	3 Servings
Fruit Group	2–4 Servings	2 Servings
Meat, Poultry, Fish, Dry Beans, Eggs, and Nuts Group	2–3 Servings	2 Servings
Milk, Yogurt, and Cheese	2–3 Servings	2 Servings
Fats, Oils, and Sweets	Eat Sparingly	Eat Sparingly

We often think we are providing nutritional meals for our families, but when we take the time to evaluate each day, we realize there are inadequacies. It is helpful to take the time to see where you need to make changes in your diet. A form is provided at the end of this chapter to help you evaluate your family's diet in light of *The Food Guide Pyramid*. Keep a record of your family's diet for three to five days in order to get a good understanding of their eating patterns. Then make the needed changes to their diets based on your observations. (See "Evaluating Menus According to *The Food Guide Pyramid*" at the end of this chapter.)

MEAL MANAGEMENT GOAL TWO: MATCHING MEALS TO THE FOOD BUDGET

Most women will find they are primarily responsible for menu planning as well as purchasing and preparing the food. Since our resources are often limited, living within the constraints of the family food budget becomes a major challenge. As the budgeting process discussed in chapter 6 suggests, approximately 15 percent of the family budget is to be spent on food-related expenses (15 percent for lower incomes—$20,000 gross; and 10 percent for higher incomes—$60,000 gross). Once the overall dollar amount is established for the food purchases, the real challenge is staying within the allotted amount. Maintaining a balanced food budget is directly related to one's management and food-shopping skills. Applying the *principle of economical,* our Wise Woman shops carefully and makes good decisions related to her food purchases. Here are some principles for helping her maintain the family food budget:

- Take time to plan your menus each week. Planning is worth the effort and will save you time and money by limiting the number of trips to the grocery store. Use the weekly store advertisements to maximize special offers.
- Use the "calendar method" for planning your menus:
  - List the days/dates for the length of time you are shopping.
  - Add weekly events impacting your menus (anything that will affect your time to prepare your meals or the type of meal you should prepare; for example, late afternoon soccer practice for the children may mean planning a quick and easy meal versus having guests for dinner that might require planning a more elaborate meal).

❑ Select meals for each day you will be home (be sure to include family favorites, and try new recipes each week).

❑ Add the cookbook name and page number to the list, if needed.

❑ Make your shopping list from your menu plan.

❑ Post it on the side of your refrigerator for easy reference.

• In addition to making your shopping list from your menu plan, keep a "running list" on the side of your fridge for items you run out of or are getting low on during the week.

• Use your shopping list to check your cupboards, refrigerator, and freezer *before* leaving for the grocery store to ensure you have all your needed supplies; doing this also prevents buying supplies you already have.

TABLE 7.2
A SAMPLE MENU PLAN

Monday (10/1)—	Jake's soccer practice—Chicken Fajitas with refried beans
Tuesday (10/2)—	Smiths coming for dinner—Chicken Manicotti, salad, rolls, and creampuffs for dessert (*Quick and Easy Cookbook,* 34 and 57)
Wednesday (10/3)—	Kids' youth group—Crock-pot Beef Stew and biscuits (*Homestyle Cookbook,* 107)
Thursday (10/4)—	Doctor's Appointment —Chicken Potpie (*Lifestyles,* 24)
Friday (10/5)—	Date night out/kids—mac and cheese; carrots
Saturday (10/6)—	Lunch out and leftovers
Sunday (10/7)—	Crock-pot roast, baked potatoes, and vegetables

Note: Do not plan to buy food for every day if you eat out regularly. You will end up buying food "twice," once at the grocery store and once at the restaurant. You also might lose perishables, such as fruits and vegetables.

- Maintain careful records of all food purchases. Know how much money is being spent on each category of food (for example, how much of the food budget is spent on meats or dairy products each month). This will allow you to modify a specific food category if you are spending too much.

- Know how much pre-prepared (such as a fully assembled lasagna) or partially prepared (such as meat in a marinade, but still needing to be cooked) food items your budget will allow you to purchase. Remember, the less work you do for yourself the higher the cost at the grocery store.

- Use coupons selectively. Coupons do not always save you money. Use coupons only for the items you buy routinely. Store brands or generic brands may be cheaper than a name brand purchased with a coupon.

- Allow plenty of time to shop. This allows you to compare prices (for example, using unit pricing). Look under the "sale" tags to determine if the item is really a sale or simply a promotion for the week (for example, the "sale" tag may say three for ninety-nine cents, but when you look under the tag the regular price says thirty-three cents each. This is not a "sale"—only buy three if you need three).

- Buy fresh fruits and vegetables in season only. Know what grade of fruits and vegetables your budget will accommodate (for example, are you on an "asparagus" or a "corn" budget?).

- Know current food costs in your area by comparing the weekly store advertisements. This will help you identify when stores really are having "good deals."

- Take advantage of store specials or sales to stock up on items *regularly* purchased.

- Buy the right "grade" of food to match quality to the intended use (for example, buying stew meats for soups versus buying lean steak).

- Know the most economical choices within each food category (for example, does your budget accommodate hamburger or steak?).
- Buy in bulk only if this is consistent with your family needs and storage ability (or you will have too much waste).
- Shop only with a list. Do not deviate from your list and avoid buying items not on your list except if it is a "need" that was forgotten.
- Shop as little as possible—the fewer number of trips made to the grocery store the better! This saves both time and money.
- Know where to shop. Some items will be more economical to buy in bulk from a discount wholesale store rather than the grocery store (if they can be stored and used before they perish).

MEAL-MANAGEMENT GOAL THREE: MATCHING MEALS TO AVAILABLE TIME

Time is a precious and limited resource. Wise Women understand how to manage and maximize their available time. The first step in managing your time as it relates to meal management is to actually understand how your time is being spent. Women will spend approximately twenty-two-and-a-half hours per week planning, preparing, and organizing family meals. The chart on the following page illustrates how time is used on food preparation:

TABLE 7.3 TIME SPENT IN FOOD PREPARATION	
Time spent in an Average Week	Average Hours per Week
Shopping for Food	1.5 hours
Putting Away Purchases	0.5 hours
Baking	2.0 hours
Cooking/Food Preparation	9.0 hours
Setting the Table	1.0 hours
Washing Dishes/Cleaning up	7.0 hours
Planning Meals	1.5 hours
Total time per week	22.5 hours

Most women do not realize how much time they are spending on food-related tasks. It is a good idea to maintain a record of the time you invest in meal management for one week so that you have an idea of how much time you are spending. You then can make decisions as to how to limit that time—for example, can you be more organized when you go shopping so that you spend less time? Can your children set the table for you? Can you "clean as you go" so that your cleaning time is less at the end of the meal? Each woman will have unique circumstances requiring unique management strategies.

A second area related to time and meal management is to learn how to organize the food preparation process so that meals are prepared and served at the desired time. I used to struggle with this. Learning how to use menu time schedules helped me organize the individual food preparation tasks so that I realistically planned enough time for each item on the menu. A menu plan allows you to plan time for preparation, cooking, and serving each of the menu items (see Table 7.4, "Sample Menu Schedule"). The steps to preparing a time schedule include the following:

1. List the items of the menu on the left side of your paper.
2. Add the jobs that are not food related (for example, setting the table or making coffee).
3. Make four columns across the top of your paper and label them:

   • Preparation for Cooking
   • Actual Cooking Time
   • Preparation for Serving
   • Total Time in Minutes

4. Rearrange the items in descending order (the item taking the longest to prepare will be at the top of the list).
5. Identify the specific times you need to start each menu item or meal task.
6. File each menu plan in a hospitality notebook to be used again in the future. (Hospitality notebooks are discussed in more detail at the end of this chapter.)

TABLE 7.4 SAMPLE MENU SCHEDULE				
Menu Items or Tasks	Preparation for Cooking	Actual Cooking Time	Preparation for Serving	Total Time in Minutes
Meat Loaf	15 minutes	45 minutes	5 minutes	65 minutes
Mashed Potatoes	10 minutes	35 minutes	10 minutes	50 minutes
Carrots	15 minutes	15 minutes	0	30 minutes
Peas	5 minutes	15 minutes	0	20 minutes
Coffee	5 minutes	5 minutes	15 minutes	15 minutes
Setting the Table/Beverages	0	0	10 minutes	10 minutes
Bread (prepared rolls)	0	0	5 minutes	5 minutes
Ice Cream (store)	0	0	5 minutes	5 minutes

A menu schedule identifies the time you need to begin preparing your meal and the order in which to accomplish each task (more experienced meal managers will know if they can accomplish two tasks at once or work a little faster, but for beginners, allow "extra" time so that the stress is eliminated). Be sure to plan around other obligations; for example, if you have to stop to pick up children from school. You may need to start some of the tasks in the morning and then finish the menu schedule later in the day (you can have the table already set or the vegetables peeled and chopped). Each woman will need to customize the way she applies the menu schedule. Here are some practical suggestions for saving time on food preparation:

- Learn quick food preparation techniques, such as stir-fry, BBQ, or soups.
- Invest in a few basic appliances that will save you time—a bread machine, Crock-Pot, and pressure cooker are good ones to start with.
- Collect recipes that can be prepared in thirty minutes or less, such as chicken fajitas.
- Collect recipes such as lasagna or pizza that can be prepared in advance and then frozen or stored in the refrigerator. This will allow you to plan ahead for a day you may have no time to cook.
- Make two recipes at one time and freeze the second one; it usually does not take much extra time to prepare two recipes at once (spaghetti sauce and chili are good choices).
- Keep "homemade mixes" made up in the refrigerator (for example, homemade biscuit mix that requires only the milk to be added at the time of preparation or the dry ingredients for muffins).
- Do the simple pre-preparation steps while you are putting the groceries away; for example, wash the fruits

and vegetables before storing—not all can be prewashed, but most can.

- Plan simple, well-balanced meals. Be realistic in what you can accomplish with your other responsibilities, such as meeting the needs of small children. You do not have to spend the whole day preparing a gourmet meal for it to be delicious and enjoyed!
- Start dinner when you are cleaning up the night before. You can check your menu plan and start some of the preparation. Doing a few simple things, such as taking out the meat to defrost, boiling chicken for casseroles, and chopping vegetables the night before, will make the following day seem like you are really ahead on your time!

MEAL-MANAGEMENT GOAL FOUR: PREPARING MEALS YOUR FAMILY WANTS AND LIKES

Depending on the eating habits of your family, the fourth goal, preparing meals the family likes, may be the most difficult to accomplish. These are a few practical guidelines the meal manager can follow to help her family enjoy the meals she prepares:

- Include "family favorites" at every meal. For example, if corn is a favorite, serve it with a vegetable that may not be enjoyed as much. All family members should be able to look at their plate and see something they really like.
- Limit the number of mixtures (or combination dishes) within each meal. For example, if the main meal is a casserole, serve whole vegetables or fruit to add variety to the meal. Make sure, even with casseroles, that every ingredient is identifiable!
- Avoid repetition or ways of preparing food. For example, do not serve fried chicken and fried potatoes at the same meal; instead, serve fried chicken with baked potatoes.

- Vary the *color* of the meal. When the meal is presented on the plate, there should be a variety of colors. For example, if you are serving chicken, avoid serving potatoes, corn, and cauliflower! Select carrots and peas to add color.
- Vary the *texture* within the meal. Texture has to do with the way things feel in your mouth. Usually meals are more enjoyable if there is variety.
- Vary the *flavors* in the meal. Using a variety of flavors will make the meal more interesting—for example, include both savory and sweet.
- Vary the *shapes* of the meal. Avoid using all the same shapes or sizes of food.
- Vary the *consistency* of the meal. Consistency is the degree of firmness or softness of the food items. Meals should include both hard and soft items—raw carrots and bread are contrasting consistencies.

Preparing meals your family wants and likes is a fun goal to pursue; I find it very rewarding to serve my family meals they enjoy. Of course, every family member will not enjoy everything about every meal—that is not a realistic goal. However, by considering these guidelines you will prepare interesting meals that look and taste good! Most family members will enjoy something from every meal.

GETTING STARTED: PRACTICAL SUGGESTIONS FOR EXERCISING HOSPITALITY

Do not neglect to show hospitality to strangers,
for by this some have entertained angels without knowing it.
HEBREWS 13:2 NASB

In addition to pursuing the four meal-management goals, there are several practical suggestions that will help you get started in becoming a gracious and confident hostess:

- Identify an older, more experienced woman whom you can learn from. Ask her if she will disciple you in the areas of hospitality, meal management, or home management (whatever your specific needs are). Perhaps you can help her on her next hospitality event. Help her with the planning, preparing, and serving. Also, ask her what she serves when she has guests in her home (these are tried recipes you know will work!).
- Start a "hospitality notebook." Start keeping a record of your hospitality opportunities. File away menus, guest lists, shopping lists, and party ideas you collect from your favorite magazines.
- Identify simple menus that work. Practice one or two menus on your family and use them for entertaining guests. As you develop your confidence, add variety to the menus you prepare.
- Work together with a friend. Instead of being responsible for the whole menu, share the responsibility. This will develop your relationship as well as help lighten the workload.
- Plan ahead. Set yourself up to be successful for practicing hospitality by keeping food on hand that can be made up quickly and easily; for example, keep brownie or cake mixes for easy and quick desserts. Also, keep your freezer stocked for unexpected guests.
- Read more about it! There are many practical books on the areas of menu planning, meal management, and hospitality. They will give you creative ideas that will continue to inspire you in your hospitality endeavors.
- Take classes that will develop your skills in ethnic cooking, cake decorating, or garnishing techniques. They will be fun and will develop your technical skills. Consider taking them with a friend.
- Be intentional. Make a list of people you would like to entertain and consult it when you are planning the family

calendar. Choose a specific time to invite individuals to your home.

THE REWARDS OF HOSPITALITY

The generous man will be prosperous,
and he who waters will himself be watered.
PROVERBS 11:25 NASB

Practicing hospitality is one of the most rewarding experiences in life. While experiencing personal rewards should never be our motivation for practicing hospitality, whenever we take the time to invest our lives into the lives of others, we will reap the rich rewards associated with loving others. True, there are many sacrifices involved in practicing hospitality, but it has been my experience that the rewards far outweigh the costs. Here are some of those rewards:

ESTABLISHMENT OF RELATIONSHIPS

Proverbs 17:17 reminds us that "a friend loves at all times." Having people into your home allows relationships to be established and grow. Allowing people to see how you really "live" brings warmth and depth to the relationship.

EXPANDED UNDERSTANDING OF GOD'S WORLD

Learning from the experiences of others will broaden your worldview; for example, inviting missionaries into your home will expose your family to the needs of other people groups around the world (see chapter 8).

ENCOURAGEMENT FROM THE FELLOWSHIP

Proverbs 11:25 can be translated, "He who refreshes others will himself also be refreshed." The principle found in this proverb is that a generous person will receive far more than he gives.

EDUCATING YOUR CHILDREN

Proverbs 22:6 exhorts us to "train up a child." One of the areas children must be trained in is in the area of having a compassionate heart for the needs of other people. Practicing hospitality as a family provides numerous training opportunities for children. Additionally, children who participate with the family in practicing hospitality will probably learn to be hospitable themselves. They will have the opportunity to converse with godly men and women who will serve as role models in addition to their parents. Finally, they will have the opportunity to develop practical skills, such as conversation or cooking skills.

EXERCISING SPIRITUAL GIFTEDNESS

As we saw earlier, 1 Peter 4:9 says that we should practice hospitality without complaint. Immediately following this statement, verse 10 tells us, "As each one has received a special gift, employ it in serving one another as good stewards of the manifold grace of God" (NASB). Hospitality provides the forum for exercising many of the spiritual gifts. Mercy, giving, exhortation, or teaching can all be exercised while practicing hospitality.

EXPERIENCING SPIRITUAL GROWTH

Philippians 2:1–4 exhorts us to "esteem others better than [ourselves]" and to "look out . . . for the interests of others." Hospitality provides us with numerous opportunities to practice serving others with humility—the same sacrificial humility Christ demonstrated. By selflessly serving others we will allow our character to become more like Christ's.

A FINAL THOUGHT . . .

God expects all Christians to practice hospitality (Romans 12:13). We are to embrace this command cheerfully and without complaint (1 Peter 4:9). Understanding the biblical definition of hospitality as loving strangers and meeting the needs of others is critical to the success of practicing hospitality (Hebrews 12:1–2). Embracing a biblical definition of hospitality prevents us from merely becoming "Christian event planners." It alleviates much of the pressure we often feel when entertaining, for biblical hospitality is simply love in action.

TABLE 7.5
EVALUATING MENUS ACCORDING
TO *THE FOOD GUIDE PYRAMID*

(Use 3–5 days for each family member)

Family Member's Name: _____

Date: _____

Food Group	Day One	Day Two	Day Three	Summary
Bread, Cereal, Rice, and Pasta Group (6–11 Servings)				
Vegetable Group (3–5 Servings)				
Fruit Group (2–4 Servings)				
Milk, Yogurt, and Cheese Group (2–3 Servings)				
Meat, Poultry, Fish, Dry Beans, Eggs, and Nuts Group (2–3 Servings)				
Fats, Oils, and Sweets (Use Sparingly)				

Needed changes to menu plans include:

_____

_____

_____

GROWING IN HOSPITALITY

1. Review these Scriptures on hospitality: Romans 12:13; Hebrews 13:2; 1 Timothy 3:2; Titus 1:8; 1 Peter 4:9. Pray about how the Lord would have you implement the command to be hospitable.

2. Identify specific "challenges" unique to you (i.e., lack of time, money, or experience). Develop a plan to overcome the challenge in relationship to practicing hospitality. For example, if you lack skill, how can you learn?

3. Make a list of people to whom you would like to extend hospitality; then identify how you will implement it. For example, your list may look like this:

NEW NEIGHBORS	Bake bread and deliver on Tuesday
GRANDMA	Invite over for dinner on her birthday
OFFICE WORKERS	Invite to church on Sunday

4. Complete a diet evaluation for each family member using the "Evaluating Menus According to The Food Guide Pyramid*" form.*

5. *Create a hospitality notebook. Ideas to include might be:*

    a. *Menu plans*
    b. *Recipes*
    c. *Shopping lists*
    d. *Calendars*
    e. *Garnishes*
    f. *Party ideas*
    g. *Guest lists*

$\mathcal{M}$y pastor's wife, Beverly LaHaye, approached me after an evening church service and asked, "Pat, would you be interested in joining a group of ladies at my home next week to discuss some issues vital to our role as Christian women?" Inwardly my mind was racing . . . there isn't anything that I would rather do! Outwardly, I graciously smiled and responded, "How thoughtful of you to include me—I would be delighted to attend." As I laid my head on my pillow the night before the meeting, sleep was long in coming as I anticipated the upcoming afternoon gathering.

The sun cast a gentle glow on the LaHayes' living room as a group of ladies gathered on the lovely summer day. We began with refreshments and the usual ladies' chatter—all the while knowing that a cause greater than "female fellowship" had drawn us together. The room silenced as Mrs. LaHaye rose and began to share with us the purpose of the gathering . . . as she watched a television interview of Betty Friedan, founder of the National Organization for Women, she realized that Friedan claimed to speak for the women of America. Beverly knew that Friedan was not accurately representing her beliefs and was confident that she was not the only woman who felt that way. A time of discussion, af-firmation of Beverly's convictions, and prayer followed.

Subsequently, a meeting to educate and alert Christian women on the Equal Rights Amendment (ERA), led by Mrs. LaHaye, was held in San Diego—with an attendance that exceeded twelve hundred! This event served to launch Concerned Women for America (CWA).

Lisa and I had the opportunity to attend the CWA Convention in October of 1997 in Washington, D.C.; as we sat in the audience we learned that CWA's membership, drawn from the fifty states, comprised well over 500,000 members. My mind drifted back to that initial gathering of women where I was first taught that . . .

EIGHT

THE WISE WOMAN DEVELOPS A WORLDVIEW

You are the salt of the earth; but if the salt has become tasteless,
how will it be made salty again? It is no longer good for anything,
except to be thrown out and trampled under foot by men.
You are the light of the world. A city set on a hill cannot be hidden;
nor does anyone light a lamp and put it under a basket,
but on the lampstand, and it gives light to all who are in the house.
Let your light shine before men in such a way that they may see
your good works, and glorify your Father who is in heaven.

MATTHEW 5:13–16 NASB

Our Wise Woman responds to her position of prominence (Proverbs 31:23–24) by choosing to be alert and abreast of current events. Her desire to implement the *principles of unselfish, economical, prepared,* and *lovable* motivate her to ask herself the question, "How broad is my world?" As professional and social opportunities emerge, she rarely finds herself lacking an accurate knowledge of topics under discussion in a group of well-informed people. Purposing to maintain relevancy with current events allows her to avoid the how-ignorant-and-uninformed-I-am syndrome. Our Wise Woman purposes to stimulate her mind by keeping her heart and eyes open to the multifaceted dimensions of life that arouse her interest, delight her soul, provide an opportunity for ministry, and tickle her curiosity. Elizabeth George challenges the Christian Woman in *A Woman After God's Own Heart* to develop "Five Fat Files." She introduces the challenge by stating:

> In addition to being our Savior, Jesus is our model for how to live a life that pleases God. When we look at His life, we see that "Jesus increased in wisdom" (Luke 2:52). One proverb (a constant challenge to me) reflects the importance of such growth: "The heart of him who has understanding seeks knowledge, but the mouth of fools feeds on foolishness" (Proverbs 15:14). Put another way, an intelligent person purposefully seeks knowledge, but fools nibble randomly, vacantly chewing on words and ideas that have no value, no flavor, and no nutrition.
>
> What are you and I feeding our mind? Are we heeding this biblical warning about the danger of "garbage in, garbage out"? May we *purposefully* seek knowledge and guard against spending precious time on things that have no value. One way I guard my mind is by following the advice of a special woman, advice which has provided fodder for teaching, books, study materials and ministry. She told me, "Liz, you've got to have five fat files!"

She then provided a workable strategy:

Create five fat files—Purchase five manila file folders.

Aim at expertise—Next, select five areas you'd like to become an expert in and label a file for each of them. A word of caution: choose areas from the spiritual realm. Remember the proverb? You don't want to feed on pursuits that have no value. Instead choose topics of eternal value. To help you determine those five areas, answer the questions "What do you want to be known for?" and "What topic do you want your name associated with?"

Fill the files—Now start putting information into your files. They'll get fat as you follow the exhortation to "read everything on [your] subject . . . articles, books, specialized magazines, and news clippings . . . attend seminars . . . teach on the subject(s) . . . spend time with those who are the best in these areas, picking their brains . . . seek and sharpen your expertise."[1]

Our Wise Woman will develop a personal worldview by cultivating her mind and elevating her thoughts. Grasping the principle of "salt and light," learning to disciple her children, and comprehending the challenge of Christian parenting are areas that will assist in its cultivation.

THE PRINCIPLE OF SALT AND LIGHT

A lamp is not brought to be put under a basket,
is it, or under a bed?
Is it not brought to be put on the lampstand? . . .
Salt is good; but if the salt becomes unsalty,
with what will you make it salty again?
Have salt in yourselves, and be at peace with one another.
MARK 4:21; 9:50 NASB

Harper's Bible Dictionary says:

Salt is one of the most commonly used seasonings in antiquity (Job 6:6). Its preservative powers made it an absolute necessity of life and, not surprisingly, endowed it with religious significance. Salt was used for Israelite worship to season incense (Exodus 30:35), and all offerings were to be seasoned with salt (Leviticus 2:13; Ezekiel 43:24). Numbers 18:19 and 2 Chronicles 13:5 find salt symbolizing the making of a covenant. Jesus, in the Sermon on the Mount, calls the people who listen to Him "the salt of the earth" (Matthew 5:13).[2]

The MacArthur Study Bible offers a useful description of the phrase "if the salt loses its flavor, how shall it be seasoned?"

> Salt is both a preservative and a flavor enhancer. No doubt its use as a preservative is what Jesus mostly had in view here. Pure salt cannot lose its flavor or effectiveness, but the salt that is common in the Dead Sea area is contaminated with gypsum and other minerals and may have a flat taste or be ineffective as a preservative. Such mineral salts were useful for little more than keeping footpaths free of vegetation.[3]

"Light is the word used in connection with joy, blessing, and life in contrast to sorrow, adversity, and death. At an early time it came to signify God's presence and favor (Psalm 27:1; Isaiah 9:2; 2 Corinthians 4:6) in contrast to God's judgment (Amos 5:18)."[4] The principle of "salt and light" is derived from combining the preserving power of the salt with the joy and blessing derived from light. Our Wise Woman's presence will produce joy and blessing and at the same time offer a savory and preserving influence.

The principle of "salt and light" radiates from the Wise Woman's home. The *principle of unselfish* allows her to cast her vision beyond her own needs to the needs of others (John 4:34–38), as well as reminding her to incorporate the model of the homes of the citizens of the ancient East that left a light burning through the night (Proverbs 31:18). The light burning indicated a haven for the distressed and signified prosperity. While perhaps not leaving a literal light on throughout the night, the Wise Woman's home is known as a haven for the physically and emotionally distressed.

The *principle of prepared* motivates her to maintain her priorities in such a way that she possesses the physical and spiritual resources to assist others (Jeremiah 17:1–8), while the *principle of lovable* challenges her to concentrate her ministry efforts first on those residing in her home and then on the application of the Titus 2:3–5 principle to those beyond her household. Our Wise Woman's home will serve as a preserving institution of society and a lighthouse to point others to the saving power of God. Rebecca Pippert's writings in *Out of the Saltshaker and into the World* reinforce evangelism as a way of life; in the preface to the book she proposes:

> Jesus tells us in the Sermon on the Mount that we are the salt of the earth. And he challenges us not to lose our savor—our saltiness. This means—among other things—that we are to be active in the world as his representatives. We are to get out of the saltshaker and into life itself. Not to be trodden down, but to be zestful witnesses to Jesus as Lord and Savior, as the one who alone gives life and meaning to a dying world.[5]

Our Wise Woman mobilizes her home to function as a saltshaker, spreading its contents to a decaying world desperately needing its preserving contents. Hospitality is a vehicle to begin the "seasoning process." The Scriptures record that God used food in special ways to carry out His will and show His grace. Esau sold his birthright for a bowl of stew (Genesis 25:29, 33; Hebrews 12:16). Jacob sent his sons to Egypt to buy grain and thus found Joseph (Genesis 41–46). Abraham and Sarah made a meal for strangers and so entertained angels unaware (Genesis 18:1–22; Hebrews 13:2). When the Israelites went to spy out the land, they came back with reports about the food (Numbers 13:26–33). The birds fed Elijah (1 Kings 17:2–7). The widow of Zarephath shared her food, which caused a supernatural multiplication (1 Kings 17:8–16). And the greatest blessing—all Christians will be guests at the marriage feast of the Lamb (Revelation 19:7–10)! The "Recipe for Successful Discipleship" provides the procedure for the mobilization process:

RECIPE FOR SUCCESSFUL DISCIPLESHIP

START
with one person who has a
desire to serve the Lord.

SIFT
in several eager Christians,
plus some who want to meet Jesus or know Him better.

BLEND
in a balanced,
interesting course of study.

ADD
a cup of prayer and a
cup of preparation.

STIR
in a tablespoon of
common sense.

DROP
in a pinch of
humor.

SKIM OFF
the religious jargon,
the dos and don'ts,
the over-emotionalism.

SEASON
with generous portions of acceptance,
genuine personal interest, and love.

REMOVE
preachiness, self-effort, and a
holier-than-thou attitude.

ALLOW
the influence of the Holy Spirit
to lift hearts to worshiping the Lord.

FOLLOW
this recipe of discipleship and it will almost never
burn, over-bake, sour, or fall flat.
—Author Unknown

The Wise Woman's home will always be a "prepared place" (John 14:2–3) for her family and a "city that is set on a hill" (Matthew 5:14) for those who observe her life.

DISCIPLESHIP OF CHILDREN

Train up a child in the way he should go,
Even when he is old he will not depart from it.
PROVERBS 22:6 NASB

Before the Wise Woman can have an impact on the world, she must take seriously her responsibility to disciple and train her children. Wise Women will acknowledge the significant opportunity for influence they have in the lives of their children.

I write as a relatively new mom who sincerely desires to be found faithful in her parenting, but in daily encounters I experience failure due to inexperience, physical fatigue, and character weaknesses such as impatience, anger, and harsh words (in other words, sin!). I write representing thousands of moms who, as my father says, experience the fact that parenting "brings out the very best and very worst in you." After reading numerous authors, seeking counsel from older, more experienced parents, and most important, searching the Scriptures for direction, my husband and I have developed principles for our parenting. They are principles we are committed to intentionally pursuing with our children. They give us a direction for our priorities, choices, and lifestyle as it relates to parenting our children. I pray that they are an encouragement to you and provide a starting point for you to build your own set of principles for discipling your children.

PRINCIPLE ONE: AS A PARENT I ACKNOWLEDGE THAT THE PURPOSE OF OUR FAMILY IS TO BRING GLORY TO GOD (PSALM 86:11–12; ROMANS 15:5–6; 1 PETER 4:11).

The discipleship of our children begins with an understanding that the primary purpose of our family is to bring glory to God. This concept is critical to the parenting process because it determines the priorities and goals for parents as we train, disciple, and love our children. Acknowledging the purpose of the family as bringing glory to God means that family priorities will be spiritual rather than material.[6] If, as the Westminster Catechism states, "The chief end of man is to glorify God and enjoy Him forever," we must establish this as a foundational principle in our family and in the hearts of our children. It is a fundamental truth needed to help our children establish a worldview of being "salt and light."

We can apply this first principle by practicing Deuteronomy 6:2–7 and Matthew 9:22 on a daily basis through using everyday life situations to remind our children all of life is spiritual and God is in all of life. Jean Fleming explains this concept by stating:

> Our days are full of opportunities to share spiritual truth with our children. We can use everyday incidents as a springboard for this. We can explain how Jesus washed away our sins as we give them a bath, or talk about the parable of the good soil as we work in

the garden, or tell them Jesus knows the number of hairs on their heads as we comb their hair. Making or slicing bread can be the setting for telling them that Jesus is the bread of life, or that man doesn't live by bread alone, or how Jesus fed five thousand people with two loaves of bread and five fishes. Seeds of truth are waiting everywhere to be planted in your child's mind.[7]

PRINCIPLE TWO: AS A PARENT, I TAKE SERIOUSLY THE RESPONSIBILITY OF BOTH TEACHING AND TRAINING MY CHILDREN SPIRITUALLY AND MORALLY (PROVERBS 22:6; EPHESIANS 6:4; 2 TIMOTHY 3:14–15).

Becoming a parent for the first time can be a frightening experience. I remember feeling incredibly unprepared when I was pregnant with my first child. Yes, I had taken child development classes, prepared the nursery, and read numerous books on parenting. Because I was an older, first-time mom, I even had a few extra years to observe the parenting strategies of friends. I still, however, felt completely inadequate and unprepared for the responsibility of becoming a mother. I have come to realize that this was an appropriate response. This "healthy fear" keeps me dependent on a daily basis for God's wisdom, strength, and forgiveness when I fail as a parent. It helps me to take the job of parenting seriously. I must recognize that if I am going to impact the world for Christ, I must begin by impacting my own children.

We must teach and train our children both spiritually and morally. Spiritual training includes knowledge of God and His word; moral training is based on spiritual training and includes developing good character or conduct as well as virtues that reflect standards of right and wrong behavior. Training differs from teaching. While both training and teaching are necessary in parenting, they have different outcomes. H. Clay Trumbull explains the differences:

It has been said that the essence of teaching is causing another to know. It may similarly be said that the essence of training is causing another to do. Teaching gives knowledge. Training gives skill. Teaching fills the mind. Training shapes the habits. Teaching brings to the child that which he did not have before. Training enables a child to make use of that which is already his possession. We teach a child the meanings of words. We train a child in speaking and walking. We teach him the truths which we have learned for ourselves. We train him in habits of study, that he may be able to learn other truths for himself. Training and teaching must go on together in the wise upbringing of any and every child. The one will fail of its own best end if it is not accompanied by the other. He who knows how to teach a child is not competent for the oversight of a child's education unless he also knows how to train a child.[8]

To summarize the importance of intentionally training and teaching our children, we could say that as parents, we should be active, not passive in our parenting goals. It takes thought, preparation, and planning to accomplish parenting goals.

Using a catechism such as *Training Hearts*[9] might be helpful in teaching doctrine to your children. For moral training, parents can identify areas of behavior to cultivate, such as honest speech or good manners.

PRINCIPLE THREE: AS A PARENT I RECOGNIZE THE BEST WAY TO TRAIN MY CHILDREN IS TO MODEL GODLY CHARACTER (1 CORINTHIANS 4:16; 11:1; EPHESIANS 5:1; PHILIPPIANS 3:17; 4:9).

How do we begin to teach and train our children? The Puritans believed that training children was accomplished by a threefold approach, including teaching sound doctrine, being an example, and disciplining one's children. Those three areas give us parameters for training our children spiritually and morally. Simply stated, we teach our children sound doctrine that is given credibility by our godly example and reinforced through biblical discipline.

Children are no fools! They will quickly see hypocrisy in the lives of their parents. If there is inconsistency between the "message" and the "messenger," they will learn to be insincere and deceptive. As parents, we must be growing in our knowledge of God and seeking God's forgiveness for areas of sin in our own lives. John MacArthur states, "True success for Christian parents is the parent's own character."[10] When we compromise God's character in our example, we compromise our children's understanding of God's fatherhood.

Carl K. Spackman suggests parents often do not model godly character in three areas.

1. We have failed to model a sense of the joy involved in living the Christian life.
2. We have failed to communicate by our example the spirit of compassion and service to the needy that is the heart of true Christianity.
3. We have failed to maintain open minds that enable us to deal lovingly with our children's questions and honest doubts.[11]

To be successful in training our children, we must model godly character. Godly character is developed by maintaining a right relationship with God through worship of His character, confession of sin, and knowledge of His word.

Here are some ways we, as parents, can model godly character:

- Seeking our children's forgiveness when we have sinned, for this clarifies the image of God to our children (for example, when we were impatient or became angry). God is not impatient.

- Working through personal areas of sin by identifying areas needing growth. Develop a plan for personal change (e.g., read a book, complete a study, begin a mentor relationship with an older woman).
- Always taking time for God personally (establish a routine time for reading His Word and praying).

PRINCIPLE FOUR: AS A PARENT I UNDERSTAND THAT I MUST DISCIPLINE MY CHILDREN IN ORDER TO DEVELOP THEIR CHARACTER (PROVERBS 3:11–12; 13:24; 22:15; 23:13–14; 29:17).

Discipline can be divided into three basic components:

First, children are required to obey (Exodus 20:12; Proverbs 6:20; Ephesians 6:1–3; Hebrews 12:9). The most basic goal of discipline is obedience. Children are required to obey because they lack maturity. MacArthur states that children lack maturity in four areas: mental maturity, physical maturity, social maturity, and spiritual maturity.[12]

Second, parents are required to discipline (Proverbs 29:15). We cannot read the book of Proverbs without clearly seeing that God expects parents to discipline our children. As parents, we have the God-given authority and responsibility to discipline our children. The purpose of disciplining our children is to develop their character, not for personal convenience or even right behavior (although right behavior will flow out of right character). Discipline is the primary tool for training our children.

Third, Scripture reveals two primary tools for discipline— communication and "the rod" (Deuteronomy 6:2–7; Proverbs 29:15). Communication allows the parents to clearly articulate the standards and boundaries for attitudes and behavior. "The rod" is the instrument for administering discipline when violations of the standards and boundaries have occurred. Tedd Tripp explains the rod: "The rod is a parent, in faith toward God and faithfulness toward his or her children, undertaking the responsibility of careful, timely, measured, and controlled use of physical punishment to underscore the importance of obeying God, thus rescuing the child from continuing in his foolishness until death."[13]

I find that while I am very committed to communicating and disciplining my children, it is very challenging to be consistent. Tiredness or laziness often creeps into my parenting. It is important, however, that I am intentional and consistent in the training and nurturing of my children so their lives are not lost to the "foolishness that is bound up in their hearts" (see Proverbs 22:15). The following principles are based on Chuck Swindoll's suggestions for remaining consistent in disciplining:

- Establish firm rules so that children understand what is right and wrong.
- When rules are broken, discipline in private.
- Clearly and briefly explain the discipline before administering the discipline.
- Console the child and restore the relationship. Affirmation and compassion are needed to restore the relationship.[14]

It is important for parents to establish practical parameters for disciplining their children. Both partners must be in agreement for discipline to be effective. Reading *Shepherding a Child's Heart,* by Tedd Tripp,[15] might be a helpful guide for beginning to establish discipline procedures and character goals for your children.

PRINCIPLE FIVE: AS A PARENT, I STRIVE TO SHAPE MY CHILD'S WILL BUT NOT CRUSH HIS OR HER SPIRIT (EPHESIANS 6:4; HEBREWS 12:5–11).

When our boys follow through in obedience to a request we have made, we intentionally use the phrase "You made a good choice." We started this at an early age to emphasize to them that they always have a choice whether or not to obey, and they are responsible for the consequences of that choice. This is the primary distinction between shaping a will and crushing the spirit. Shaping of the will allows the choice to remain a result of personal character. In other words, your child obeys because he is choosing to do the right thing.

Trumbull clearly defines the difference between breaking and training a child's will when he states, "The term 'will' as here employed applies to a child's faculty of choosing or deciding between two courses of action. Breaking a child's will is bringing the pressure of external force directly upon that will, causing the will to give way under the pressure of that force. Training a child's will is bringing such influences to bear upon the child that he is ready to choose or decide in favor of the right course of action."[16]

Crushing the spirit removes the choice and requires conformity due to pressure or force from the parent. Examples of crushing a child's spirit include:

- punishing for disobedience and childish "accidents" in the same fashion;
- verbally demeaning him or her, and
- punishing while angry.

All are examples of parents provoking their children rather than training them (Ephesians 6:4). Parents are responsible for training the will of their children so that they make right choices because they understand the consequences of their actions. This requires that parents know each of their children individually and acknowledge that they are uniquely created by God (Psalm 139).

There are many areas in which parents could crush their children's spirit. As parents, we need to think through the specific ways we might be violating our children and make the needed changes. For example, do you

- carefully select your tone of voice and choice of words when your children disobey (to reinforce their personal responsibility of choice and the consequences that will follow their choice)?
- nurture your children's curiosity for life by allowing them to ask questions with freedom?
- differentiate between willful acts of disobedience and unintentional accidents?
- allow your children to fail without becoming angry?

PRINCIPLE SIX: AS A PARENT I SEEK TO DEAL WITH THE HEART ISSUES, NOT JUST BEHAVIOR ISSUES (PROVERBS 4:23; 22:15).

As parents, we should want to avoid raising legalistic children. Legalism focuses on merely external compliance or behavior. Rather, we want to develop internal desires to do what is good and right because of their desire to honor God. Legalism, as it relates to behavior, fears man because the motivation for behavior is to please others or to avoid conflict with others. The contrast to legalism is nurturing the heart that encourages children to do what is right because they love God. In other words, behavior flows out of the heart (Mark 7:21; Luke 6:45). Tedd Tripp explains this concept by stating:

Parents often get sidetracked with behavior. If your goal in discipline is changed behavior, it is easy to understand why this happens. The thing that alerts you to your child's need for correction is his behavior. Behavior irritates and thus calls attention to itself. Behavior becomes our focus. You think you have corrected when you have changed unacceptable behavior to behavior you sanction and appreciate. "What is the problem," you ask? The problem is this. Your child's needs are far more profound than his aberrant behavior. Remember, his behavior does not just spring forth uncaused. His behavior—the things he says and does—reflects his heart. If you are to really help him, you must be concerned with the attitudes of heart that drive his behavior.[17]

It is so easy to become focused solely on trying to conform the outward behavior of our children; we want them to act appropriately. We should, however, be primarily focused on the character of our children's heart. God values character above all. Fleming says, "Man cares about externals, but God cares about inner qualities. Man values beauty, brains, wealth, and power; God values a pure heart. Integrity and faithfulness have greater value to God than success."[18]

Our primary goal as parents, therefore, becomes helping our children to see their own sinfulness, their need to repent, and ultimately their need for a Savior.

A practical exercise for parents desiring to focus on heart issues is to read through Proverbs. Parents can generate a list of character traits or behavior patterns that need to be taught to their children. (You are identifying character goals rather than behavior goals.)

PRINCIPLE SEVEN: AS A PARENT, I MUST TEACH MY
CHILDREN HOW TO BE "IN" BUT NOT "OF" THE WORLD
(MATTHEW 5:14; JOHN 15:19; 2 CORINTHIANS 10:3;
1 JOHN 2:15).

It is Christ's command to be a witness to the world, which requires interacting with people in the world. Because of our concern for nurturing our children's morality, we often believe that
sheltering them from the world is the best means to protect their
moral character. However, just protecting them from the world
does not assure their moral purity because sin or immorality is
primarily an expression of an internal reality—our children are
sinners. Therefore, the primary focus should be on educating our
children's hearts from the principles found in God's Word, teaching them to love truth, and to discern evil. Spackman offers this
advice: "To help our children come to an enduring faith in Christ
we must, in every possible way inculcate them with the truth of
God's Word. As a part of this inculcation, we must repeatedly in-
oculate them against the man-centered philosophies and god-
less lifestyles of the world."[19]

Isolating ourselves from the world may also isolate us from
the people God intended us to reach. We may find ourselves
violating the Great Commission found in Matthew 28 to "go
out into the world and teach"—Christ's example was to live
truth out in the midst of sinners. We do want to protect our children as they mature into adults and are ready to confront the
sin found in the world. As children mature in age physically,
parents should help them mature spiritually so they are able
to be "in" the world but not "of" the world.

A practical suggestion for helping our children be "in" the
world, but not "of" the world, is to develop with our children
biblical criteria for watching television or movies, reading
books, or listening to music.

PRINCIPLE EIGHT: AS A PARENT, I RAISE MY CHILDREN TO MANIFEST GOD'S LOVE TO THE WORLD (MATTHEW 9:36–38; 28:19–20; 2 CORINTHIANS 5:16–20).

My husband and I are concerned that our children will become indifferent and uncompassionate concerning the needs of others because of the affluence, comfort, and privileges they experience just because they are "middle-class Americans." One of the most critical jobs a parent undertakes is to raise children who understand that "life is not just about them." Instead, life is about reaching out to a lost world, the majority of whom are poor and defenseless (James 2:1–9).

We have to confront the values of our culture. The American dream conveys that it is a right to accumulate material possessions for personal benefit. Our job, as parents, is to teach our children that Christ modeled a lifestyle of simplicity, making people a priority over possessions. Simply put, we should help our children understand the motto "Less, not more, and others, not self." Children raised with this value have the potential to become adults who are more willing to follow Christ wherever He may lead. They are willing to leave home, family, friends, career, or other material gain to pursue Christ's priority, which was needy people. In addition, God's heart for the nations is evident throughout Scripture. He invites us to participate in His redemptive plan to share the gospel with people from every tribe, tongue, and nation. A mature Christian, growing in the image of Christ, must manifest Christ's interest in reaching the world (Matthew 28:19–20; Acts 1:8). Your home can become a place where you celebrate the uniqueness of the cultures of people God loves. You can raise up children who are "world Christians."

RAISING WORLD CHRISTIANS

For God so loved the world, that He gave
His only begotten Son, that whoever believes in Him
should not perish, but have eternal life.
JOHN 3:16 NASB

There are many simple things we can do on a daily basis that will help broaden our children's worldview, expose them to the needs of others, and teach them to be compassionate to people different from themselves. Some ideas to stimulate your thinking:

- Doing volunteer work as a family at a local shelter for the homeless or for abused women, or for other similar organizations
- During the Christmas holiday, participating in preparing packages for needy children (there are numerous organizations that deliver Christmas gifts each year)
- Reading books such as *Growing Compassionate Kids,* by Jan Johnson[20]
- Subscribing to *National Geographic*
- Buying your children a globe
- Putting up a world map somewhere in your home (a child's room or the family room)
- Buying "world" place mats for your children to see at the dinner table
- Inviting international students from a local university into your home
- Preparing ethnic meals for your family
- As a family, learning a foreign language
- Inviting missionaries to stay in your home while they are on furlough
- "Adopting" a missionary child the same age as your children (they can write, send birthday presents, and spend

time together when the missionary child is home on fur-
lough)
- Collecting missionary prayer cards from your church,
  placing them in a small photo album, and praying for a
  different family each day
- Reading and praying through *Operation World*, by
  Patrick Johnstone,[21] or *You Can Change the World*, by Jill
  Johnstone[22] (a children's version of *Operation World*)

A FINAL THOUGHT . . .

We know we cannot save the souls of our children; the
Scripture says that only by God's grace can anyone come to
know and love Him (Ephesians 2:8–9). We can, however, provide an influence in our children's lives that will position them
to be sensitive to God's Word and work in their lives. This primarily is how women with children will influence their world,
by raising up a godly generation who will continue to be "salt
and light" (Philippians 2:12–16). As you invest in your children, you should be involved yourself in ministering to the
needy and evangelizing the lost. You must "practice what you
preach." Your children will learn by your example how to care
for and minister to the poor and lost of our world.

GROWING IN THE
ABILITY TO DEVELOP
A WORLDVIEW

1. *Evaluate John 10:10 in light of the question, "How broad is your world?"*

2. *Provide a scriptural rationale for the primary reason for entertaining unbelieving friends and acquaintances.*

3. *Read through the Proverbs as a parent. Identify specific commands and character traits parents should instill in their children. Use a chart format like the one below to keep a record of the principles identified.*

PROVERBS REFERENCE	I must teach my child . . .

4. *Select and put into practice one or more of the "application ideas" from the principles for "Discipling your Children."*

5. *Read missionary biographies (Hudson Taylor, Amy Carmichael, John and Betty Stam) together as a family to help your children develop a compassion for other people.*

As a Christian woman and trained as a Home Economist, I never expected to be single past my mid-twenties. However, the Lord had a much different plan for me and has gently matured my attitude toward singleness, as well as the purpose of marriage. Rather than marriage simply providing a "live-in date," I know now that I should marry only if our united lives would be more effective for the Lord than either of us are in our single state.

As a single professional I established Home Economics departments in two Christian colleges, and I have had the joy of watching numerous young women mature into useful instruments for our Master's kingdom. Though I have no children of my own, I have spiritual children and grandchildren all over the world. My single status allows me to provide the nurturing that my students need without neglecting my own family. I daily have the joy of experiencing what Paul wrote about in 1 Corinthians 7:32–34!

My greatest challenge in experiencing contentment in my single state is members of the body of Christ who cannot understand how someone who can cook and sew, as well as implement effective management and financial skills, is not married. Their insistence that "Mr. Right" will one day come along discounts the possibility that it is the Lord's will for me to minister to others, as a single, using my spiritual gifts, talents, and educational background.

A consistent encouragement to me is the report that Boaz had of Ruth in Ruth 3:11. He observed her behavior from a distance and formed conclusions about her character. Should the Lord have as His plan a union for me in the future, I would want that individual to give the same report of me: "All my people in the city know that you are a woman of excellence" (NASB). This focus reminds me that regardless of her marital status . . .

THE WISE WOMAN ACCEPTS HER UNIQUE POSITION IN THE BODY OF CHRIST

*For just as we have many members in one body
and all the members do not have the same function,
so we, who are many, are one body in Christ, and
individually members one of another.
Since we have gifts that differ according to the grace given to us,
each of us is to exercise them accordingly."*

ROMANS 12:4–6 NASB

Edith Schaeffer, in her classic work *What Is a Family?*, describes the family as a mobile. Her captivating imagery presents a description of the diversity of the family:

A family is the most versatile, ever-changing mobile that exists. A family is a *living* mobile that is different from the hand-crafted mobiles and the art-museum mobiles, different from the mobiles of lakes and trees and from the mobiles of birds, fish and animals—different from any mobiles of machine, animal or plant. A family is an intricate mobile made up of human personalities.

In so many ways a family is a mobile—an artwork that takes

years, even generations, to produce, but which is never finished. The artwork of this mobile called "family" continues, and imagination, creativity, originality, talent, concern, love, compassion, excitement, determination and time produce diversity, which is a challenge to any intelligent human being who has been given understanding of how to begin in the studio of life itself.

A family is a grouping of individuals who are *affecting* each other intellectually, emotionally, spiritually and physically. No two years, no two months, or no two days is the exact same blend or mix within the family, as each individual is changing.[1]

Likewise, the family of God is a mobile. Romans 12:4–8 teaches that God sovereignly gives the body of Christ a unified diversity. A variety of circumstances including singleness, single motherhood, childlessness, and widowhood necessitate the establishment of diverse homes. Our Wise Woman cultivates an appreciation of these homes within the family of God.

THE WISE WOMAN THRIVES IN HER SINGLE STATE

For in Him all the fullness of Deity
dwells in bodily form,
and in Him you have been made complete,
and He is the head over all rule and authority.
COLOSSIANS 2:9–10 NASB

"Overall, there are significantly more unmarried women than men: 89 single men for every 100 single women."[2] This imbalance suggests that a percentage of Christian women will not marry. As our Wise Woman applies the *principle of trustworthy* (Proverbs 31:11) she is able to live in today's world with or without a husband. Paul addresses the practical advantages of singleness in 1 Corinthians 7:7–9, 25–40. A primary reason for remaining single, according to Paul, is the special freedom and independence afforded to the individual. Our Wise

Woman uses her days of singleness to concentrate on becoming complete in Christ. The spiritual maturity resulting from this focus prepares her for the future plan her heavenly Father has for her (Jeremiah 29:11–13).

Our Wise Woman's choice to become complete in Christ eliminates the need of looking to other people and other situations to meet her needs. Only spiritual maturity, not professional achievement, marriage, children, or ministry success, will stimulate spiritual completeness to flourish in the Wise Woman's life.

Several concepts of completeness emerge as the Wise Woman pursues spiritual maturity:

- Her growth commences by "holding fast" to Christ (John 17:3; Ephesians 2:1; Colossians 2:19; and 1 Peter 1:23).
- She is capable of doing what God has called her to do (2 Timothy 3:17).
- She acknowledges Christ as her authoritative head (Ephesians 1:22–23).
- She doesn't doubt in the dark what she believed in the light (Romans 5:10; Ephesians 1:13; Philippians 1:6; Hebrews 7:25).
- She continues to cultivate completeness though temporal situations change (1 Corinthians 15:58; Colossians 1:10; 2:6–7).
- She makes completeness in Christ her life's goal (1 Corinthians 9:24–27; Philippians 3:13–14; 1 Timothy 6:12; Hebrews 12:1–2).
- Her strength to deal with Satan's temptations develops as she matures in Christ (Ephesians 6:10–20; 1 Peter 5:7–9).
- Her value system is in the proper perspective (Matthew 6:19–21, 33; Colossians 2:20–23).
- She recognizes she is equipped to become involved in the work of the ministry (1 Corinthians 12:12–31; Ephesians 4:7–16).

- Her completeness in Christ and effective ministry occur only with the combination of divine assistance + personal responsibility (Philippians 4:13)!
- She acknowledges that dying to self and the rudiments of the world are part of the process (Galatians 2:20; Colossians 2:20; 1 Peter 1:2–4).
- Her knowledge of God reminds her that He will not take second place *and* achieve His completeness in her (Deuteronomy 10:12–13; 30:6; Matthew 22:37–39; Mark 12:29–31) at the same time.
- She acquires a humble faith as the process is carried to completion (Colossians 2:20).
- She is confident that as she walks uprightly there is no good thing that her heavenly Father will withhold from her (Psalm 84:11).

Our Wise Woman in progress is focused on her Lord—and the more she focuses on Him, the more she demonstrates her love toward Him (1 John 2:3–6). The world says others' affirmation of her confirms or negates her value as a person. God's Word states that as His daughter, she is loved even when no human affirms her (Jeremiah 31:3). A number of biblical references affirm that she is loved:

- She is God's special treasure . . . chosen by Him (Exodus 19:5; 1 Peter 2:9).
- She was created in the image of God (Genesis 1:27).
- She was created for His glory (Isaiah 43:7).
- She is one in whom "[His] soul delights" (Isaiah 42:1 NASB).
- He keeps her as the "apple of His eye" (Deuteronomy 32:10).
- She is precious in His sight (Isaiah 43:4).
- Her loving, heavenly Father created her, formed her, redeemed her, called her by name, and claims her as His very own (Isaiah 43:1).

• When she was at her worst, God gave, out of a heart of love, His very best for her (Romans 5:8).

As our Wise Woman embraces Her heavenly Father's love for her, her actions reflect biblical characteristics:

• She thinks and meditates on the fact that she is loved by God (Philippians 4:8–9).
• As God's child, she acknowledges that nothing can separate her from His love (Romans 8:35).
• She purposes to respond to the situations of life with her will rather than her emotions (Psalm 119:7). The psalms direct our reactions to our will, not our emotions.
• She purposes to know the love of Christ (Ephesians 3:17–19).
• Her aim is to make love a habitual practice (1 John 4:7–10).

The bit of prose entitled "On His Plan for Your Mate" clearly communicates the Wise Woman's approach to God's will for her life regarding singleness.

ON HIS PLAN FOR YOUR MATE

Everyone longs to give themselves completely to someone—to have a deep, soul relationship with another, to be loved, thoroughly and exclusively.

But God, to a Christian says, "No, not until satisfied, fulfilled, and content with being loved by Me, with giving yourself totally and unreserved to Me; to have an intensely personal and unique relationship that I have planned for you.

"You will never be united with anyone until you are united with Me. Exclusive of anyone or anything else, exclusive of any other desires or longings.

"I want you to stop planning, stop wishing, and allow Me

to give you the most thrilling plan existing—one that you cannot imagine. I want you to have the best. Please allow Me to bring it to you.

"You just keep watching Me, expecting the greatest things. Keep experiencing the satisfaction that I am. Keep learning and listening to the things I tell you. You just wait. That's all. Do not be anxious—don't worry. Don't look around at the things you think you want. You just keep looking off and away, up to Me, or you'll miss what I want to show you.

"And when you are ready, I'll surprise you with a love far more wonderful than any you would dream. You see, until you are ready, and until the one I have for you is ready (I am working at this moment to have you both ready at the same time), until you are both satisfied exclusively with Me and the life I have prepared for you, you won't be able to experience the love that amplifies your relationship with Me, and is thus, the perfect love.

"And dear one, I want you to have this perfect love. I want you to see, in the flesh, a picture of your relationship with me, and to enjoy naturally, completely the everlasting union of beautiful perfection, and love that I offer you.

"Know that I love you utterly; believe it and be satisfied."

—Author Unknown

Our Wise Woman understands that marriage is not a condition for salvation, a command, or the standard for everyone. Reflecting on 1 Corinthians 7:17–24, she willingly accepts the position into which God has placed her and is content to wholeheartedly serve Him there rather than live in a state of limbo until "Mr. Right" appears (1 Corinthians 7:32; Philippians 4:11; Hebrews 13:5). The teachings of Jesus in Matthew 19:12 suggest that He believed singleness was a good thing. As we study the Scriptures we find a number of single individuals who positively impacted our Father's kingdom, including the apostle Paul, Lazarus, Mary, Martha, and the Lord Jesus

Himself. If singleness was an acceptable state for the Son of God, how can we reject it?

THE WISE WOMAN
NOURISHES THE SINGLE MOTHER

Pure and undefiled religion
in the sight of our God and Father is this:
to visit orphans and widows in their distress.
JAMES 1:27 NASB

"And they lived happily ever after . . ." is the idyllic conclusion to romantic writings from children's fairy tales to adult novels. In a perfect world with perfect people, living happily ever after is the result of a perfect union. In a sinful world with sinful people, divorce and death shatter the notion of such a union. The U.S. Census Bureau reports that "children who live in a household with one parent are substantially more likely to have family incomes below the poverty line than are children who grow up in a household with two parents."[3] Their report, *America's Children, 1998*, offers a variety of sobering statistics:

- "In 1997, 68 percent of American children lived with two parents, down from 77 percent in 1980."
- "In 1997, almost a quarter (24%) of children lived with only their mothers, 4% lived with only their fathers, and 4% lived with neither of their parents."
- "The percent of children living with two parents has been declining among all racial and ethnic groups."
- "Among the factors contributing to the increase in children living with just one parent is the sharp rise in the percentage of all births that were to unmarried mothers."
- "The rise between 1960 and 1996 in the nonmarital birthrate is linked to an increase in the proportion of women of childbearing age who are unmarried (from 29% in

1960 to 47% in 1996), concurrent with an increase in nonmarital cohabitation. About 20–25% of unmarried women aged 25–44 years were in cohabiting relationships in 1992–94. At the same time, childbearing within marriage declined: births to married women declined from 4 million in 1960 to 2.7 million in 1996, and the birthrate for married women fell from 157 per thousand in 1960 to 84 per thousand in 1996."[4]

Regrettably, Christians are included in these statistics, thus creating another category of the diverse home—that of the single mother. Our Wise Woman will choose to nourish the single mother.

Single is defined as "pertaining to the unmarried state."[5] The Wise Woman first nourishes the single mother by redirecting her to the biblical teachings addressing singleness. As she chooses to follow the instruction of the apostle Paul in 1 Corinthians 7:8–9, her first consideration is to determine whether she can best fulfill the Lord's plan for her by remaining unmarried. While not a popular choice, Paul does teach in 1 Corinthians 7:27, "Are you bound to a wife? Do not seek to be loosed. Are you loosed from a wife? Do not seek a wife." The word *husband* would be substituted for *wife* by the single mother. Multiple Scriptures provide comfort and encouragement to the single mother. As well, instruction is provided to the church in relation to their approach to her:

- Those who exploit or abuse widows and orphans will incur God's wrath (Exodus 22:22–24).
- The Covenant Code (Exodus 22:22) and the Deuteronomic Code (Deuteronomy 16:11, 14; 24:17), provided for the welfare of orphans, protected their rights of inheritance, enabled them to have a portion of the tithe crops and allowed them to share in the annual feasts.

- God administers justice for the orphan and widow (Deuteronomy 10:18).
- Old Testament tithing principles included providing for widows and orphans in the third and sixth years of the seven-year sabbatical cycle (Deuteronomy 14:28–29).
- God exercises special concern for the fatherless (Psalms 10:18; 27:10; 68:5; 146:9; Hosea 14:3).
- A characteristic of a noble man in the ancient Near Eastern world was his care of the fatherless (Job 29:12–13).
- God promises to meet the needs of His children out of His infinite resources (Psalm 23:1; 1 Corinthians 9:8; Philippians 4:19).
- Christians demonstrate the purest form of religious faith by caring for orphans and widows (James 1:27).

Our Wise Woman will possess a tender heart toward the single mother and will apply the *principle of unselfish* in nurturing her. Realizing that the single mother can and should be a contributing member of the local church, the Wise Woman challenges her to invest a portion of her talents and resources in its ministry (1 Corinthians 12:12–26). The piece of prose entitled "God's Path" is a reminder that every member of the church can make a contribution to its prosperity.

GOD'S PATH

A water bearer in India had two large pots. Each hung on each end of a pole, which he carried across his neck. One of the pots had a crack in it, and while the other pot was perfect and always delivered a full portion of water at the end of the long walk from the stream to the master's house, the cracked pot arrived only half full. For a full two years this went on daily, with the bearer delivering only one and a half pots full of water in his master's house. Of course, the perfect pot was proud of its accomplishments, perfect to the end for which it was made. But the poor cracked pot was ashamed of its own imperfection, and miserable that it was able to accomplish only half of what it had been made to do.

After two years of what it perceived to be a bitter failure, it spoke to the water bearer one day by the stream. "I am ashamed of myself, and I want to apologize to you."

"Why?" asked the bearer. "What are you ashamed of?"

"I have been able, for these past two years, to deliver only half of my load because this crack in my side causes water to leak out all the way back to your master's house. Because of my flaws, you have to do all of this work and you don't get full value from your efforts," the pot said.

The water bearer felt sorry for the old cracked pot, and in his compassion he said, "As we return to the master's house, I want you to notice the beautiful flowers along the path."

Indeed, as they went up the hill, the old cracked pot took notice of the sun warming the beautiful wild flowers on the side of the path, and this cheered it some. But at the end of the trail, it still felt bad because it had leaked out half its load, and so again it apologized to the bearer for its failure.

The bearer said to the pot, "Did you notice that there were flowers only on your side of the path, but not on the other pot's side? That's because I have always known about your flaw, and I took advantage of it. I planted flower seeds on your side of the path, and every day while we walk back from the stream, you've watered them. For two years I have been able to pick these beautiful flowers to decorate my master's table. Without you being just the way you are, he would not have this beauty to grace his house."

Each of us has our own unique flaws. We are all cracked pots. But if we will allow it, the Lord will use our flaws to grace His Father's table. In God's great economy, nothing goes to waste. So as we seek ways to minister together, and as God calls you to the tasks He has appointed for you, don't be afraid of your flaws.

Acknowledge them, and allow Him to take advantage of them, and you, too, can be the cause of beauty in His pathway. Go out boldly, knowing that in our weakness we find His strength, and that "In Him every one of God's promises is a Yes."

—Author Unknown

THE WISE WOMAN IS
CONTENT WITH CHILDLESSNESS

"For I know the plans that I have for you," declares the Lord,
"plans for welfare and not for calamity
to give you a future and a hope."
JEREMIAH 29:11 NASB

One in four couples will not be able to conceive a child of their own.[6] Approximately 2.3 million couples in the United States are infertile.[7] Infertility is on the rise due to sexually transmitted disease, people marrying older, and delayed childbearing. In addition to these issues there are numerous physical conditions, including male health issues, which may impact a woman's ability to conceive. Unless you have struggled to conceive children personally, the statistics on infertility are usually surprising. Most couples assume they will be able to conceive in a timely manner and have as many children as they desire. The statistics for infertility and childbirth within the United States, however, tell a different story for many women. The fact is that many couples struggle with issues of infertility, and many women bear the pain of being childless.

I remember a day, not too many years ago, when I was sitting in The Master's College dining room with Pat. We had just begun our lunch when one of our students asked to join us.

She was very friendly and obviously desirous of spending the lunch hour conversing. After a few moments she looked directly at me and asked, "Mrs. Tatlock, why don't you have children? Don't you want to have kids?" While this was a very innocent and honest question for a student to ask, time stood still for a moment and my mind began to race. How do I answer this question? Do I give her the generic Christian answer, "It is all in God's timing" (not to make light of this truth, but it was a habitual response to a question I heard on a weekly basis). Or do I tell her the truth—that my husband and I at that point were unable to conceive a child. Yes, I desired to be a mom, but God had chosen to withhold children from His plan for our lives. Did I really want to get into all the details again? I was so tired of responding to the questions. I usually felt obligated to share some of the facts because the Christian community is typically a very ungracious community for a married woman without children. Most assumed that I was "career oriented" and that was the reason why we did not have children.

While I don't remember the exact response to the questions at lunch that day, I do remember that this young college student did not know that just a few short hours earlier, before breakfast that day, I had been at my infertility doctor's office. I had taken my routine blood test and once again been told, "I'm sorry, Mrs. Tatlock, you are not pregnant again this month." The blood tests always followed a rigorous regimen of stomach injections, medications, and numerous doctors' visits. I had been treated for infertility for almost two years when this conversation occurred. Why do I share this story? I share this because it illustrates two points: First, like many women, I never thought I would have to deal with the issue of childlessness and infertility. Second, it illustrates the insensitivity many people, even Christians, have toward women who are childless.

Scripture uses the word *barren* to describe women without children. Psalm 113:9 states, "He grants the barren woman a home, like a joyful mother of children. Praise the Lord!" God is very concerned with the pain of women who cannot bear their own children. Scripture gives us the stories of several barren women including Sarah (Genesis 21:2), Rebekah (Genesis

25:21), Rachel (Genesis 30:1), and Elizabeth (Luke 1:7). Just as God had a unique plan for each of these women, God has a unique plan for women currently facing the issue of childlessness. This plan may or may not include children. Women who face childlessness are forced to apply the principles of contentment and acknowledging God's sovereignty (see chapter 3). In addition to these concepts she can take comfort in the following principles and thoughts:

- Your genes and your ability to bear children do not determine God's blessing. God's blessing is based on His grace, and it extends to all who are a part of God's family (James 1:17).
- An infertile woman can still please God in her marriage and family. See Luke 1:6–7; Elizabeth was a barren woman, but she and her husband were both righteous in the sight of the Lord.
- You are not an incomplete woman without children of your own. Our primary focus for our lives as women can still be lived out to the fullest, that is "to love the Lord your God with all your heart, soul, and mind" (Matthew 22:37–39).
- Refuse the idol of motherhood. While motherhood will be the primary calling for most women, it should not be the *source* of joy and contentment (John 15:11; Philippians 3:1; 4:4).
- Refuse self-pity, which leads to anger and bitterness (Recall Hannah's story in 1 Samuel 1).
- Cultivate a heart of thankfulness for God's many blessings (Psalms 7:17; 30:12; 100:4; 1 Thessalonians 5:18).
- Maximize, as a good steward, the extra time you have because you do not have children; just as single women can invest more of their life into service for the Lord, so can women without children.

- You and your husband are the family unit; children, if the Lord chooses to give them, simply extend the household you have already established (Genesis 2:24).
- Take comfort in God's promises. For example, Psalm 126:5, "Those who sow in tears shall reap in joy" (see also 2 Corinthians 12:9 and James 1:2–8).
- Be gracious with your responses to those who lack understanding of your circumstances. A gracious woman retains her honor (Proverbs 11:16).
- Don't presume on God's will for your life. He may or may not have it as a part of His plan for your life to bear children. Be open to the Lord's perfect and best plan for your life (Psalm 31:24; Jeremiah 33:3; 1 Peter 1:21).

Although most women would agree they desire to have children one day, we, as with all of life's circumstances, do not know if this is God's plan for our lives. In light of this, a Wise Woman will be quick to acknowledge God's sovereign control of her life and the lives of her potential children (Ephesians 1:11). She will not become God's counselor by assuming she must have children to be a fulfilled and happy woman (Psalm 8; Romans 11:33–36). Rather, she will rejoice in the truth that she is a complete woman because of her relationship with Christ (2 Peter 1:3).

The Divine Weaver

My life is but a weaving
Between my Lord and me;
I cannot choose the colors
He worketh steadily.

Ofttimes He weaveth sorrow
And I in foolish pride,

Forget that He seeth the upper,
And I the under side.

Not till the loom is silent
And the shuttles cease to fly,
Shall God unroll the canvas
And explain the reason why.

The dark threads are as needful
In the Weaver's skillful hand,
As the threads of gold and silver,
In the pattern He has planned.
—Author Unknown

THE WISE WOMAN CARES FOR WIDOWS

Honor widows who are widows indeed. . . .
If any woman who is a believer has dependent widows,
she must assist them and the church must not be burdened,
so that it may assist those who are widows indeed.
1 TIMOTHY 5:3, 16 NASB

Once again, if we consider current statistics, most women will become a widow sometime during their lives. For most it will be at the end of their lives, based on the reality that women often outlive men. For others, however, it will be in the midst of a "normal" life that one day is cut short by our standards. God is very concerned with the needs of widows (Psalms 68: 5 and 146:9) and clearly established guidelines for their care in the New Testament church (1 Corinthians 7:8; 1 Timothy 5:4). In James 1:27, James describes the more sincere type of Christian faith as being measured by compassion for orphans and widows—two especially needy groups of people within the body of Christ. Our Wise Woman understands the needs of orphans and widows, is eager to help meet their physical needs, and provides emotional and spiritual encouragement.

My own family has experienced the unique challenges that widows face. Several years ago my father-in-law was killed in a car accident. Obviously, this unexpected event changed all of our lives forever. However, the impact on the lives of the children (by God's grace they were all grown adults) and extended family members pales in comparison to the impact it had on my mother-in-law. When we decided to include a discussion on widows for this book, I asked my mother-in-law, Diana Tatlock, if she would be willing to write about her experience. She responded positively and several weeks later a six-page, single-spaced narrative arrived in the mail! She gave me permission to edit her letter; it gives us a glimpse of the pain of widowhood. Furthermore, it illustrates the needs widows have and contains practical advice for adjusting to widowhood.

Monday, July 21, 1997, was the day my life was dramatically changed forever. The day began with my husband, Larry, awakening me by kissing me and telling me he loved me as he prepared to leave for an out-of-town trip. He wanted me to accompany him on the trip as I often did; however, I decided to stay home and get in some extra hours at work.

I had a great morning at work, things were going smoothly and I was enjoying what I was doing. It was a beautiful summer day filled with sunshine in a small town in southern Alberta, Canada. We had moved there ten years earlier from California when my husband was contracted to teach at Prairie Bible College. I had absolutely no forebodings or dark shadowy feelings of anything being wrong that day. All seemed well.

After lunch, I was returning to my office when I saw my pastor and a police officer walking down the hall toward me.

There had recently been some vandalism outside our build-ing so I thought that might be why the police officer was in the building. The two men, however, followed me into my office. The police officer asked, "Are you Diana Tatlock, wife of Larry Tatlock?" Our pastor proceeded to say, "Larry was in an accident this morning." I waited for the conclusion of the sentence—was Larry in a hospital somewhere? The po-lice officer, who is also a Christian, finished the sentence, say-ing, "And he has gone home to be with the Lord."

Immediately shock settled down upon me—a shock that would last a long time. I felt compelled to call my children. Someone offered to call them for me, but I desperately wanted to do the calling myself. The problem was, when I actually heard the voices of my children on the phone, I couldn't talk to them beyond saying Dad was gone.

In the days, weeks, months, and now years that have fol-lowed the death of my husband (whom I had been married to for 33 years), I found the role of being a "widow" very difficult. I experienced the stages of grief (typically described as the ten stages of grief, including: shock, emotional release such as crying, preoccupation with the deceased, symptoms of some physical and emotional distresses, anger, guilt, de-pression, withdrawal, the reentry to relationships, reso-lution, and readjustment to reality). Episodes of grief come and go like the waves of the ocean; I have started to re-build my life again. The Lord taught me many lessons that I refer to as:

PRACTICAL TIPS FOR WIDOWS

- Don't try to face your loss alone. Thankfully accept the loving help of those around you.
- Don't be afraid to show your grief.
- Do talk freely of your loss.

- Don't suppress your grief or feel guilty about experiencing the different stages of grief. The grief will manifest itself in some way either now or later. Acknowledge the necessity of grieving.
- Don't try to rush through your grief. Grief will come and go in different stages and different waves.
- No one who is truly your friend expects you to be as strong as you think they do.
- Reach out to God for your strength and help. He will never leave you or let you down.
- God's Word is a great source of comfort.
- Your loss is not a result of some sort of punishment for something you have done wrong.
- Seek the advice of those who know what you are experiencing.
- Seek sound financial and life-decision-making advice from qualified people.
- Join a grief share group.
- Grief can feel unending.
- Closure is crucial.
- God has a plan for your life, even through the storm. He will use this storm to strengthen you so that His plan can be accomplished in your life, if you let Him.

I have literally lived in the Psalms during my time of grief. At times the pain and sorrow have seemed more than I could bear. Psalm 86:6–7 says, "Give ear, O Lord, unto my prayer; and attend to the voice of my supplications. In the day of my trouble I will call upon thee: for thou wilt answer me" [KJV]. I experienced many emotions over the past several years—fear, sorrow, pain, loneliness, anxiety, anger, and hopelessness, to name a few. But through it all there has run a thread of peace, hope, comfort, strength, and even joy that was given to me by my heavenly Father. I have learned spiritual lessons and had my eyes opened to Scriptures that I would never have learned or seen had not God chosen for me to journey through such difficult paths. How could life ever be normal again? It won't ever be the same again, but God can and will lead me in new paths, new experiences, new joys, new victories, and new blessings because He promised that He will. He has given me hope, even though I don't always feel that way; there is a future and a plan for my life that will go beyond my losses and bring me peace and happiness. To God be the glory.

And God Said

I said, "God, I hurt."
And God said, "I know."

I said, "God, I cry a lot."
And God said, "That is why I gave you tears."

I said, "God, life is so hard."
And God said, "That is why I gave you loved ones."

I said, "God, my loved one died."
And God said, "So did mine."

I said, "God, it is such a loss."
And God said, "I saw mine nailed to a cross."

I said, "God, but your loved one lives on."
And God said, "So does yours."

I said, "God, it hurts."
And God said, "I know."[8]

THE WISE WOMAN RESPONDS TO DEMANDS

The Lord will give strength to His people;
The Lord will bless His people with peace.
PSALM 29:11 NASB

We do not know what the Lord will allow us to face during our life. Some will face challenges due to life circumstances such as physical illnesses, loss of spouse in death, or financial calamities. Other challenges will be related to your status as a single woman or single mother. We do not have control over the circumstances God allows us to encounter during our life; we do, however, have the ability to choose our response to life events.

The challenge for most women, including myself, is learning how to respond rather than react to life's demands. Responding indicates you are thoughtfully managing the events God has sovereignly allowed to enter your life. The following principles give a starting point for responding rather than reacting to difficult life circumstances.

DEAL WITH THE HEART ISSUES

Whenever life becomes challenging or God allows circumstances that are difficult to understand, there is a tendency in our lives to react inappropriately. Because of our sin we may become angry, experience self-pity, or develop resentment or bad attitudes toward our life circumstances. A proper response is to deal honestly with the emotions of our heart and to confess any known sin. When we are sorry for our sin (Psalm 38:18) and seek a clean heart (Psalm 51), God grants forgiveness (1 John 1:9–10). Scripture is clear; we will not prosper if we cover our sin (Proverbs 28:13).

COMMUNE WITH GOD

There is a temptation to eliminate personal time with the
Lord when life becomes busy and stressful. We often feel that
we do not "have the time" to pray and read God's Word. Ironi-
cally, the very thing we eliminate is the very thing we need to
respond appropriately to life's demands. We need to "renew our
minds" daily so that we can draw upon the encouragement,
strength, and sound thinking Scripture develops in our hearts.
It is imperative that we protect our personal time with the Lord.
We should begin and end our days reflecting on God's Word.
As Psalm 92:2 reminds us, it is a good thing "to declare Your
lovingkindness in the morning, and Your faithfulness every
night." In the middle of our day we can meditate on God's Word.
Meditating simply means to reflect or ponder on. The world's
definition of "meditation" means to empty your mind. A biblical understanding of meditating means to fill your mind (with
God's Word). You can meditate on the person of God (Psalm 63),
the works of God (Psalm 77), and the words of God (Psalm 1).

COMMUNICATE WITH OTHERS

God never intended us to live in isolation from other believers. Rather, He commands us to "bear one another's burdens"
(Galatians 6:2). The strong are to help the weak with the goal of
edification (Romans 15:1). Unfortunately, many women often
have not established meaningful relationships prior to a challenging life event in order to have a trusted individual to help them
"bear their burdens." Additionally, many of us allow our own
pride to prevent us from honestly sharing our needs. Either situation prevents us from honestly seeking the support of other
women who can help us both spiritually (for example, praying for
us) and physically (preparing a meal or cleaning our house). A
proper response allows others to help "bear our burdens."

SEEK GODLY COUNSEL

In addition to allowing people to "bear our burdens" there will be numerous times where godly counsel is needed (Proverbs 11:14). Mentors, pastors, and individuals with expertise in a particular area (such as finances) will be needed to ensure we are making good decisions and choices. Wise Women will acknowledge their need for counsel and be quick to seek it from the appropriate individuals. Proverbs 15:22 reminds us that our plans will fail for lack of counsel.

LIST AND PRIORITIZE ALL DEMANDS

The Wise Woman understands the time spent getting organized is time well spent (see chapter 4, "Priorities, Decision-making, and Planning"). You need to know what obligations are making demands on your time and energy before you can devise a plan that will help you manage your commitments. The goal is to seek God's wisdom (Proverbs 8:11; Proverbs 9:10). Seeking God's wisdom means we are applying biblical principles (our knowledge) to everyday life circumstances.

RECOGNIZE THE SUPERWOMAN SYNDROME

Women need to recognize they "cannot do it all" (and are not meant to do it all). We all have limited time, energy, and resources (such as finances). It is very easy to succumb to the world's view of women that places demands on us that God never intended us to bear. For example, it is not uncommon for women who work full-time to continue to have full responsibility for household operations (the cleaning, grocery shopping, and cooking, for example). A question that may help you determine your priorities would be, "In light of eternity, what are my priorities?" Identify the important priorities of your life and begin to focus your time and energies on these specific areas. It may take some time to eliminate obligations that do not align with your priorities, but eventually you will be able to invest your time and energies on the areas you have identified.

DEVELOP MANAGEMENT STRATEGIES

Everyone will have unique circumstances requiring unique management strategies. We are responsible for giving thought to our plans while at the same time trusting the Lord (Proverbs 19:21 and 16:9). There are, however, several management strategies that will benefit most women endeavoring to manage the demands in their lives:

- *Eliminate the "extras."* Reduce current demands (if possible). If you cannot eliminate anything in your schedule, definitely do not take on additional responsibilities! Learn to say "no" graciously. Just because you are qualified to do a job, does not mean you should be the individual to complete the task! Remember your priorities.
- *Delegate where possible.* When it is appropriate we should allow others to help with our responsibilities. There are many times when a family member or friend can be helpful, for example, allowing children to do household chores or coteaching a Bible study instead of assuming the full workload. Often it is our own pride that does not allow us to "give up" a responsibility. We should evaluate the reason why we do not allow others to help us. Proverbs is very clear that pride brings strife and leads to ruin (Proverbs 13:10; 16:18).
- *Take time before committing.* Instead of accepting a new commitment when it is first presented, there is much value in taking time to think before you obligate yourself. This allows you to consider your family calendar, physical

stamina, and other commitments already in process (away from the pressure of the individual or opportunity). This is the principle of "considering the cost of the tower before building it" seen in Luke 14:28.

- *Address demands as they arise.* Procrastination will not make our demands go away. Procrastination presumes on the future (Proverbs 27:1), a future which we are not guaranteed (Proverbs 27:1; James 4:13–17). It is much more difficult to play "catch up" than to do tasks as they arise. For example, housecleaning is not difficult if it is maintained on a weekly basis. It is only difficult when things pile up. The same principle applies to other areas: organizing the finances, physical exercise, or making phone calls. Simple tasks can become stressors when they are not completed as they arise.

- *Dovetail.* This we've mentioned before, but it is no less important for that. One of the most effective management strategies is to accomplish two things at once. For example, you can spend time with a friend while you are eating lunch or running errands. You can "renew your mind" while cleaning the house by listening to sermons. There are numerous times we can multiply our time by planning activities concurrently.

- *Maximize your most effective time slots.* Most women will not have the luxury of solely being "a morning" or "a night" person (meaning we will have too many things to accomplish not to be busy during both the morning and evening hours!). We can, however, maximize the time slots in which we function best. For example, I am a "morning person," so I plan the activities that require the most energy and "brain power" for the morning hours (cleaning the house, paying the bills, or writing a portion of this book). I save activities that require little of each for the evening (for example, folding laundry).

- *Take action.* All the planning in the world will not accomplish tasks or eliminate demands unless you actually complete the work! Laziness often compounds demands in our lives. Proverbs 18:9 reminds us laziness is the brother of waste, and Proverbs 6:9–11 tells us that laziness leads to want and wrath. In order to respond to demands we must be willing to work hard and be faithful with the obligations and responsibilities God has allowed.

CONSIDER THE NEEDS OF OTHERS

It is easy to neglect the needs of others when we ourselves are feeling overwhelmed with life. It is important, however, to once again remember our priorities. People are more important than tasks. Reaching out to others while experiencing personal difficulties can actually be an encouragement and remind us that everyone has a burden to bear. For example, a young mother might think she is unable to continue dealing with a stubborn child, until she reaches out to call another mother whose child is dying of cancer. She gladly renews her commitment to persevere under her difficult circumstances because they do not seem as difficult anymore. We should be looking out for the interests of others before our own needs are met (Philippians 2:1–4).

TAKE CARE OF YOURSELF PHYSICALLY

We seem to be tempted to eliminate first the things that are most helpful in responding to life's demands. We already mentioned the temptation to eliminate time in God's Word. Another area we are often tempted to eliminate when we are under pressure is our physical health. We start eating poorly and stop exercising and sleeping. This is a practical area that we can address on a daily basis to help us respond to challenging life events. We must remind ourselves our bodies are the temple of God; and we must continue to care for His temple, even when life is difficult (1 Corinthians 6:19).

ACKNOWLEDGE GOD'S SOVEREIGNTY

Every circumstance of our lives God has allowed to pass through His sovereign hands (see Chapter 3); we must respond with joy to the trials He allows in our lives (James 1:2–8). God's grace is sufficient (2 Corinthians 12:9). There is no circumstance in our lives that we will not be able to handle (1 Corinthians 10:13) through His strength. When we question our ability to handle life's difficult circumstances, we are questioning God's sovereign control in our lives. We place ourselves in a position of counselor to God, as Romans 11:33–36 reminds us. We are to respond to life with a confidence that is a result of embracing God's sovereignty rather than questioning it (Psalm 8).

A FINAL THOUGHT . . .

A Christian woman's joy is not dependent on her life circumstances. The Psalms are full of promises identifying the Lord as both our joy and strength; Psalm 28:7: "The LORD is my strength and my shield"; Psalm 46:1: "God is our refuge and strength"; Nehemiah 8:10: "The joy of the LORD is your strength." A Wise Woman accepts with confidence her unique position in the body of Christ, and chooses to draw her strength from God's Word.

GROWING IN ACCEPTING
ONE'S UNIQUE POSITION
IN THE BODY OF CHRIST

1. *Read Jeremiah 31:3; Romans 5:6, 8; Romans 8:35, 37–39; and 1 John 4:7–21. Using the verses, write one-sentence prayers of thanksgiving for God's love.*

2. *Renew your thoughts by memorizing and meditating upon Philippians 4:8. Do you choose to control your thinking according to the guidelines listed in Philippians 4:8? Explain.*

3. *Study the lives of Naomi and Ruth (Book of Ruth), the widow of Zarephath (1 Kings 17), the daughters of Zelophehad (Numbers 27:1–5), Esther (Book of Esther), Anna (Luke 2:36–37), and the woman who gave two pennies in the temple (Mark 12:41–44 and Luke 21:2)— women who were widows or orphans. Create a chart like the one below; record the attitudes these women had toward their situation and God's provision for them.*

WOMAN	VERSE	ATTITUDE	GOD'S PROVISION
NAOMI	Book of Ruth	Bitter in the beginning of her widowhood. (Continue to develop this section.)	Ruth stayed with her and provided for her needs. (Continue to develop this section.)

4.   Consider how you can practically live out James 1:27 (NASB): "This is pure and undefiled religion in the sight of our God and Father, to visit orphans and widows in their distress, and to keep oneself unstained by the world."

5.   Evaluate how you are responding to life's demands. Identify where changes need to be made in order for you to respond rather than react to your life circumstances.

I first attended "Enriched Living Workshops" in Indiana in 1974 to gain a spiritual foundation for the character portion of the college-level Home Economics Department Pastor LaHaye asked me to develop. Verna Birkey was the seminar leader and her teaching provided the catalyst I needed to get the research for the character curriculum underway. Now, more than twenty-five years later, she continues to "cheer me on." Kind notes and copies of her books provide the stimulus to "press on" in my mentoring of young women. I was blessed beyond measure when she agreed to write an endorsement for Becoming a Woman Who Pleases God! The greatest impact on my life is her consistent desire to grow into Christlikeness (2 Peter 3:18), to share her talents with others, to "train the younger women" (Titus 2:3–5 NIV), and to "walk worthy of [her] calling" (Ephesians 4:1–3).

The young women I have mentored are Verna's "spiritual grandchildren"; I look forward to our reunion in heaven when she has the opportunity to meet each one. Every woman needs at least one mentor. I am eternally grateful to Verna for serving as an "older woman" in my life and for teaching me by example that . . .

THE WISE WOMAN PRACTICES THE TITUS 2 PRINCIPLE

Older women likewise are to be reverent in their behavior,
not malicious gossips nor enslaved to much wine,
teaching what is good, so that they may encourage
the young women to love their husbands,
to love their children, to be sensible, pure, workers at home,
kind, being subject to their own husbands,
so that the word of God will not be dishonored.

TITUS 2:3–5 NASB

My commitment to mentoring comes from my early years as a young professional when there was an absence of older women who were willing to lend a helping hand. Many offered criticism; few offered help. I vowed that if I survived, I would be willing to help others on their spiritual and professional journeys. The young women whom I have mentored serve our Lord throughout the world. I love the times when I answer the phone to find one of them on the other end of the line. Their personal visits are always a blessing and their e-mails, cards, and letters often arrive to encourage and minister to me on challenging days. I am looking forward to our reunion in heaven and count it a privilege to be "the older woman" in their lives!

The mentoring strategy outlined in Titus 2:3–5 provides the method for our Wise Woman to activate the *principles of trust-worthy, unselfish, prepared, prudent, lovable* and *God-fearing. The MacArthur Study Bible* provides a definition of the role of the older woman to the younger woman described in Titus 2:3–5 by stating "their own example of godliness (v. 3) gives older women the right and the credibility to instruct younger women in the church. The obvious implication is that older women must exemplify the virtues (vv. 4, 5) that they 'admonish.'" The biblical rationale for mentoring is clearly articulated in Titus 2:5, "That the word of God may not be blasphemed." Dr. MacArthur writes:

> This is the purpose of godly conduct—to eliminate any reproach on Scripture. For a person to be convinced God can save from sin, one needs to see someone who lives a holy life. When Christians claim to believe God's Word but do not obey it, the Word is dishonored. Many have mocked God and His truth because of the sinful behavior of those who claim to be Christians.[1]

Despite the fact that Titus 2:3–5 is an instruction, not a suggestion, to Christian women, few are willing to mentor. Excuses range from "I don't know that much" to "No one cares what I have to say"; however, when an older woman hides behind these excuses she is sinning by failing to obey a clear instruction from her heavenly Father. Remembering that an excuse is not a substitute for obedience (1 Samuel 15:22), our Wise Woman joyfully practices this heavenly instruction!

PUTTING TITUS 2:3-5 INTO ACTION

Be imitators of me, just as I also am of Christ.
1 CORINTHIANS 11:1 NASB

As Lisa and I discussed how Titus 2:3–5 is practically applied to a mentor/mentoree relationship, we agreed that it must move beyond a one-on-one Bible study. She commented, "If mentoring is defined only as teaching or studying a book together, the importance of relationship and community so critical to Christ's definition of ministry is missed. It is relationship that makes the Christian life critically alive. As image bearers we are created and redeemed for relationship. This is God's desire. His call to delight in Him, seek Him, and enjoy Him can be understood first as the mentor models this kind of relationship." We believe that mentoring relationships can be either formal or informal and have some practical suggestions for each to share with you.

FORMAL MENTORING SUGGESTIONS

Be diligent to present yourself approved to God as a workman who does not need to be ashamed, accurately handling the word of truth. (2 Timothy 2:15 NASB)

- Reading and discussing a Christian women's book together (for example, *Lies Women Believe and the Truth that Sets Them Free* by Nancy DeMoss, *Loving God with all Your Mind* by Elizabeth George, or *The Excellent Wife* by Martha Peace).[2]
- Completing a study on a book of the Bible (perhaps the book of James or the book of Philippians).
- Reading and discussing a commentary (such as one on Titus).

291

- Memorizing Scripture or keeping a prayer journal and then spending time talking and praying together each week.

INFORMAL MENTORING SUGGESTIONS

So that you will not be sluggish, but imitators of those who through faith and patience inherit the promises. (Hebrews 6:12 NASB)

- Discussing questions raised by the younger woman (questions can be related to relationships, skills, or life experiences).
- Working on projects together, such as planning events or holidays to learn practical skills in management (set goals; then work together to accomplish them).
- Simply spending time together talking and letting the younger woman see your life and family.
- Sharing your knowledge about practical home management (menu planning, cleaning house, or paying the bills).

Whether formal or informal, "The Seasons of Mentoring Cycle" begins when younger and older women regularly spend time together.

THE SEASONS OF MENTORING

There is an appointed time for everything.
And there is a time for every event under heaven.
ECCLESIASTES 3:1 NASB

Season is defined as "a period of the year marked off by prevalent climatic conditions."[3] In Hebrew or Greek no particular word designates season, but several words are used for a specific period of time described by such things as weather, agricultural cycles, and annual festivals. These include the time of rain (Deuteronomy 11:14), the heat of summer (Psalm 32:4), threshing and sowing (Leviticus 26:5), blossoming of the fig tree (Matthew 24:32), and the Feast of Unleavened Bread or Passover (Exodus 23:15; Luke 2:41; 22:1). As Ecclesiastes 3:1–8 depicts the seasons and times appointed by God, so mentoring will flow from one season to another. Committed mentors and mentorees possess a willingness to remain faithful to the relationship as it proceeds through the "Seasons Cycle."

THE SEASON OF ACQUAINTANCE

Older women likewise are to be reverent in their behavior, not malicious gossips nor enslaved to much wine, teaching what is good. (Titus 2:3 NASB)

The *Season of Acquaintance* is characterized first by discussing the expectations of the relationship and how it differs from discipleship. When discipling, one meets with someone regularly to learn how to study the Bible, explore theological issues, pray, and use her spiritual gifts. Discipleship usually begins with a request by the younger woman desiring discipleship and is often a more formal agreement—"We will meet each Tuesday morning from 10:30 to 11:30 and study or talk about such and such." Mentoring is much less formal. It is not to be a dependent relationship but simply a growing friendship that emerges as time is spent with a woman who possesses the character, knowledge, skills, expertise, and experience the younger woman desires to assimilate into her life. Our wise heavenly Father brings a variety of temperaments together to sharpen one another in the mentoring relationship (Proverbs 27:17). Sometimes the mentor and mentoree will be very similar; other times they will be very different, as is the case with Lisa and me. Regardless of the temperaments of the younger and older woman, the *Season of Acquaintance* begins with respect for the older woman and a desire to learn from her life experiences.

It is generally best for the younger woman to take the initiative in asking to spend time with the older woman. The younger woman may have more than one mentor—one woman may excel in home or financial management, another in discipling her children, another in her profession, and yet another in Bible knowledge. This "composite mentor" emerges as the young woman asks questions of and takes the initiative to spend time with several women.

A mentor relationship is obviously of great value to the younger woman, but it can be equally rewarding to the older woman. Lisa and I both find that participating in a mentoring relationship provides accountability for our own spiritual maturity. We are stimulated, refreshed, encouraged, and challenged to view circumstances from a different perspective when we are willing to share our lives with others. Though it may be best for the younger woman to initiate the mentor relationship, the older woman can demonstrate that she is available. As the relationship grows, it gradually shifts to the *Season of Tutoring or Coaching*.

THE SEASON OF TUTORING OR COACHING

So that they may encourage the young women to love their husbands, to love their children, to be sensible, pure, workers at home, kind, being subject to their own husbands. (Titus 2:4–5 NASB)

The *Season of Tutoring or Coaching* suggests that the younger and older woman know one another, their individual interests, their future goals, and their previous experiences. The younger woman's struggles and victories with sin, the joys and difficulties of career and relationships, and the need for spiritual maturity provide the catalyst for her to probe the depths of the older woman's treasure chest of wisdom (Proverbs 16:31). The *Season of Tutoring or Coaching* transitions to the

Season of Counseling and Guidance as the relationship matures. As with each of the seasons, it is impossible to place a time frame on this season or to assume that the "Seasons Cycle" will continue.

THE SEASON OF COUNSELING AND GUIDANCE

That the word of God will not be dishonored. (Titus 2:5 NASB)

The older woman is to be open, vulnerable, and modeling behavior that reflects her spiritual age. Her goal is to become so filled with God that He will make her a woman of great spiritual power (Proverbs 31:26). It is not an option on the older woman's part to be willing, for, as Titus 2:3–5 teaches, Scripture commands it.

The older woman may need to limit the number of younger women she can mentor at any one time, but she is to be approachable and open to the leading of the Holy Spirit. Paul mentions, in the Titus passage, several things the older women should be modeling for the younger women. They should be reverent in the way they live, not slanderers, not addicted to much wine, teaching what is good, so that the younger women learn to love their husbands and their children, be sensible and chaste, home lovers, kindhearted, willing to adapt themselves to their husbands, and a credible advertisement to the Christian faith, thus ensuring that the Word of God will not be *discredited.*

Several words describe the behavior of the younger and older woman during the *Season of Counseling and Guidance*— the younger woman is teachable, as the older woman is discerning (she acts like a Wise Woman). Essentially, the younger woman desires to absorb the wisdom of the older woman and allows her to teach her. Proverbs is filled with counsel to acquire wisdom (Proverbs 3:13; 4:5, 7; 16:16; 19:18)! And

Proverbs 24:7 is a reminder to the younger woman that "wisdom is too lofty for a fool." Applying the *principle of unselfish*, the older woman is quick to discern whether her response will be active or passive. She offers counsel when she is asked and possesses the discernment to offer assistance when she is not.

Nourishment is characteristic of the *Season of Counseling and Guidance*. Verna Birkey writes in *Women Connecting with Women*, "Nourishment, then, is something that feeds my soul hunger so that life will be full, healthy and growing, instead of fainting and ebbing away."[4] The older woman offers nourishment through encouragement, admonition, and reproof.

Encourage is derived from the Greek word *protrepo*, meaning to urge forward or to persuade. The older woman acknowledges that though the younger woman is benefiting from her experience, one day she may surpass her. The older woman's attitude is like that of John in relation to the Lord Jesus, "He must increase, but I must decrease" (John 3:30); she becomes the younger woman's strongest cheerleader!

Admonition is in Greek, *nouthesia*, meaning "training by word," whether of encouragement, or, if necessary, by reproof or remonstrance. Colossians 3:16 instructs believers "to let the word of Christ dwell rightly in them, so that they might be able to teach and admonish one another and to abound in the praises of God."[5] The older woman will be careful to use the Word of God as a source for any admonition.

Elegmos, the Greek word for *reproof*, refers to conviction or rebuke. Second Timothy 3:16–17 provides the biblical pattern for reproof: "All Scripture is given by inspiration of God, and is profitable for doctrine, for reproof, for correction, for instruction in righteousness, that the man of God may be complete, thoroughly equipped for every good work." Martha Peace presents an "Example of an Older Woman Encouraging a Young Woman" in *Becoming a Titus 2 Woman* (Table 10.1).

TABLE 10.1
EXAMPLE OF AN OLDER WOMAN
ENCOURAGING A YOUNG WOMAN

---

1. Use Scripture to **teach** her biblical principles on receiving reproof. Proverbs 15:31–32 (for more information on receiving reproof see *The Excellent Wife*).

2. **Reprove** her in a kind but clear manner. Give specific examples. For example, "Sue, I know it is very difficult when your children are young, but I believe I have noticed a pattern of sin in your life when you are correcting your children. Sometimes you speak to them in a harsh, angry tone of voice."

3. Explain how she can **correct** this fault. "It might help if you discipline them the *first* time you give them an instruction and they do not obey. If you keep telling them, you are much more likely to become angry and they are much more likely not to take your instruction seriously. Also, it may help to practice what you are going to say to them aloud. Before you speak, think something like, 'Love is patient. I *can* show love to my child by instructing her, speaking in a gentle tone of voice.'"

4. Training in righteousness is a process that must occur over and over until it becomes part of the younger woman's character. It takes time and practice. Meanwhile, the older woman should continue to biblically, lovingly, and patiently encourage the young woman.[6]

Often the mentoring relationship remains at the *Season of Counseling and Guidance.*

THE SEASON OF FRIENDSHIP

A friend loves at all times. (Proverbs 17:17 NASB)

Should the mentoring relationship continue, one day the *Season of Counseling and Guidance* gently fades into the *Season of Friendship.* Just as the difference between the final day of winter and the first day of spring is subtle, so is the transition that marks the disappearance of intergenerational boundaries when the relationship turns to friendship.

Characteristic of the *Season of Friendship* is the willingness on the part of women to share intimately. The older woman should be willing to share at the same level of disclosure that the younger woman is sharing, and both exercise caution as they move slowly into intimate sharing. Vulnerability is evidenced as convictions, joys and disappointments, weaknesses, failures and fears, victories and successes are shared.

Listening to one another wholeheartedly is an attribute of the *Season of Friendship.* Focusing on the woman speaking, continuing to listen rather than interrupting, asking appropriate questions, responding to her emotions, and allowing her to talk the topic through reflect the respect that is characteristic of this season of mentoring. When differences in opinion occur, as they most assuredly will, the maturity of the relationship requires the women to willingly confront and talk through the situation. Proverbs 27:6 reminds the women that "faithful are the wounds of a friend." Both will value the relationship more than being right or having the last word—and at times they will agree to disagree.

The *principle of trustworthy* is evident in the *Season of Friendship.* The first quality listed in Proverbs 31:12 for the Wise Woman is that of "doing good." The women will do all that is within their power to improve the other's life and challenge the other to her fullest potential. They will not compete, but rather assist one another in doing the work and will of God. Purposing to not "do evil" will involve defending the person. Using 1 Corinthians 13 as a foundation for the relationship will ensure that betrayal, gossip, talking of her faults, injuring her reputation, stretching the truth to or about her, breaking promises, using what she shared against her, or undermining her potential with criticism is lacking. This shared bond of commitment assumes that the women will never make acceptance of the one conditional upon compliance, cooperation, or confirmation of the standards or wishes of the other.

Love and reciprocal contribution encourage the *Season of Friendship* to flourish (Ecclesiastes 4:9–12). Warmth, communication of mutual concern and respect, and a willingness to accept one another demonstrate the presence of love. Each contributing to the maintenance of the relationship furthers its growth. Neglecting to invest time and effort communicates a lack of care and interest. Extending kindness to one another, forgiving one another (Ephesians 4:32), bearing with weaknesses and idiosyncrasies (Galatians 6:2), and reassuring one another will ensure that there are no weeds in their Mentoring Garden. The poem "Tribute" paints a beautiful picture that reflects the *Season of Friendship.*

Tribute

I love you not only for what you are,
but for what I am when I am with you.
I love you not only for what you have made of yourself,
but for what you are making of me.
I love you for the part of me that you bring out.

I love you for putting your hands into my heaped-up heart, and passing over all the foolish and frivolous and weak things which you cannot help dimly seeing there, and for drawing out into the light all the beautiful, radiant belongings that no one else had looked quite far enough to find.

I love you for ignoring the possibilities of the fool and weakling in me, and for laying firm hold on the possibilities of good in me. I love you for closing your eyes to the discords in me, and for adding to the music in me by worshipful listening.

I love you because you are helping me to make of the lumber of my life not a tavern, but a Temple, and of the words of my every day not a reproach but a song.

I love you because you have done more than any creed could have done to make me good, and more than any fate could have done to make me happy. You have done it just by being yourself. Perhaps that is what being a friend means after all.

—Author Unknown

THE SEASON OF SPIRITUAL REPLICATION

I have no greater joy than this, to hear of my children walking in the truth. (3 John 4 NASB)

The *Season of Spiritual Replication* introduces spiritual children into the mentoring relationship. As a new younger woman desires to be mentored, the existing younger woman becomes the mature woman or spiritual mother while the older woman transitions to the role of spiritual grandmother. The truth of 3 John 4 is evident in the lives of both the now-mature and older woman as the "Seasons Cycle" replicates itself. The roles of the mature and older woman reverse in the *Season of Spiritual Replication*—the mature woman charts the direction and the older woman supports her. When asked, the older woman merges into the intergenerational relationship; when she is not, she receives pleasure in viewing it from a distance. Using care not to usurp the mature woman's position, the older woman shares her spiritual mentoree's joys and sorrows. As she "rejoices with them that do rejoice, and weeps with them that weep" (Romans 12:15), the spiritual legacy of the Wise Woman mirrors the words of the apostle Paul in 2 Timothy 1:3–5 NASB:

> *I thank God, whom I serve with a clear conscience the way my forefathers did, as I constantly remember you in my prayers night and day, longing to see you, even as I recall your tears, so that I may be filled with joy. For I am mindful of the sincere faith within you, which first dwelt in your grandmother Lois, and your mother Eunice, and I am sure that it is in you as well.*

PRINCIPLES OF MENTORING
I exhort you therefore, be imitators of me.
1 CORINTHIANS 4:16

Becoming a Woman Who Pleases God began with eleven principles describing the Wise Woman of Proverbs 31:10–31 that shape her character, thus preparing her to assume the Titus 2:3–5 mandate. The *Principles of Mentoring* provide a foundation by which our Wise Woman lives out the mandate.

- Mentoring is a direct instruction from our heavenly Father, not a suggestion!
- Sometimes the mentor and mentoree will be very similar; other times they will be very different. Tim LaHaye

writes in *I Love You, But Why Are We So Different?*: "In every field I know, from electricity to chemistry, pluses are attracted to negatives. In the human realm, introverts are usually attracted to extroverts. They don't realize it at the outset, but people are subconsciously attracted by the other person's strengths that correspond with their weaknesses."[7]

- A mentor is someone the younger woman trusts—a person who operates in an environment of love, not power.
- A Titus 2 mentor provides the mentoree with the freedom to follow God; she leads by modeling, not coercion.
- There are no mentor/mentoree combinations that are the same.
- Confidentiality is the foundation of a strong mentoring relationship.
- Mentoring involves give and take, sharing and tackling goals together. It is a ministry of presence, empowering women with love and insight that is more caught than taught.
- A mentor asks probing questions that help the mentoree discover the "why" behind the challenges that are being faced.
- Biblical mentoring is about character formation.
- The mentoring relationship takes time to develop.
- Mentoring from a biblical perspective is helping a sister focus and make choices rather than its being a counseling session.
- The *Season of Life* of both the younger and older woman impacts the style of mentoring.
- The mentor and mentoree purpose to cherish their current *Season of Life* and maximize it, rather than resent it.
- The younger and older woman consistently communicate their expectations to one another.

- The younger woman is to adjust her schedule to the older woman's.
- The older woman is to model flexibility for the younger woman.
- Mentoring is to be creative and intentional.
- The mentor and mentoree must be willing to allow one another to see their "real" life.
- The mentoring relationship will not always proceed through the entire "Seasons Cycle."
- Time and shared experiences move the mentoring relationship through the "Seasons Cycle."
- Confidence, know-how, and healing grow out of healthy relationships when the mentor and the mentoree purpose to confess their sins, pray, and trust one another.
- A mature mentor relationship means the women have earned the right to say things that might otherwise seem too personal.
- The mentor learns and practices "The Mentor Alphabet."

THE MENTOR ALPHABET
A MENTOR . . .

ACCEPTS YOU AS YOU ARE.
BELIEVES IN "YOU."
CALLS YOU JUST TO SAY, "HI."
DOESN'T GIVE UP ON YOU.
ENVISIONS THE WHOLE OF YOU (EVEN THE UNFINISHED PARTS).
FORGIVES YOUR MISTAKES.
GIVES UNCONDITIONALLY.
HELPS YOU.
INVITES YOU OVER.
JUST TO "BE" WITH YOU.
KEEPS YOU CLOSE AT HEART.

Loves you for who you are.
Makes a difference in your life.
Never judges.
Offers support.
Picks you up.
Quiets your fears.
Raises your spirits.
Says nice things about you.
Tells you the truth when you need to hear it.
Understands you.
Values you.
Walks beside you.
X-plains things you don't understand.
Yields her right to be in control and
Zaps you back to reality.

—*Author Unknown*

HARVESTING THE FRUIT OF MENTORING

I have no greater joy than this,
to hear of my children walking in the truth.
3 JOHN 1:4

Becoming a Woman Who Pleases God *is the fruit of a mentoring relationship that began at the* Season of Acquaintance *and now derives pleasure from the* Season of Spiritual Replication. *The* Season of Acquaintance *began for us when Lisa's parents assumed the responsibility of a singles' Sunday school class to fulfill a Christian service graduation requirement at a Christian college. Her father, recently retired from the military, was acquiring a degree to prepare himself to serve as a missionary. Lisa, then a high school student, displayed an interest in the Home Economics major at Christian Heritage College where her father was enrolled. I was a member of the Sunday* school class and the chair and professor of the Home Economics Department.

The Season of Acquaintance *transitioned to the* Season of Tutoring or Coaching *when Lisa enrolled at Christian Heritage College five years later and chose to major in Home Economics. The* Season of Tutoring or Coaching *included classroom instruction and academic advisement, as well as strengthening the relationship built on the underpinning of respect that began during the* Season of Acquaintance. *She was careful to refrain from abusing the rapport that was established prior to the professor-student relationship. The* Season of Tutoring or Coaching *extended beyond college graduation, as she was advised to, and chose to, pursue a graduate degree. I relocated to The Master's College to begin a Home Economics Department at the invitation of Dr. John MacArthur. The year Lisa completed her master's degree I needed a second full-time faculty member and invited Lisa to apply for the position. As Lisa joined the Home Economics faculty, the* Season of Tutoring or Coaching *matured into the* Season of Counseling and Guidance.

As a new professional, Lisa was careful to draw upon my wisdom and experience while developing her own identity. Time, shared experiences, courtship, marriage, the building of a strong college-level Home Economics Department, and the completion of a doctoral degree characterized the ebb and flow of this season.

A pregnancy and subsequent changes in Lisa's personal and professional responsibilities subtly moved the Season of Counseling and Guidance *into the* Season of Friendship. *The spiritual, professional, and personal contribution we each made to the other's life was the motivation to maintain our relationship. Though daily interchange with each other changed, the intimate sharing during times of fellowship confirmed the depth and breadth of our relationship.*

The national search for Lisa's full-time replacement ushered in the Season of Spiritual Replication. *Erin, the candidate most qualified to fill the position, was a graduate of The Master's College Home Economics Department and a former student of both Lisa and me. As Lisa assumed the role of mentor to Erin, I slipped into the role of spiritual grandmother, sharing the joys and sorrows of her mentoree while at the same time urging them both on to "love and good works" (Hebrews 10:24).*

ꝯ ꝯ ꝯ

A FINAL THOUGHT . . .

The fruit of the mentoring harvest differs for each mentor/ mentoree combination. Few will build a college Home Economics Department or co-author a book; however, because of God's faithfulness (Philippians 1:6), all will bequeath a rich heritage to subsequent generations because committed Christian women chose to obey the biblical mandate of Titus 2:3–5.

GROWING IN THE
MENTORING PROCESS

1. List individuals who have been mentors in your life.
Provide specific examples of how they provided light for
the road ahead spiritually, in a college or career choice, etc.
Write a note to each of them, thanking them for their investment in your life.

2. Study the book of Proverbs and record the counsel to
acquire wisdom. Proverbs 3:13; 4:5, 7; 16:16; 19:18; and
24:7 will provide a foundation for your study.

3. Describe whom you are accountable to in areas such
as:

    a. sexual purity
    b. Bible study
    c. additional areas of personal need—be specific

4. What are some practical ways an older, single woman
could be a mentor to a younger woman:

    a. in the career world?
    b. in her walk with the Lord?

5. Identify several individuals whom you could mentor
at your current age. Describe how you might foster the
relationship.

SCRIPTURE
GRIDS

The scriptural principles upon which chapters of this book are built are given in the ten Scripture Grids on the next several pages.

CHAPTER 1
THE WISE WOMAN BUILDS HER HOME
PROVERBS 14:1

Subtitle	Reference
The Wise Woman Learns from the Wisdom of Others	Psalm 111:10
Eleven Principles of the Wise Woman	Proverbs 31:29
The Principle of Virtuous	Proverbs 31:10
The Principle of Trustworthy	Proverbs 31:11–12
The Principle of Energetic	Proverbs 31:13–16, 19–20, 24, 27
The Principle of Physically Fit	Proverbs 31:17
The Principle of Economical	Proverbs 31:18
The Principle of Unselfish	Proverbs 31:19–20
The Principle of Prepared	Proverbs 31:21–22, 27
The Principle of Honorable	Proverbs 31:25
The Principle of Prudent	Proverbs 31:26
The Principle of Lovable	Proverbs 31:28–29
The Principle of God-Fearing	Proverbs 31:30
The Reward	Proverbs 31:25, 31

CHAPTER 2
THE WISE WOMAN ACKNOWLEDGES
THE STRATEGIC POSITION OF THE HOME
GENESIS 2:21–24

Subtitle	Reference
A Portrait of Twenty-first-Century Family Life	2 Timothy 3:1–7
Leaving and Cleaving	Genesis 2:24
Threats to Leaving and Cleaving	1 Corinthians 1:10
Protection for "Oneness"	Philippians 2:2
The Purposes of Marriage	Ephesians 5:22–23

CHAPTER 3
THE WISE WOMAN DEVELOPS A HEART OF CONTENTMENT
JOHN 14:1–3

Subtitle	Reference
Cultivating a Welcoming Environment	Matthew 5:13–16
Attributes of the Welcoming Home	Psalm 57:1
Maintaining a Diligent Heart	Proverbs 4:23
Embracing Flexibility and Forgiveness	1 Peter 5:5–6
Developing a Heart of Contentment	Philippians 4:11–12
Confidence in God's Sovereignty	Ephesians 1:11
God's Goodness	Psalm 31:19
God's Work	Psalm 106:2
Practicing the Principle of Contentment	Hebrews 13:5

CHAPTER 4
THE WISE WOMAN MANAGES HER HOME
PROVERBS 24:3

Subtitle	Reference
Embracing a Biblical Motivation for Home Management	James 1:22
Understanding the Biblical Mandate for Home Management	Proverbs 31:27
The Principle of Prudence	Proverbs 8:12
Implementing Effective Methods of Household Management	Colossians 3:23
The Principles of Planning and Organization	Proverbs 16:3–4
Organizing Household Cleaning	Proverbs 14:23
The Principle of Goal Setting: Reflecting Priorities	Psalm 20:4
The Principle of Decision Making: Wisdom Applied	Proverbs 16:20
Decision-Making Model	James 4:15

CHAPTER 5
THE WISE WOMAN CREATES A GRACIOUS HOME
PROVERBS 11:16

Subtitle	Reference
Growing in Graciousness	Proverbs 11:22
Responding Graciously to Invitations	Luke 6:31
Speaking Graciously	Proverbs 15:23
Displaying Gratitude	1 Thessalonians 5:18

CHAPTER 6
THE WISE WOMAN PRACTICES STEWARDSHIP
PHILIPPIANS 4:11–12

Subtitle	Reference
Principles of Financial Management	Psalm 37:16
Developing Financial Management Skills	Matthew 25:21
Basic Budgeting Principles	Proverbs 27:23–24
Principles for Partnering on Finances	Proverbs 21:5
Principles of Time Management	Psalm 90:12
Principles of Scheduling	Proverbs 16:9
Women and Work	Proverbs 3:13–15
Fundamentals of Entrepreneurship	Proverbs 31:24

CHAPTER 7
THE WISE WOMAN PRACTICES BIBLICAL HOSPITALITY
ROMANS 12:13

Subtitle	Reference
The Attitude of Hospitality	2 Corinthians 9:7
The Challenges of Hospitality	Philippians 4:19
Meal Management Goals	1 Corinthians 10:31
Getting Started: Practical Suggestions for Exercising Hospitality	Hebrews 13:2
The Rewards of Hospitality	Proverbs 11:25

CHAPTER 8
THE WISE WOMAN DEVELOPS A WORLDVIEW
MATTHEW 5:13–16

Subtitle	Reference
The Principle of Salt and Light	Mark 4:21; 9:50
Discipleship of Children	Proverbs 22:6
Raising World Christians	John 3:16

CHAPTER 9
THE WISE WOMAN ACCEPTS HER UNIQUE POSITION IN THE BODY OF CHRIST
ROMANS 12:4–6

Subtitle	Reference
The Wise Woman Thrives in Her Single State	Colossians 2:9–10
The Wise Woman Nourishes the Single Mother	James 1:27
The Wise Woman is Content with Childlessness	Jeremiah 29:11
The Wise Woman Cares for Widows	1 Timothy 5:3, 16
The Wise Woman Responds to Demands	Psalm 29:11

CHAPTER 10
THE WISE WOMAN PRACTICES THE TITUS 2 PRINCIPLE
TITUS 2:3–5

Subtitle	Reference
Putting Titus 2:3–5 Into Action	1 Corinthians 11:1
Formal Mentoring Suggestions	2 Timothy 2:15
Informal Mentoring Suggestions	Hebrews 6:12
The Seasons of Mentoring	Ecclesiastes 3:1
The Season of Acquaintance	Titus 2:3
The Season of Tutoring or Coaching	Titus 2:4–5
The Season of Counseling and Guidance	Titus 2:5
The Season of Friendship	Proverbs 17:17
The Season of Spiritual Replication	3 John 1:4
Principles of Mentoring	1 Corinthians 4:16

NOTES

Chapter 1: The Wise Woman Builds Her Home

1. J. I. Packer, *Knowing God* (Downers Grove: InterVarsity, 1973), 68–72.

2. *The New Bible Dictionary,* s.v. "wisdom."

3. John MacArthur, *The MacArthur Study Bible* (Nashville: Word, 1997), notes at Proverbs **1:1 proverbs** and Proverbs **1:2 wisdom.**

4. *Random House Webster's College Dictionary,* 2d ed., s.v. "principle."

5. Clovis Gillham Chappell, *Feminine Faces: Sermons on Women of the Bible* (Grand Rapids: Baker, 1974), 21.

6. Charles Hummel, *Tyranny of the Urgent* (Downers Grove: InterVarsity, 1967), 12–15.

7. "The Love Chapter for Mothers," by Dianne Lorang, originally appeared in *Virtue* magazine. Publication date unknown.

Chapter 2: The Wise Woman Acknowledges the Strategic Position of the Home

1. Charles Swindoll, *Come Before Winter* (Dallas: Word, 1985), 310.

2. Charles Swindoll, *Strengthening Your Grip: Essentials in an Aimless World* (Dallas: Word, 1982), 253.

3. D. W. Nelson, "Kids Count Overview" (1995). Found at www.aecf.org/kidscount/kc1995/overview.htm.

4. Ellen Blum Barish, "Stepfamilies: Multiple Marriages Lead to Blended Families," *Star-News Online,* Wilmington, North Carolina, 2000. Found at www.wilmingtonstar.com.

5. "Population and Family Characteristics. America's Children" (1999).

6. Found at www.tvturnoff.org//factsandfig4page.htm.

7. Found at www.divorceinfo.com/statistic.htm.

8. Found at www.divorceinfo.com/statistic.htm.

9. "Child Abuse," *Encyclopaedia Britannica.* Found at www.britannica.com.

10. "Statistics on Domestic Violence," Women Against Abuse. Found at www.libertynet.org/waasafe/stats.html.

11. Found at www.tcpalm.com/stuart/opinions/v20snels.shtml/Income.

12. Found at www.census.net/familystatistics/children.

13. D. W. Nelson, "Kids Count Overview" (1995).

14. Stanley K. Henshaw, "Abortion Services in the United States, 1991 and 1992," *Family Planning Perspectives* 26 (1994): 101.

15. Found at www.newportnewstimes.com/2000/nt-news0408/general/nt-news01.html.

16. Found at www.bfl.org/abortion-stats/htm.

17. Found at www.census.gov/press-release.

18. Michele Menfeld, "Single Parent Central" (2000). Found at www.singleparents.com.

19. John MacArthur, *The MacArthur Study Bible* (Nashville: Word, 2000), discussion at Genesis **2:4 leave . . . be joined to.**

20. Terms taken from unplublished notes, John R. Baird (1978), Faith Baptist Church, Rokeby, Tasmania, Australia. Used by permission.

21. *Thorndike and Barnhart Advanced Dictionary,* 2d ed. (1974), s.v. "communication."

22. John MacArthur, *The MacArthur Study Bible* (Nashville: Word, 2000), notes at Romans **12:2 do not be conformed.**

23. H. Norman Wright, *More Communication Keys for Your Marriage* (Ventura, Calif.: Regal, 1982), 26.

24. N. Wilson, "A Beautiful Doorway," *Agenda* 9, no. 3 (1998): 15.

25. Ibid.

26. *The True Significance of the Marriage Covenant* (Oak Brook, Ill.: Institute in Basic Life Principles, 1997), 9.

27. *What Is the Promise of Marriage?* (Grand Rapids: Radio Bible Class, 1992), 12–13.

28. Gary Thomas, *Sacred Marriage* (Grand Rapids: Zondervan, 2000), 13.

29. Ralph P. Martin, Colossians: *The Church's Lord and Christian's Liberty* (Grand Rapids: Zondervan, 1972), 130.

30. *The True Significance of the Marriage Covenant,* 13.

Chapter 3: The Wise Woman Develops a Heart of Contentment

1. Verna Birkey, *God's Pattern for Enriched Living* (Kent, Wash.: Enriched Living, 1989).

2. *Random House Webster's College Dictionary,* ed., s.v. "refuge."

3. Steve Goodier, "Three Messages of Strong Families," *Steve Goodier's Newsletter* (2001), found at www.bestinspiration.com.

4. Birkey, *God's Pattern for Enriched Living,* 2.

5. Henri J. M. Nouwen, *Lifesigns: Intimacy, Fecundity, and Ecstasy in Christian Perspective* (New York: Doubleday, 1986, 1989), 36–37.

6. John MacArthur, guest speaker for "Philosophic and Professional Issues in Home Economics," Fall 2001.

7. John MacArthur, *The MacArthur Study Bible* (Nashville: Word, 1997), note at Genesis **1:8 This Book of the Law; meditate.**

8. Ibid., note at Psalm **1:2 his delight . . . in the law.**

9. *Harper's Bible Dictionary,* 1985, s.v. "humility."

10. *Harper's Bible Dictionary,* 1985, s.v. "forgiveness."

11. *Thorndike and Barnhart Advanced Dictionary,* 2d ed. (1974), s.v. "contentment."

12. Paul Enns, *The Moody Handbook of Theology* (Chicago: Moody, 1989), 647.

13. Ibid., 106.

14. A. W. Pink, *The Sovereignty of God* (London: Banner of Truth Trust, 1978), 18–19.

15. Elizabeth George, *Loving God with All Your Mind* (Eugene, Oreg.: Harvest House, 1994), 187.

16. Enns, *The Moody Handbook of Theology,* 204.

17. Thomas Manton, quoted by A. W. Pink, *Gleanings in the Godhead* (Chicago: Moody, 1975), 55.

18. Ibid., 55.

19. C. H. Spurgeon, quoted by A. W. Pink, *Gleanings in the Godhead*, 57–58.

20. John MacArthur, *The MacArthur Study Bible* (Nashville: Word, 1998), note at Romans **8:28; good.**

21. Cynthia Heald, *Abiding in Christ* (Colorado Springs: NavPress, 1995), 53.

22. Martha Peace, *Becoming a Titus 2 Woman* (Bemidji, Minn.: Focus, 1997), 5–14.

Chapter 4: The Wise Woman Manages Her Home

1. Elizabeth B. Goldsmith, *Resource Management for Individuals and Families* (Belmont, Calif.: Wadsworth, 1996), 4.

2. Elizabeth B. Goldsmith, *Resource Management for Individuals and Families,* 2d ed. (Belmont, Calif.: Wadsworth, 2000), 9.

3. Martha Peace, *Becoming a Titus 2 Woman* (Bemidji, Minn.: Focus, 1997), 114.

4. John MacArthur, *Different by Design* (Wheaton, Ill.: Victor, 1994), 70–71.

5. Dorothy Patterson, "The High Calling of Wife and Mother in Biblical Perspective," in John Piper and Wayne Grudem, *Recovering Biblical Manhood and Womanhood* (Wheaton, Ill.: Crossway, 1991), 377.

6. Samuel Smiles, *Happy Homes* (Chicago: U.S. Publishing House, 1888), 21.

7. Emily Barnes, *More Hours in My Day* (Eugene, Oreg.: Harvest House, 1994), 39.

8. An expression used by Martha Peace in *Becoming a Titus 2 Woman* (Bemidji, Minn.: Focus), 1997.

9. University of Michigan News and Information Services. Found at www.umich.edu/~newsinfo/releases/2001/mar01/r030501f.html.

10. Don Aslett, *Is There Life After Housework?* (Studio City, Calif.: Twin Tower Enterprises, 1986).

11. The Soap and Detergent Association, *Cleaning 101* (2000). Found at www.sdahq.org.

12. Elizabeth B. Goldsmith, *Resource Management for Individuals and Families* (Belmont, Calif.: Wadsworth, 1996), 214.

13. Betty B. Swanson, *Introduction to Home Management* (New York: Macmillan, 1981), 41.

14. Doug Sherman and William Hendricks, *How to Balance Competing Time Demands* (Colorado Springs: NavPress, 1989), 127–30.

15. Donna Otto, *Get More Done in Less Time* (Eugene, Oreg.: Harvest House,1995), 50.

16. Sherman and Hendricks, *How to Balance Competing Time Demands*, 86.

Chapter 5: The Wise Woman Creates a Gracious Home

1. *Harper's Bible Dictionary*, s.v. "gracious."

2. Elisabeth Elliot, transcript of the radio program *Gateway to Joy*, broadcast 8 July 1999. The title of the program, "An Overflowing Cup," was taken from a chapter in Elliot's book *Keep a Quiet Heart* (Ann Arbor, Mich.: Vine, 1995). Philip E. Howard Jr.'s book *New Every Morning* was published by Zondervan in 1969. It is now out of print. The transcript was found at www.backtothebible.org.

3. Elizabeth George, *A Woman's High Calling* (Eugene, Oreg.: Harvest House, 2001), 32.

4. "Only One Childhood." Copyright (c) 1998 Linda Ellis. All Rights Reserved. Found at two Web sites: (1) www.thelaboroflove.com/prose/poems/onlyone and (2) www.lindaslyrics.com.

5. D. De Haan from *Our Daily Bread*.

6. Priscilla Maurice (1810–54), in Mary Wilder Tileston, *Joy and Strength* (Minneapolis: World Wide Publications, 1929), 260.

7. Elisabeth Elliot, transcript of the radio program *Gateway to Joy*, broadcast 8 July 1999.

Chapter 6: The Wise Woman Practices Stewardship

1. *Thorndike and Barnhart Advanced Dictionary*, 2d ed. (1974), s.v. "contentment."

2. E. Thomas Garman and Raymond E. Forgue, *Personal Finance* (Boston: Houghton Mifflin, 2000), 3–5.

3. Larry Burkett, *The Word on Finances* (Chicago: Moody, 1994), 19.

4. Crown Ministries, *Small Group Financial Study* (Longwood, Fla.: Crown Ministries, 1986), 15.

5. Larry Burkett, *Personal Finances* (Chicago: Moody, 1991), 59.

6. Charles Hummel, *The Tyranny of the Urgent* (Downers Grove, Ill.: InterVarsity, 1967), 8.

7. Elizabeth George, *Loving God with All Your Mind* (Eugene, Oreg.: Harvest House, 1994), 54.

8. Charles Swindoll, *Come Before Winter* (Portland, Oreg.: Multnomah, 1985), 24.

9. Sharon Carr, *Home Business 101* (Old Tappan, N.J.: Revell, 1989), 66.

10. Ibid., 67.

11. Donna Partow, *Homemade Business* (Colorado Springs: Focus on the Family, 1992), 11.

12. John MacArthur, *God's High Calling for Women,* cassette tape series (Panorama City, Calif.: Grace to You, 1986).

13. Partow, *Homemade Business,* 11–12.

14. Ibid., 12.

15. Lindsey O'Connor, *A Christian's Guide to Working from the Home* (Eugene, Oreg.: Harvest House, 1997) 39–40.

16. Larry Burkett, *Women Leaving the Workplace* (Chicago: Moody, 1995), 200–201.

Chapter 7: The Wise Woman Practices Biblical Hospitality

1. *Thorndike and Barnhart Advanced Dictionary,* 2d ed. (1974), s.v. "hospitality."

2. *Vines Expository Dictionary of Biblical Words,* s.v. "philoxenia."

3. Ibid., s.v. "entertain."

4. Alexander Strauch, *The Hospitality Commands* (Littleton, Colo.: Lewis & Roth, 1993), 37–38.

Chapter 8: The Wise Woman Develops a Worldview

1. Elizabeth George, *A Woman After God's Own Heart* (Eugene, Oreg.: Harvest House, 1997), 174–76.

2. Paul J. Achtemier, *Harper's Bible Dictionary* (San Francisco: Harper & Row), s.v. "salt."

3. John MacArthur, *The MacArthur Study Bible* (Nashville: Word, 1997), discussion at **5:13 if the salt loses its flavor, how shall it be seasoned?**

4. *The New Bible Dictionary,* s.v. "light."

5. Rebecca Pippert, *Out of the Saltshaker and into the World* (Downers Grove, Ill.: InterVarsity, 1979) 11–12.

6. Leland Ryken, *Worldly Saints* (Grand Rapids: Zondervan, 1986), 74.

7. Jean Fleming, *A Mother's Heart,* rev. ed. (Colorado Springs: NavPress, 1996), 37.

8. H. Clay Trumbull, *Hints on Child Training* (Eugene, Oreg.: Great Expectations, 1890), 1–2.

9. Starr Meade, *Training Hearts* (Phillipsburg, N.J.: Presby. & Ref., 2000).

10. John MacArthur, *Successful Christian Parenting* (Nashville: Word, 1998), 17.

11. Carl K. Spackman, *Parents Passing on the Faith* (Wheaton, Ill.: Victor, 1989), 170.

12. MacArthur, *Successful Christian Parenting,* 230–31.

13. Tedd Tripp, *Shepherding a Child's Heart* (Wapwallopen, Pa.: Shepherd, 1995), 130.

14. Charles R. Swindoll, *The Strong Family* (Grand Rapids: Zondervan, 1991), 105–106.

15. Tripp, *Shepherding a Child's Heart.*

16. Trumbull, *Hints on Child Training,* 20.

17. Tripp, *Shepherding a Child's Heart,* 20.

18. Fleming, *A Mother's Heart,* 45.

19. Spackman, *Parents Passing on the Faith,* 39.

20. Jan Johnson, *Growing Compassionate Kids* (Nashville: Upper Room Books, 2001).

21. Patrick Johnstone, *Operation World* (Grand Rapids: Zondervan, 1993).

22. Jill Johnstone, *You Can Change the World* (Grand Rapids: Zondervan, 1993).

Chapter 9: The Wise Woman Accepts Her Unique Position in the Body of Christ

1. Edith Schaeffer, *What Is a Family?* (Grand Rapids: Baker, 1975), 17.

2. Bryan Strong, Christine DeVault, and Barbara Sayad, *The Marriage and Family Experience* (New York: Wadsworth, 1998), 172.

3. *America's Children 1998,* Electronic data tape (Washington, D.C.: Forum on Child and Family Statistics [producer and distributor], 1998), 4.

4. Ibid., 5–6.

5. *Random House Webster's College Dictionary,* s.v. "single."

6. Transcribed videotape on adoption presented on *Straight Talk from the Family Research Council,* broadcast aired Wednesday, 13 March 1996. For more information, write Family Research Council, 700 Thirteenth Street NW, Suite 500, Washington D.C.

7. Ibid.

8. This poem appears on a number of Web sites and is always listed as "author unknown."

Chapter 10: The Wise Woman Practices the Titus 2 Principle

1. John MacArthur, *The MacArthur Study Bible* (Nashville: Word, 1997), footnote at **2:5 discreet,** section **not be blasphemed.**

2. Nancy Leigh DeMoss, *Lies Women Believe and the Truth that Sets Them Free* (Chicago: Moody, 2001); Elizabeth George, *Loving God with All Your Mind* (Eugene, Oreg.: Harvest House, 1998), and Martha Peace, *The Excellent Wife* (Bemidji, Minn.: Focus, 1997).

3. *The New Bible Dictionary,* s.v. "season."

4. Verna Birkey, *Women Connecting with Women* (Enumclaw, Wash.: WinePress, 1998), 54.

5. *Vine's Expository Dictionary of Old and New Testament Words,* s.v. "admonition."

6. Martha Peace, *Becoming a Titus 2 Woman* (Bemidji, Minn.: Focus, 1997), 58–59.

7. Timothy LaHaye, *I Love You, But Why Are We So Different?* (Eugene, Oreg.: Harvest House, 1991), 31–32.

BECOMING A WOMAN WHO PLEASES GOD TEAM

ACQUIRING EDITOR:
Elsa Mazon

COPY EDITOR:
Anne Scherich

BACK COVER COPY:
Julie-Allyson Ieron, Joy Media

COVER DESIGN:
Ragont Design

INTERIOR DESIGN:
Ragont Design

PRINTING AND BINDING:
Versa Press Incorporated

The typeface for the text of this book is
Sabon